AT THE SIGN OF THE PLOUGH

AT THE SIGN OF THE PLOUGH

275 Years of Allen & Hanburys and
the British Pharmaceutical Industry
1715-1990

BY

Geoffrey Tweedale

JOHN MURRAY

© Glaxo Pharmaceuticals UK Ltd 1990
First published in 1990
by John Murray (Publishers) Ltd
50 Albemarle Street, London W1X 4BD

Designed by Lorraine Abraham
Typeset by Dorchester Typesetting Group Limited

Printed and bound in Great Britain
by Butler & Tanner, Frome and London.

British Library Cataloguing in Publication Data
Tweedale, Geoffrey
    At the sign of the plough: Allen and Hanburys and the
    British pharmaceutical industry, 1715-1990.
    1. Great Britain. Pharmaceutical industries. Companies,
    history
    I. Title
    338.7'616151'0941
    ISBN 0-7195-4786-5

*The endpapers show the analytical and manufacturing laboratories
of the old Plough Court pharmacy.*

CONTENTS

PREFACE

The British pharmaceutical industry is now a major contributor to the national economy (aside from its impact on personal well-being). By 1987 the pharmaceutical industry, in net terms, was the second largest manufacturing sector donor to the UK balance of trade. It was also the country's fastest growing "high-technology" industry in the period 1987-8. Moreover, the drugs industry – whether it be publicity about a major new advance in cancer therapy, headlines about methods to combat AIDS, or controversy over the side-effects of certain drugs – is constantly in the news. Yet the pharmaceutical firms which contribute to these developments have been little studied historically. Plenty of attention has been lavished on the great doctors and scientists, whilst the business of manufacturing drugs has been largely ignored. Thus historians have been guilty of perpetuating the snobbery of the old medical hierarchy, which dismissed those engaged in such activities as mere tradesmen.

To be sure, Allen & Hanburys has been more fortunate than most. In 1927 a member of the firm, Ernest Cripps, published *Plough Court: The Story of a Notable Pharmacy 1715-1927*, based upon many original records. This was later extensively revised with the help of Major Desmond Chapman-Huston and appeared in 1954 as *Through a City Archway: The Story of Allen & Hanburys 1715-1954*. Eleven years later Simon Stander produced an unpublished London University dissertation, which retraced the firm's Quaker beginnings in great detail. Unfortunately, neither of these studies included the dramatic advances of recent years: advances which have brought closer the realisation of one of man's oldest dreams – the conquest of disease through the use of drugs. So when Colin Martin, the public relations manager of Allen & Hanburys, asked me to write a revised and updated history of the firm, I readily accepted. This book is the result.

It charts the history of Allen & Hanburys from its foundation in 1715 to the present day, when it has continued its progress as part of the Glaxo organisation. I have taken the opportunity to rewrite completely the previous histories of Cripps and Chapman-Huston. Whilst shamelessly pillaging these books for basic information, especially on the biographical side, I have suppressed much of the personal detail (which so fascinated these authors) and attempted to give a more detailed and rounded portrait of Allen & Hanburys' business activities. For example, readers will find no information here on Elizabeth Sanderson Hanbury (1793-1901), to whom Cripps and Chapman-Huston devoted a whole chapter in their book, not because she was associated with the running of the firm, but because she lived into her one hundred-and-eighth year. On the other hand, they will find more detail about the firm's capital, turnover, profits and general business development, and a more thorough description of its products.

The aim throughout has been to provide a readable, concise account of Allen & Hanburys. It is not a comprehensive survey: time constraints have imposed some limitations and, due to my own predelictions and the nature of the source material, I have not dealt extensively with the social history of the firm and its labour relations. Nor has it been possible to describe the firm's overseas activities in the detail they perhaps deserve. Inevitably, very recent events must await detailed treatment at a later date and modern drug advances have been so rapid that sometimes no more than an impressionistic account can be given.

Nevertheless, the story presented here is a remarkable one: it tells how a small Quaker apothecary's shop, founded in the City of London in 1715, emerged in recent times as one of the industry leaders within its specialised field; and how its product line evolved from the dispensing of medieval plant medicines to the manufacture of science-based synthetic drugs. In short, the history of Allen & Hanburys is synonymous with the development of the British pharmaceutical industry.

I am grateful to Colin Martin for patiently co-ordinating the writing of this study; and to Roger Hudson of John Murray (Publishers) Ltd for smoothly guiding its publication. John Saxton and Jonathan Hyde granted access to the relevant archival material, with the former also answering numerous questions on the historical background and providing indispensable help in choosing the illustrations. I am especially grateful to those members of the company who, over a series of splendid lunches, freely answered detailed questions and commented on my early drafts. These included: E.K. Samways, who gave me the benefit of his long association with the company; and Dr. Roy Brittain and Dr. David Jack, who explained Allen & Hanburys' part in the development of Glaxo Group Research.

Charles W. Robinson gave me further useful insights into the pharmaceutical business. Kate Arnold-Forster at the Royal Pharmaceutical Society of Great Britain helped me locate obscure references and illustrations. I am also grateful to my friend Dr. Richard Davenport-Hines for recommending me to the company. Others to whom I owe much include my parents, Dr. Paul Tweedale and Mary Titchmarsh.

Geoffrey Tweedale
Didsbury, Manchester, 1989

William Allen FRS (1770-1843), by H.P. Briggs RA, presented to the Pharmaceutical Society by Jacob Bell. (Courtesy Royal Pharmaceutical Society of Great Britain)

INTRODUCTION

Of Pills, Potions and Medical Men: Allen & Hanburys and the Beginnings of the Pharmaceutical Industry

The science of medicine (which has been termed the *"ars conjecturalis"*) is involved in so much mystery, that even doctors occasionally disagree; and a patient, worn out by an obstinate disorder, is not unlikely to be attracted by the professions and promises of those who propose a new system, or advertise, as a wonderful discovery, a remedy which they describe as a specific.

Jacob Bell, *A Concise Historical Sketch of the Progress of Pharmacy in Great Britain* (London, 1843), p. 91.

Pharmacy began when primitive man first employed herbs for dressing wounds, treating infections and relieving pain. Today pharmacy is still concerned with the preparation of natural medicaments, though now the research and manufacture of synthetic drugs by scientific methods, and their mass production and distribution are more important. The beginnings of pharmacy as a specialisation, and so too of Allen & Hanburys, can be traced to the seventeenth and eighteenth centuries.

When people fell sick at that time the choice of medical personnel available to treat them was, like the gamut of mortal diseases, very wide.[1] The reasonably well off might have access to three kinds of medical practitioners. At the top was the physician, who would diagnose the complaint, hopefully prescribe suitable remedies and medicines (which the apothecary would then dispense) and provide attendance and physic. Physic called itself a liberal profession; the physician was expected to be a learned man, whose ability to read Latin and Greek was at least as important as his grasp of medicine. Physicians to the well-born were expected to have a gentlemanly bearing, with a wig, a golden-headed cane, which contained the reputed preventive against infection, and a coach. The prominent physicians crowded into the capital, where fellows and licenciates of the Royal College of Physicians, founded in 1518, monopolised practice. Outside the metropolis, physicians practised in smaller numbers in corporate towns and cathedral cities where the better class of patients could be found.

Lower in status than the physician was the surgeon. His job, involved as it was with the treatment of external complaints (such as lancing boils), the setting of broken limbs and the occasional removal of them, was clearly a manual craft rather than a "science". The common use of the knife meant that surgeons and barbers rubbed shoulders together in the Barber Surgeons Company of London established in 1540 (the two did not separate until 1745).

The position of the apothecary (who, incidentally, must not be regarded as the forerunner of the modern dispensing chemist) was somewhat similar to the surgeon. The physician regarded the apothecary as his underling: the physician prescribed, the apothecary dispensed; one treated the rich, the other the poor. Moreover, the apothecary's education was a "mechanical" one, which was stigmatised because of his association with mere "trade". The whole apparatus of the pharmacy – the shop, the stock of drugs, the shelves of bottles, the noisome making up of medicines, and their sale over the counter – all these bore the unmistakeable imprint of shopkeeping. Naturally, much rivalry developed between these two branches of the medical profession. Apothecaries, knowing as much about drugs as physicians did, often prescribed on their own account (a happy arrangement for the poorer patient, since it cut out the physician's stiff fee). In the London of the late seventeenth century it was the apothecary and not the physician who performed the function of the general practitioner. It was stated in 1796 that, with regard to London: "In this city where a physician attends one patient, an apothecary attends twenty; and, in the country, the proportion is more than doubled."[2] The lower status of the apothecary was therefore no hindrance to making money. There is evidence that the prices charged by medical practitioners in the eighteenth century rose significantly, perhaps by as much as a hundred percent in the period 1740 to 1850 and then remained on the whole constant throughout the rest of the century. According to Adam Smith in his *Wealth of Nations* (1776): "Apothecaries' profit is become a by-word, denoting something uncommonly extravagant", though he added, "This great profit, however, is frequently no more than the reasonable wages of labour."[3]

The apothecaries, too, had their own society to protect their business activities. Like the other medical groups, it had developed during the Middle Ages (see opposite). At first the apothecaries had been associated with the Spicers, Pepperers & Grocers, before receiving a separate charter in 1617 as the Society of Apothecaries of London. A year later, the first London *Pharmacopoeia* was issued by the Royal College of Physicians of London, enforceable on all apothecaries throughout England. Since apothecaries began to act as general medical practitioners by giving advice and supplying medicines, this brought them into conflict with the physicians and many legal battles resulted. Moreover, the members of the Society of Apothecaries were eager themselves to control those outside their own membership, especially the charlatans and purveyors of bad medicines. For, while the College of Physicians was legally entitled to appoint censors to search apothecaries' shops – a privilege still exercised as late as the early nineteenth century[4] – the right of the Society of the Apothecaries to destroy bad medicines in apothecary and chemist shops had never been recognised. Consequently, there grew up a large body of these people – according to the Society of Apothecaries some 700 apothecary and chemist shops existed in London in the mid-nineteenth century – who had few qualifications

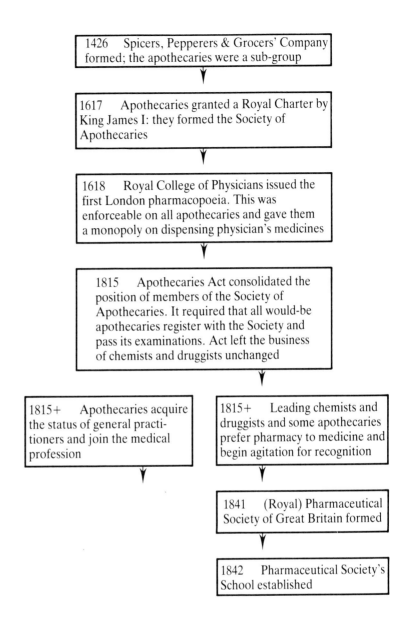

1426   Spicers, Pepperers & Grocers' Company formed; the apothecaries were a sub-group

1617   Apothecaries granted a Royal Charter by King James I: they formed the Society of Apothecaries

1618   Royal College of Physicians issued the first London pharmacopoeia. This was enforceable on all apothecaries and gave them a monopoly on dispensing physician's medicines

1815   Apothecaries Act consolidated the position of members of the Society of Apothecaries. It required that all would-be apothecaries register with the Society and pass its examinations. Act left the business of chemists and druggists unchanged

1815+   Apothecaries acquire the status of general practitioners and join the medical profession

1815+   Leading chemists and druggists and some apothecaries prefer pharmacy to medicine and begin agitation for recognition

1841   (Royal) Pharmaceutical Society of Great Britain formed

1842   Pharmaceutical Society's School established

for treating the poor. According to one commentator:

> In the same street may be seen two shops, fitted up exactly alike. The windows of each are adorned with coloured show-bottles, cut smelling-bottles, medicine-chests, tooth-brushes, and perchance a few proprietary medicines. One of these shops belongs to a member of the College of Surgeons, and a licenciate of the Apothecaries' Company; the other is the establishment of a Chemist and Druggist who is probably a member of no society, and who is not obliged by *law* to know the difference between jalap and rhubarb, much less to distinguish fungus haematodes from a cancer, or peripneumonia from pleurisy. Both these establishments are in the eyes of the public "doctor's shops". The proprietor of each is presumed to know the nature and uses of the articles in which he deals, and the diploma of the Apothecary is looked upon by the poorer classes more as a symptom of a longer bill than as a test of higher qualification.[5]

CHAP. XXIII.

Of PILLS.

1. *Pilulæ de Agarico,* Pills of Agarick.

College.) ℞ *Agarick Trochiscated ʒiii. Roots of blew flower-de-luce, Maſtich, Horehound, A. ʒj. Turbith ʒv. ſpecies Hieræ Picræ Galeni ʒſs. Troches Alhandal, Sarcocol, A. ʒij. Myrrh ʒj. Sapa, a ſufficient quantity to make a maß of Pills.*

Salmon.) It purges Flegm and Watery Humors from the Lungs, Breaſt and Joynts, curing Coughs, Phthiſicks, Aſthma's, Dropſies and Gouts. Doſe à ʒſs. ad ʒj.

2. *Pilulæ Aggregativæ* five Polychreſtæ, Pills having many Virtues.

College.) ℞ *of Citron Myrobalans, Rhubarb, A. ʒſs. Inſpiſſate juyces of Maudlin, of Agrimony, of Wormwood, A. ʒij. Diagrydium ʒv. Agrick, Troches Alhandal, freſh Polypody, A. ʒij. the beſt Turbith, Aloes, A. ʒvj. Maſtich, red Roſes, Sal Gem, Epithymum, Aniſeeds, Ginger, A. ʒj. with Syrup of Damask Roſes, make a Maſs of Pills, S.A.*

Salmon.) It purges all humors from the Head, Bowels and Joynts; opens Obſtructions of the Liver, Spleen and Meſentery, are good againſt Hypochondriack Melancholy, Agues, Dropſies, Jaundice and Gout.

Doſe à Əij ad iv.

3. *Pilulæ Alæphanginæ,* Aromatick Pills of Aloes.

Colledge.) ℞ *of Cinnamon, Cloves, Cardamoms the leß, Nutmegs, Mace, Calamus Aromaticus, Carpobalſamum, or Juniper-berries, Schænanth, yellow Sanders, Goats rue, red Roſes, A. ʒſs. being großly beaten, let the Tincture be extracted with S.V. in a glaſs Veſſel cloſe ſtopt: being ſtrained, in this Tincture ℔iij. macerate fine Aloes ℔j. to which being diſſolved add Maſtich and Myrrh in pouder, A. ʒſs. Saffron ʒij. Balſam of Peru ʒj. at laſt the ſuperfluous humidity being evaporated over warm aſhes, or in a Bath make it into a maß of Pills.*

Salmon.) It purges Choler excellently, & cleanſes the Head, Stomach and Bowels of groſs and putrified humors: it ſtrengthens the Ventricle, cauſes a good Digeſtion, excites Appetite, ſtays Vomiting, ſtrengthens the Brain, and is excellent againſt Vertigo's, Megrims, Lethargies, and other the like indiſpoſitions. Doſe à Əij ad jv. or ʒjſs at night going to Bed, 'tis an excellent and gentle Purge.

4. *Pilulæ de Aloe lota,* Pills of waſhed Aloes.

College.) ℞ *Aloes (waſhed in juyce of red Roſes) ʒj. Agarick Tro-*

Pages from the London Dispensatory *(1682), the earliest pharmacopoeia extant in the Allen & Hanburys' archive. Pharmacists relied on these books for the standard formulations for drugs.*

Pharmacopœia Londinensis.

Or, the NEW

LONDON

Difpenfatory

In VI. BOOKS.

Tranflated into Englifh for the Publick Good, and
Fitted to the whole A R T of Healing.

ILLUSTRATED.

With the Preparations Virtues and Ufes of all
Simple Medicaments, Vegetable, Animal and Mineral :
Of all the Compounds, both Internal and External : and
of all the *Chymical Preparations* now in Ufe,

Together with fome choife Medicines added by the Author.

As alfo,

The PRAXIS of CHYMISTRY,

As its now Exercifed, fitted to the meaneft Capacity.

The Second Edition corrected and amended : whereto is added a Table of *Difeafes :* & another of the Colledge's Errors :

By *WILLIAM SALMON*, Profeffor of Phyfick.

London, Printed for *Th. Dawks*, *Th. Baffet*, *Jo. Wright*, and
R. Chifwell 1682.

Naturally, the members of the Society of Apothecaries campaigned vigorously for the right to regulate the activities of the unqualified fringe of the trade. In the early nineteenth century they had some success. The Apothecaries Act, which was passed in 1815, made some progress towards the professionalisation of pharmacy. It specified that henceforth the normal qualification of an apothecary should be possession of a licence issued by the Society of Apothecaries (the LSA), which involved an apprenticeship, attending stipulated courses, alongside some hospital experience, and passing examinations. Many apothecaries found it useful also to become members of the Royal College of Surgeons, this dual qualification – LSA, MRCS – becoming the hallmark of the surgeon-apothecary or "general practitioner", a phrase increasingly in use from the 1830s.

But at this point the profession began dividing again – into those concerned with medical practice and those more with manufacture. In the early nineteenth century, the apothecaries shed pharmacy and became medical practitioners. But a few of their number and several chemists and druggists (who also had no wish to be associated with the quacks and charlatans) chose not to become medical practitioners: instead they concentrated on dispensing or manufacturing drugs. In London, a group of such men, notably Bell, Bevan, Howard, Morson, Savery and others, strove to create a new profession of pharmacy. There was a large demand for their services and plenty of room for specialisation:

> In the metropolis, and some other large cities, not only are the three grand divisions [medical, surgical and pharmaceutical] observed in the case of many individuals, but each "genus" is subdivided into a number of "species"; for instance, in Pharmacy, we have *Operative Chemists*, *Dispensing Chemists*, *Manufacturing Chemists*, *Wholesale Druggists*, *Saline Chemists and Druggists* who give their attention to *particular classes of preparations* – others who cultivate the sale of *horse and cattle medicine*s – others who are *between wholesale and retail*, and supply Apothecaries with drugs.[6]

In the eighteenth and early nineteenth century these men were called upon to treat a wide range of disease. It seems clear that it was the fevers which dominated the physician's case-load at this time. Malaria was one important hazard, which was prevalent in this period in the marshlands of Kent and Essex, the Fens, and south of the Thames in London. Usually the diagnosis of such conditions was far from precise and many different illnesses were classed as fevers or agues. Specific eruptive infections – smallpox, chickenpox, measles and scarlet fever – were often confused with each other, while some such as mumps were not recognised as specific disorders. Many of the fevers of this time are thought to have been a mixture of typhus and typhoid, together with relapsing fever amongst the Scots and immigrant Irish. These dreaded diseases often spread in epidemics, which usually left the patient dead within two or three weeks and his medical attendant helpless. Next to fevers, the biggest killers were the diarrhoeal diseases, amongst the new-born, and phthisis, a wasting disease (usually pulmonary consumption), that affected adolescents and young adults. Often these illnesses were exacerbated by chest and throat infections, which could be severe and life-threatening.

In these circumstances, what was the effectiveness of the medical treatment of the day? A glance at many of the medicines available in the early days of Allen & Hanburys would incline one to believe that many of the drugs were mere placebos. Unhappily, not all of them can have been entirely innocuous and the published Pharmacopoeias of the time contain some hair-raising recipes, that fully justified one contemporary physician's comment that these books "were loaded with a miserable farrago of useless trash".[7] Remedies from the animal kingdom were especially favoured as witness the following ingredients from a Pharmacopoeia of 1653 (with sardonic asides from a later translator):

> *The fat, grease, or suet of a duck, goose, eel, bore, heron, thymallos* (if you know where to get it), *dog, capon, bever, wild cat, stork, hedgehog, hen, man, lyon, hare, kite, or jack* (if they have any fat I am persuaded 'tis worth twelve-pence the grain), *wolf, mouse of the mountains* (if you can catch them), *album Graecum, east and west benzoar, stone taken from a man's bladder, viper's flesh, the brain of hares and sparrows, the rennet of lamb, kid, hare, and a calf and a horse too* (quoth the colledg.) [They should have put the rennet of an ass to make medicine for their addle brains.] *The excrement of a goose, of a dog, of a goat, of pidgeons, of a stone horse, of swallows, of men, of women, of mice, of peacocks, etc., etc.*[8]

One of the earliest medical books in Allen & Hanburys' archive is the *Pharmacopoeia Bateana* (1699), in which the preface proclaims that the original author, Dr. Bate, was "one of the greatest Masters of his Art in the Universe . . . [whose work] . . . exceeds in its Benefits and Usefulness to Mankind, (we speak it without flattery) all the Dispensatories this day extant, in what language foever". It recommended mercurials for venereal disease and noted, approvingly, that "these Metallicks, rarified like Fire, acquire such a penetrating force, that they pass through the whole habit of the Body".

Nevertheless, people were enthusiastic medicine- and pill-takers in the eighteenth century. Indeed, one commentator called this "The Golden Age of Physic". The oft-expressed view that tablet and medicine addiction is a vice of twentieth-century patients finds no support in the historical evidence. To understand why, one needs to know something about how our ancestors viewed sickness, disease and the medical profession.

In the seventeenth and eighteenth century, illness and death were bound to loom large in people's lives. The death rate was strikingly high through most of the seventeenth century, and though it declined some-what after the 1740s, it rose again during the early decades of industrial-isation in the nineteenth century, and only began a sustained decline after 1830. Life expectancy was perhaps around 35 years for males in the mid-seventeenth century and had only risen to about 45 by 1890.[9]

Illness, not surprisingly, is a constant theme in the letters, books and journals of the period. However, it seems to have been regarded rather differently than it is today, when periods of sickness in industrialised nations are seen as (usually) no more than a temporary interruption to the course of a normally healthy lifestyle. Today disease is regarded as an alien entity, which strikes at random from outside, and is dealt with by the surgeon and bacteriologist, who we trust to put matters right. Before the development of modern medicines and surgery, however, the sufferer's reaction to disease was far more complex. The contemporary assumptions as to what caused illness were varied. To some, it was due to a lack of proper diet, exercise, evacuations, adequate sleep, and the like; while many saw the divine hand of Providence at work, with sickness a direct manifestation of God's higher purpose; to others, it meant that there was some imbalance of the body's four "humours" (blood, phlegm, black bile and yellow bile), which might require some adjustment to the quantity or consistency of the blood to correct.

The humoral principle of disease was at the centre of the Galenic system of medicine, which still exerted a profound influence at this time. Galen (129-199) held that it should be possible to administer herbs with opposing qualities in order to cure disease. Inevitably, this required the compounding of several plants in complex formulations that later became known as "galenicals"; while the plants with the appropriate properties became known as the so-called "simples".

But much speculation was involved and disease was very much a personal matter. Not surprisingly, when people fell sick, they formed their own diagnosis and then applied their own remedies. Of course, self-medication is a universal characteristic, but it enjoyed something of a heyday in the eighteenth century. People routinely dosed themselves with tonics, gave themselves purges and emetics, willingly allowed barber-surgeons to let their blood, and applied leeches as part of a self-imposed regimen. Whether one was ill or not, it was thought wise at least once a year (usually in the Spring) to take "physic". Though drugs were expensive, it seems to have been common to stock domestic medicine-cabinets with bottles of shop-bought (or home-made) balsams, purges, vomits, pain-killers and the latest in patent and proprietary powders. Many of these medicines were imbibed in the belief that the more unpleasant the illness, the stronger and more unpleasant should be the remedy.

In these circumstances, medicine and pharmacy were a market place, where everyone from the be-wigged Oxbridge physician to the village crone who brewed herbs in her garden, competed for the trade of a clamouring public. In William Hogarth's "Marriage A-la-mode", painted in the 1740s, the French quack (with his dubious nostrums for "social diseases"), the apothecary (with his clyster syringe and bottle of medicant), and the licensed physician (with his cane and sword) all make their appearance – in Hogarth's eyes, a ridiculous and ineffectual one. By far the most successful, in the short term, were the quacks and charlatans, who enjoyed something of a vogue at this time. As the Pharmaceutical Society was to lament in the nineteenth century:

it cannot be denied that even doctors sometimes disagree . . . a fact which proves that the art and science of medicine is not based upon fixed and unerring principles, but is in some instances involved in no little obscurity. The public know very well that this is the case, and are aware that valuable remedies have not unfrequently been discovered by quacks and other persons not in the profession. It is therefore difficult to control the prejudices of

(above) William Hogarth, Marriage à-la-mode III, *c. 1742-3, provides a harrowing look at eighteenth-century quackery. The nobleman is visiting a quack doctor, who specialises in "social diseases". (Courtesy National Gallery)*

(below) The quack doctor, 1814. The eighteenth and early nineteenth century was the heyday of the quack and charlatan. (Courtesy Royal Pharmaceutical Society of Great Britain)

London Pub. July 1. 1814. at R. Ackermann's, 101. Strand.

I have a secret art to cure
Each malady, which men endure.

patients; and not only the Chemists, but Hydropathists, Homoeopaths, and Quacks and Imposters of every description enjoy a certain proportion of the confidence of the public.[10]

The lives of some of these quack doctors make entertaining reading.[11] There was, for example, Martin van Butchell, active in London after 1770, who practised as a quack doctor and *Super* dentist, and who achieved notoriety by having his wife embalmed and displayed in a glass case in his living room. There was also James Graham, the "Emperor of Quacks", who became notorious in London after 1770 as one of the most extraordinary charlatans of his day. He established a "Temple of Health" in a fine house in the Royal Terrace, Adelphi, where he gave advice and sold nostrums, such as his "Elixir of Life" and "Imperial Pills". One room had a "Grand Celestial Bed" on which "children of the most perfect beauty could be begotten" for a fee of 500 guineas a night. Graham later became something of a nuisance, since he would half-madden himself with ether and then run outside, stripping himself naked to clothe beggars. Later he went completely mad, before his sudden death in 1794 at the age of forty-nine.

Most of these quacks achieved fame and often great wealth by inventing and patenting a medicine. Many of these became household words. One of the most popular remedies of the seventeenth century was Daffy's Elixir, said to have been originally mixed in about 1660 by the Reverend Thomas Daffy, the rector of Redmile. It apparently contained senna, jalap, aniseed, caraway seeds and juniper berries, macerated in alcohol. Dover's Powder owed its renown to Thomas Dover, an English doctor and adventurer, who had enjoyed some success as a buccaneer, and eventually began practising in the Strand. His specific first appeared in the London *Pharmacopoeia* of 1788. Dover, who also had a fondness for prescribing metallic quicksilver, liberally laced his powder with opium, though the cocktail also included, *inter alia*, saltpetre and tartar. The recommended dosage was a large one and Dover was reputed to have stated that some apothecaries advised their patients to make out their wills before swallowing a large dose.

Dr. Robert James (1705-1776), a lifelong friend of Dr. Johnson, took out a patent on his fever powder in 1747 and it was sold by him and Francis Newbery. The main constituent of the powder was antimony; and James also had a mercury pill to offer. Indeed, he often combined the two and then, it is said, followed it up with a large dose of bark. There are several accounts of the effects of James's powders and it seems certain that in at least one documented case, that of the writer Dr. Oliver Goldsmith, the concoction was fatal.

Being a quack was no barrier to Royal patronage. Joshua Ward (1685-1761) arrived on the scene in spectacular fashion by wrenching George II's dislocated thumb back into place; for which he received initially a kick in the shins and some strong Germanic oaths, but later a horse and carriage and a room at Whitehall. He made the most of his many remedies, which included "White Drop" and a "sweating powder". He was consulted by the dying Henry Fielding, who admitted that his potions had little effect and that "Mr. Ward declared it was as vain to attempt sweating him as a deal board".[12] Fielding was fortunate, since Ward's drops and powders contained mercury, arsenic and opium. Later it was declared in the courts that his mixtures were harmful and that he had only a slight knowledge of pharmacy. But this did little to dent his popularity and the 1748 Apothecaries Act specifically exempted him. After amassing a fortune the recipes were bequeathed to John Page, who published them as *Receipts for Preparing and Compounding the Principal Medicines Made Use of By the Late Mr. Ward* (1763).

Shrewd marketing rather than medical knowledge was the main factor in a successful career in quackery. James Morison (1770-1840) stressed a single cause and a single cure (his Morison Pills) for every disease, lambasted the ignorance and evil of members of the medical profession, and used books, pamphlets and hand-outs to expound the virtues of his product. According to one source, he was making £80,000 a year towards the end of his life and left £500,000 at his death.

In the nineteenth century, the pharmaceutical "establishment", as represented by the Pharmaceutical Society, was quick to highlight the idiocy of the more fraudulent practitioners. Jacob Bell, one of the founder members of the Pharmaceutical Society, in his history of pharmacy cites the case of St. John Long, whose embrocation was supposed to consist of a mineral acid, mixed with a spirit of turpentine. It was also alleged to contain arsenic, but this was conjecture since its originator did not allow the recipe out of his hands. Near the end of 1830 a Miss Cassian, who had symptoms of consumption, died while under the influence of his mixture. Her sister, who had shown no symptoms, was brought before St. John Long, who recommended the same treatment by way of prevention. She died, too, though St. John Long continued to practice as an "infallible consumption doctor", until he himself fell victim to the disease.

The system which acquired the greatest notoriety was homoeopathy, devised by Dr. Samuel Hahnemann (1755-1843) of Dresden in 1796. Hahnemann's drug therapy was based on the unproven principle *similia similibus curantur* (like cures like) – in other words, the precise opposite of the Galenic approach, which induced a condition different from the cause of the disease (allopathy). Hahnemann administered doses so inconceivably small as to be invisible to the naked eye and immeasurable by the usual methods. This approach, which perhaps had the merit that it rescued the patient from the more bizarre contemporary nostrums, failed dismally, yet today it still has adherents in the field of unorthodox medicine. Another treatment which was aimed at the patient rather than the disease was the discovery by Priessnitz, of Graeffenburg, of the virtues of cold water. Remarked Jacob Bell: "It is now discovered that patients may sit in a cold-bath for a considerable time, envelope themselves in wet sheets, and retire to a dripping bed, not only with perfect safety, but with a very beneficial effect!"[13]

Not surprisingly, few of these nostrums would pass scrutiny today and many seem to have actually hastened rather than hindered death. Generally, it seems clear that medicine in the period from 1700 to the beginnings of the twentieth century could do little to reduce mortality from the most lethal diseases, particularly those spread by epidemics. As we shall see, not until the coming of sulphonamides and antibiotics in the 1930s and 1940s did the medical profession have the means reliably to combat such infectious diseases. Nevertheless, the picture is not entirely gloomy. Aside from the role of the physician and pharmacist as a source of assurance and comfort – a role which should never be underestimated – some progress in drug treatment was evident. In fact, not all the patent medicines were as lethal as those described above (indeed, it might be argued that such drugs in the long run were counter-productive, even for the charlatan) and even quacks were involved in real breakthroughs. Many of today's leading manufacturing and retail chemists – Beechams and Boots are perhaps the best examples – had their beginnings on the medical "fringe".[14]

A glance at the pharmacopoeias of the seventeenth and eighteenth centuries shows that the apothecaries derived most of their drugs from roots, barks and leaves and that "chemical medicines" (such as arsenic and antimony) were comparatively few. In retrospect, if one makes the generous assumption (doubtless, too generous in many cases) that the drugs were carefully compounded and not over-prescribed, many of these vegetable preparations were very efficaceous and were the forerunners of many modern drugs. Perhaps the best example is "Fever Bark" or "Jesuit's Powder", which was found on the eastern slopes of the Andes in about 1630. The way in which this tree bark found its way to Europe as an anti-malarial specific is one of the most extraordinary tales in the history of pharmacy. Imported by the Jesuits and given the name "quina", it was introduced in England in the mid-seventeenth century, where its use was hindered by the antagonism towards the Jesuits. A shrewd quack, however, Robert Talbor, achieved international fame and a large fortune by popularising the bark as a treatment for fevers, while carefully concealing its Jesuitical origins. Talbor eventually struck a bargain with Louis XIV of France to part with his remedy for a large sum of money and an annual pension – but on condition that the secret would only be revealed after Talbor's death. When that occurred in 1681, Louis XIV arranged for the remedy to be published in a small volume that appeared a year later, disclosing that Talbor had used "Jesuit's Bark" infused in wine. An English translation was published in London in 1682 as *The English Remedy, or, Talbor's Wonderful Secret for Curing Agues and Feavers*. In 1753 Linnaeus classified the family of trees from which the bark was obtained as *Cinchona*, from which quinine, the anti-malarial drug, was isolated in France in 1820.

The sources of such drugs tended to be obscure and frequently legends grew up surrounding their discovery. The fact they had usually been found by explorers and traders in the New World, often from the Indians or the Incas, added to the mystique. Besides quinine, other vegetable drugs were soon added to the apothecary's armoury. There was, for example, *ipecac*, a Brazilian treatment which was based on a jungle shrub *Cephaelis ipecacuanha*. It contained an alkaloid, emetine, which was later found to be an important remedy for amoebic dysentery. An array of plants was soon found that catered for the eighteenth-

"Fever Bark" or "Jesuit's Powder" (the source of the anti-malarial drug quinine) was one of the most important medicines used in the eighteenth century. It was derived from the bark of certain South American trees. This illustration shows sections of bark in John E. Howard, Illustrations of the Nueva Quinologia of Pavon, with Coloured Plates by W. Fitch *(London: Lovell Reeve & Co, 1862). (Courtesy Royal Pharmaceutical Society of Great Britain)*

century obsession for purging and cleansing the system: there was jalap (*Ipomoea purga*), a purgative root from Mexico; manna, a gum laxative from the Mediterranean; *cassia*, or senna, a mild cathartic from a North African shrub; and rhubarb, another treatment for bowel "disorders", which was obtained from the Chinese plant, the *Rheum*, and should not be confused with English rhubarb, which has no cathartic properties. For those who required a more "soothing purge", castor-oil from the seeds of an African or Indian plant proved increasingly popular in the eighteenth century. Other plants, such as Virginian snakeroot from North America, were valued both for their digestive attributes, and also as all-round medicines for such common ailments as rheumatism. Friar's balsam (sometimes known as Jesuit's Drops, or Turlington's Drops) also came into vogue at this time. It contained storax, an old remedy for asthma, bronchitis and catarrh, though controversy raged over its source

13

and ingredients. Resin from the *Styrax benzoin*, a large, quick-growing tree from the Far East, was the eventual primary constituent; the benzoin was mixed with alcohol and used as an emollient mixture. Other vegetable drugs included sassafras and guaiacum, which were vaunted as a cure for syphilis. If all else failed, there was the opium poppy, which provided the most efficient pain-killer known to man. Not all these drugs, though, came from abroad. In 1785, a Birmingham doctor, William Withering, discovered that dropsy could sometimes be cured by a preparation of foxglove leaves first shown to him by "an old woman of Shropshire". Later it was realised that it was the drug's action in stimulating the heart that was responsible for the cure. In the two hundred years since then chemists have been unable to find a better drug to replace the foxglove. Its extract, digitalis (or the man-made equivalent digoxin), is still one of the major treatments for heart failure.

Quinine, digitalis, opium, smallpox vaccination (which although introduced at the end of the eighteenth century really belongs to the nineteenth), alongside the somewhat debatable use of mercury for syphilis – this list of major advances is not a long one, yet they are harbingers of the momentous changes that were to occur in pharmacy in later years. The picture was not entirely without hope. And Allen & Hanburys, as it came into existence at the beginning of the eighteenth century, was at the heart of these developments.

It was in London that the business that became Allen & Hanburys was founded.[15] In December 1715, the year after George I ascended the throne, Silvanus Bevan (1691-1765), then aged twenty-four, opened an apothecary's shop in Old Plough Court, off famous Lombard Street. The premises were leased to him by a Quaker merchant, Salem Osgood. Bevan had gained his freedom of the Society of Apothecaries in July of that year, since it was noted in the court minutes that "Mr. Silvanus Bevan servant to Mr. Mayleigh wanting six or seven months of his time paid £6 9s. and is to be freed".[16] It is not known who Thomas Mayleigh was – possibly an apothecary in Cheapside – but the entry certainly signifies that Bevan had served seven laborious years of apprenticeship. His final examination would have concerned his knowledge and "Election of Simples", and his preparation, dispensing, handling, commixing and compounding of medicines. Once he had satisfied the examiners in these respects, he was at liberty within the City of London "to have, keep or furnish an Apothecary's Shop, or to prepare, make, mingle, work, compound, give, apply, minister, utter, put forth, sell or set on sale, any medicines or otherwise by any other ways or means exercise the Art of an Apothecary".

Little is known about the background of Silvanus Bevan, except that his forebears had been merchants and townsmen of some influence in Swansea. That, and the crucial fact that he was a Quaker. This was to have such a profound impact on the firm in its early days, that it is worth examining this aspect in some detail.

As a Quaker, Bevan automatically became a member of possibly the most influential, wealthiest and clannish group in the business life of the day. Like the Jew's, the Quaker's life revolved in a complex manner around three primary considerations: religion, family, and business. In Bevan's day, and until well into the nineteenth century, it remained necessary to belong to the Church of England in order to enjoy the full rights of citizenship and swim in the mainstream of political, university and governmental life. Devout Quakers objected to this and so, like the Roman Catholics, Jews, Unitarian and other Dissenting sects, they remained partly isolated from English life.

The Quakers' equivocal standing in the eyes of the law and in public opinion did not stop them prospering in business. In fact, it has become a historical commonplace that the growth of industry was strongly linked with the rise of groups which dissented from the Church of England.[17] The Quakers may have been shut off from the traditional routes to worldly wealth, but this left them free to concentrate singlemindedly on what was left – an expanding economy, which offered plenty of scope for advancement. The Quakers made the most of it: thus in relation to their membership – about 60,000 in 1700 and probably only a third of that figure by 1800 (or 0.2 percent of the population) – the influence of successful Quaker businessmen was out of all proportion to their numbers. In the eighteenth century members of the Society of Friends played a prominent part in the development of corn-milling, foodstuffs, brewing and banking; and the Quaker families of the Darbys, Reynolds, Lloyds and Huntsmans came to direct the destinies of the iron and steel industries at a period of rapid change. Quaker principles presented no obstacle to getting rich; indeed, they emphasised precisely those virtues of hard work and sober habits that might be expected to contribute to that end. Discipline in business, as in all other matters, was strict for the Quakers and any Friend who was declared bankrupt could expect to have his affairs closely inspected. Allied with an often superior education, these were formidable business virtues.

The Quakers also insisted on honest dealing and so it comes as no surprise to discover that they were also very active in the field of pharmacy, where their guarantee would have been an important, even life-saving, consideration in a market where adulterated medicines prolif- erated. Not only Allen & Hanburys, but also such famous pharmaceutical firms as John Bell & Co, Corbyn, Stacey & Co and Howards had strong links with the Society of Friends.[18] These linkages could have endless ramifications. Among the people who Silvanus Bevan took into his business in the early days was William Cookworthy, a far-sighted chemist and a clever linguist from a West Country Quaker family which had been ruined by the South Sea Bubble in 1720. Cookworthy later achieved prominence as the discoverer of China clay in Cornwall. Silvanus's own Quaker links were strengthened when, shortly before opening his shop in London in December 1715, he married Elizabeth Quare at a Friends' Meeting House in the City. His wife was the daughter of none other than the Royal clockmaker to King George I, Daniel Quare, which ensured that a "large party from the Court" was present at the ceremony and doubtless brought Silvanus many useful contacts.

Why Bevan came to London is not known, but probably it had something to do with the opportunities it offered as the pharmaceutical capital of the country. This was signified by the fact that while there were only nine apothecaries between Holborn and Aldgate when Silvanus began business, shortly after there were within the area no less than thirty-nine druggists and two chemists; and eighteen of these were within half a mile of Plough Court and three in adjoining Lombard Street. Silvanus had chosen an excellent location. His shop was in the centre of the commercial world in a street famous for its banks; it was within easy reach of the coaching inns and a stone's throw from wharf and canal agents; nearby were the coffee houses; close by too were the major hospitals; and these locational advantages were to grow in the nineteenth century when the Post Office was erected in Lombard Street.

Bevan occupied No. 2 Plough Court, which in those days was a cul-de-sac that was reached by a passage from Lombard Street. Bevan's residence faced this passage and could be seen by those passing along Lombard Street. In the forecourt of the building was a yard and from there access could be had to the spacious cellars beneath the building. The address appears to have been well-suited as an apothecary's shop. It was a lofty three-storied building with offices and good-sized rooms, in one of which Alexander Pope, the poet, was born in 1688. (Plough Court still exists, as a thoroughfare off Lombard Street, though the old buildings have long since been obliterated by high-rise banks. A blue plaque commemorates Pope's birth-place.) There are no accounts of Bevan's shop at this time, but it was perhaps not too different from the description of one we have from a later date:

> A strong, pungent smell which masks even that of the malodorous lane, betokens the shop of the apothecary. Above the door swings a signboard, emitting groans like some wounded animal, upon which may be discerned by the feeble light from a green lantern suspended over it, the figure of a golden Phoenix with outstretched wings. Inside, the shop is a throng of people: women buying worm-seed for their children or treacle to drive out the measles, serving men waiting for their masters' electuaries or clysters, maids anxious to buy Hungary Water to beautify the complexion, Lac Virginis or perfumes for my lady's chamber, which the apprentice behind the counter is busy preparing. In a little room at the back of the shop, a woman is seated in a stout oak chair waiting to be bled . . . for the apothecary was ready to perform any operation, from the cutting off of a wen to the amputation of a leg. From the heavy beams that cross the ceiling of the shop, strange objects hang. Here an alligator with open mouth, there a gaping sunfish with staring eyes, and other mysterious creatures, together with strings of poppy-heads, chamomile, centuary, sage and mint in bunches to dry. The walls are lined with shelves bearing an array of Delft jars of blue and white . . . [and] . . . on a desk are the great books and ledgers in parchment covers, while the counter is belittered with phials, pots and boxes of remedies ready for sale, such as the "Elixir Proprietatis", the "true Venice Treacle", the "Vatican Pills" and "Fioraventi's Balsam".[19]

It was still the empirical age of medicine. There seems no doubt that Silvanus Bevan soon acquired a laboratory for making many of his preparations; one of his assistants later commented that Bevan had "a still" for evaporating liquids. However, a copy of an early Pharma-copoeia actually used in the shop at about this time – the

Timothy Bevan (1704-1786). Together with his brother, Silvanus, Timothy Bevan established the early fortunes of the firm. He was a strict Quaker, with a reputation for being "cross and difficult to please".

Pharmacopoeia Londinensis (1677) – recommends some rather curious substances, which ranged from the commonplace (earthworms and dung) to the fantastic (horn of unicorn and the moss growing on a human skull). Some time before 1730 Bevan issued a wholesale list, *A Catalogue of Druggs, and of Chemical and Galenical Medicines, Prepared and Sold by Silvanus and Timothy Bevan in Plow Court, in Lombard Street, London*, which discarded some of the more ludicrous remedies (perhaps because they were in short supply!). But the list still included such specifics as *mumia* (or Egyptian mummy), human skull, and a Venice treacle which contained vipers.

This catalogue shows that by this time Silvanus had been joined in business by his younger brother, Timothy Bevan (1704-1786). It is written in the minutes of the Apothecaries' Society for 11 March 1731 that "Mr. Timothy Bevan, who as he says has been bred an Apothecary in the country and has been some time with his brother, Mr. Silvanus Bevan, a member of this Company desires his Freedom . . . by Redemption; ordered that on payment of £25 and 40s. to the Garden and the usual Fees and passing an Examination, he be made free". Soon after, Timothy became a Freeman of the Society and the two brothers went into partnership, appearing in a London directory as "Silvanus and Timothy Bevan, Apothecaries, Lombard Street".

Silvanus epitomised the ease with which apothecaries could enter the field of medicine. Increasingly, he practised as a physician and became known as Dr. Bevan. His interest in the subject is evinced by a letter he sent in 1743 to the Royal Society (of which he had been elected a Fellow in 1725), entitled, *An Account of an Extraordinary Case of the Bones of a Woman Growing Soft and Flexible.* He also took a keen interest in smallpox inoculation, corresponding on the subject with Dr. James Jurin, a well-known physician of his day, who also supported the practice of inoculation.

Silvanus Bevan became a rich man and lived in some style at Hackney at this time. At the age of seventy in 1761 he was reported by a visitor to be:

> living well on good food and drinks . . . In the house [were a] variety of curious paintings and rich old china, and a large library containing books on most subjects . . . He says his intellects are as strong as ever, and that he has as much pleasure in reading a book now as he was when a young man. He was bred a chymist and apothecary, but has practised as a physician for many years. Now he is retired from all business. He is a batchellor [sic], and his brother, who has a family of children keeps on the trade at the old shop in Lombard Street. Was introduced into [the] Royal Society by Sir Isaac Newton (so said William Jones gynt) visits and is visited by most great men of taste, also by the Ministry, being one of the principal leading men among the Quakers.[20]

Meanwhile, at Plough Court Timothy does not seem to have been interested in the practice of medicine, and when Silvanus died in 1765 at the age of seventy-four, the style of the firm became "Timothy Bevan and Sons, Druggists and Chymists, Plow Court". These two sons of Timothy's first marriage (confusingly named Silvanus and Timothy) were not destined to promote the affairs of the drug house. Silvanus left within two years to pursue a career with one of the notable banking families of the country, Barclays, and to become a partner in a brewery – by no means an unusual combination for a Quaker. Timothy died in 1773, predeceasing his father.

The elder Timothy appears to have carried on the business alone and lived mainly at Plough Court, where he seems to have lived up to the popular conception of a Quaker. A thin man, of medium height, Timothy had an uncommonly sallow complexion, which was hardly enlivened by a white wig and light drab. According to one Quaker diarist: "he was of a temper the very opposite of cheerfulness and affability, [so that] in all his deportment you seemed to hear the language of 'Stand Off!'."[21] In 1775 he retired to Hackney, handing over the business to the younger son of his second marriage, Joseph Gurney Bevan (1753-1814). Timothy still continued to visit Plough Court occasionally until his death at Hackney. Future expansion was firmly now in the hands of one man – Joseph Gurney Bevan – who as we shall see was to effect a sharp break with the firm's apothecarial roots.

1

JOSEPH GURNEY BEVAN TAKES COMMAND

I hope I shall always endeavour to vend good Drugs & genuine medicines & I intend to be properly paid for them . . . I would rather decline having [my products] brought into an improper comparison with those traders in Medicine whose only maxim seems to be to sell things *Cheap.*

J. G. Bevan to William Harvey, 28 April 1778.

From 1775, when Joseph Gurney Bevan took control of the business, we are allowed our first real sight of the pharmacy at Plough Court. A series of letter-books survive, which give an unprecedented insight into eighteenth- and early nineteenth-century life and constitute a unique record of the firm.[1] Usually written and signed by a partner (or sometimes a clerk), the letters in the books were regarded as the original document, and the letter was then transcribed again for despatch to the correspondent. Those were leisurely days and often not more than one missive was dispatched in a day. The letter, though, might occupy two foolscap sheets and Bevan was frequently discursive.

Like his father, Timothy, Joseph Gurney Bevan was a staunch Quaker and many of the letters begin: "Esteemed friends"; "Dear brother". The months at the head of the letter are always numbered, never named – another Quaker practice. When he was seventeen years old, we are told, Joseph was "under serious impressions of mind [and] one of the first things he thought it his duty to make a change in was the use of the heathen names of the month".[2] He also foresook the fashionable apparel of his youth, which had so grieved his mother, and reverted to the sombre raiment favoured by other Friends.

Joseph not only adopted his father's beliefs, he also inherited a firm which manufactured and sold drugs wholesale and retail. But this was by no means his only business. The young Bevan spent much of his time shipping bales of textiles to Europe – usually employing a complicated system of codes to facilitate their dispatch and collection – on behalf of Friends and correspondents in East Anglia. Peter Colombine, James Tuthill or Gurney & Ellington sent down bales of cloth from Norwich by coach (if urgent) or by wagon and Bevan undertook to secure a ship for them to various Mediterranean ports. Destinations included Cadiz, Gibraltar, Malaga, Seville, Bilbao and San Sebastian. The connection with the Gurney family through his mother had given Bevan this East

Anglian contact. It proved to be a profitable, if minor, sideline; in some of the years before the American War of Independence terminated the trade Bevan's profits were over fifty percent. Many of the other letters concern Bevan's dealings in stocks and annuities for his family and Friends. He also transacted business in relation to his property in South Wales. After the 1770s, however, Bevan spent less and less time on the woollen side of the business and eventually dropped it entirely as conditions forced him to concentrate increasingly on his pharmaceutical trade.

Announced Joseph in one of the earliest letters in 1777: "I have lately succeeded my Father Timothy in business, who has for many years been established in an extensive trade for Medicines". Bevan had no pretensions as a medical man and, apart from requesting the occasional botanical specimen on behalf of his friends, never discussed scientific or medical matters in his letters. Indeed, it was during Bevan's management of the business that a significant break was made with the firm's apothecarial origins. Joseph Bevan made no attempt to become a member of the Apothecaries' Society or even of the Grocers' Company; in fact, he joined no London company until 1789, when at the age of thirty-five he chose the Woolmen's Company, which had close links with the Society of Friends.[3] Bevan was now firmly along the route towards being a manufacturing and wholesale chemist.

Nevertheless, it is also true that the firm had a reputation for prescribing as well as dispensing medicines. Bevan's correspondence contains references to all the most celebrated herbs, barks, roots and leaves of the period, alongside the relatively less popular "chemical medicines" – alum, arsenic, antimony, calomel, cream of tartar, magnesia, several salts and nitric and sulphuric acid. Occasionally, Bevan sold genuine patent medicines. In 1779, on behalf of one of his West Indian clients, he applied unsuccessfully to Newbery for a certificate to manufacture James's Powder. Hence Bevan employed an apothecary. On one occasion in 1780 he enquired as to the character of one Charles Rugge: "I want his character as an Apothecary . . . The place in my shop for which he applied is to make up prescriptions & serve retail customers to whom advice is also frequently wanted to be given – He will also now and then be required to go out to see patients who are customers at the shop."

Bevan thus did not work alone. Moreover, much of the work concerning the bales of wool and cloth and medicines was taken up by a clerk. During the 1770s and 1780s this man was a clerk named Graham, who was kept very busy dealing with correspondence, and packing and dispatching orders. During the periods of Bevan's absence – and he was frequently away in the autumn – almost the whole of the administration was in Graham's hands, though his master still had overall responsibility and took care of the pricing of the goods on his return. When Graham was ill in October 1779 it was therefore a great hindrance to Bevan, even though business was not brisk. To one customer he wrote by way of apology: "Graham has been confined above a fortnight with the Gout."

Assistance of a different kind was received from Joseph Jewell (1763-1843), who began at Plough Court as a porter. Jewell was an extraordinary character, who started work as a farmer's boy in Berkshire at the age

Strychnos Nux vomica

Published by Phillips & Farden, April 1807.

Joseph Bevan derived most of his drugs from plants. For example, strychnine was produced from the seed of the berry of the Strychnos Nux Vomica, *illustrated here in William Woodville,* Medicinal Botany: Containing Systematic and General Descriptions with Plates of All the Medicinal Plants *(London: John Bohn, 1832). (Courtesy Royal Pharmaceutical Society of Great Britain)*

of eight. After joining Bevan in about 1790, he soon began to help in the laboratory under his master's guidance and eventually ended his career as a partner with Luke Howard, another noted Quaker pharmacist, who was to play an important future role in Allen & Hanburys.

Bevan evidently took over a flourishing trade. The home market for drugs was a large one and the firm was well situated in the heart of the commercial capital of the world. Bevan's largest single group of domestic customers were druggists and merchants, such as Horner & Fawkes, who exported or retailed their own preparations. The London Hospital and St. Thomas's Hospital were also regularly supplied with drugs by Bevan. Additionally, he dealt with the "country" trade outside the capital, where Friends and relations were a useful outlet. Sometimes the arrangements were reciprocal; Bevan supplied various drugs in return for some kind of

London 17th 1mo 1777

James Suthill & Son

Enclosed 4 Letters in a frank

Peter Colombine & Sons London 18th 1mo 1777

Esteemed friends. I have yours of the 16th inclosing a bill value £27:17:8 which is to your credit. The Bilboa Ship is full & the Capt. has refused the bale. I mentioned to you she was a small vessel and likely to be soon full from the great quantity of goods excluded from the N:a S:a del Rosario. The present ship is also one Nill. the San Joseph y San Joachin Juan de Balliboan of 90 Tons. The bale must not be shipped yet. If you have orders for Bilboa I think you cannot depend on longer time than a month to send them by this vessel. The Nephew is to continue in loading all the month. I am your obliged friend

J G Bevan

A page from Joseph G. Bevan's letter-books, showing a letter sent in 1777.

22

raw material. The correspondence with fellow Quakers has a genteel ring. In 1782 he wrote to a customer in Kettering for payment, but added: "I desire thee not to straiten thyself." This personal character to the correspondence was to disappear as Bevan became increasingly involved with the export trade.

Abroad the problems Bevan faced as a young man were to be formidable, especially those stemming from the disruptions caused by the American War of Independence. Exports of pharmaceutical products at this period to Continental Europe were limited and therefore the state of the transatlantic trade was crucial to Bevan. It had formed one of the mainstays of his father's business. Thus it was not long before Bevan was picking up the threads of this trade. In 1776 he wrote to one customer in the West Indies: "My father having resigned his business to me, has put in my hands the order contained in your favour of the 15th of 6 month; which I have accordingly executed and shipped."

Many of Bevan's customers were located in the troubled American colonies, particularly the urban centres of Philadelphia and New York, but the majority of his drug's trade was with the West Indies. Here most of his customers were medical practitioners – apothecaries, surgeons and physicians – though Bevan also dispatched to wholesale druggists. Many of these West Indian physicians styled themselves as "Dr." and were addressed as such by Bevan in his letters. But not too much should be made of this. The title of "doctor" was freely bestowed at that time (and indeed much later) and merely denoted a medical practitioner. Apo-thecaries sometimes called themselves "doctor" or were known as such to signify respect. It was all very vague and even Bevan, who, interest-ingly, had a policy of charging wholesalers less than practitioners, admitted: "it is difficult for me to know where to draw the line between a simple practitioner & a druggist – some practitioners order largely as Druggists and many Druggists practise physic – ."

The economic status of Bevan's customers in the West Indies also appears to have varied a good deal. Some evidently practised medicine as a sideline and had extensive plantations and other investments. Others appear to have been apothecaries and surgeons out to seek their fortune in a land where the climate and opportunities seemed to be so bright. All estates needed a doctor to keep slave labour healthful and efficient as well as to tend to the needs of the owner. The openings for the charlatan were also, of course, correspondingly great and one con-temporary writer lamented the activities of a Mr. Apozem in the islands, who apparently spread "depopulation far and wide" with the aid of laudanum, mercury and opium, and whose "maxim it was that the dead tell no tales".[4]

Though Bevan never sold to Mr. Apozem, his dealings with the West Indian trade were to stretch his gentle patience to the limit. On taking over the business he was soon writing to claim outstanding debts. To one he corresponded: "I must also put thee in mind on behalf of my Father that thy account with him is yet unsettled & as he has retired from business it is particularly desirable that he should have his debts collected." To another, in Antigua: "As I have been witness to the long delay that my father has experienced in his dealings with thou, I must beg leave to mention, now in the beginning of ours, that it will by no means suit me to wait so long and therefore I would suggest that thou would on thy side use the punctuality becoming a man of business; & on mine endeavours will not be wanting to supply the commissions in a satisfactory manner."

The slight misgivings evident in this letter highlight the chief characteristic that was to mark all Bevan's transatlantic dealings during the 1780s and 1790s – the difficulty of obtaining payment for his goods. Bevan's terms were reasonable enough and standard for the time: a year's credit from the date of the invoice, with 5 percent rebate for prompt payment; and 5 percent interest on any outstanding account after the first year. He normally expected payment in bills of exchange drawn on a house in England or in the form of merchandisable produce, such as ginger, rum or sugar. Usually Bevan preferred swift payment and was not prepared to tie up his money in bonds or mortgages in the West Indies.

Nor did he care to become involved in any other aspects of the transatlantic trade. Inevitably, his connection with the developing economies of the New World brought with it requests for many items besides drugs. At various times Bevan sent surgical instruments, medical books, spirits and, on one occasion, a complete chimney piece and window glass! The firm at this time did not manufacture medical instruments and so these had to be bought from specialist manufacturers, of which there were several in London. Trusses, catheters and scapels were sometimes dispatched by Bevan alongside his drugs, though he once had to admit defeat when he was asked to supply an ivory syringe "so large as a pint"! Usually, Bevan supplied such items reluctantly, replying to a New York request for lancets and mortars in 1777: "I am obliged by the offer of thy consignments, but I rather desire to stick to my own business of a Chemist & Druggist . . . and only supply either medicines or necessaries connected with them." The reluctance increased as the debts of his customers rose. To Thomas Brown, in Montego Bay, a customer who was to die leaving Bevan saddled with an unpaid bill totalling £1,800, he wrote:

> As to Brandy, Wax Candles, & Sugar Candy I must remark, as I did before respecting Tea, it is entirely out of my line to go largely into these articles . . . [but] . . . if the debt on account of medicinal articles & their appurtenances were reduced & kept in a proper degree of proportion to the annual supplies, if then I was furnished with *money* to purchase some other articles, I might have no objection to make.

These requests also had to run the gauntlet of Bevan's Quaker censorship. In 1778 he refused to send Brown any pistols, since he was "a member of a Society one of whose most conspicuous tenets is the disallowance of Arms". Any books that were to be sent across the water were carefully inspected by Bevan for "vanity or evil". For example, he declined to send a pocket dictionary to Barbados because he found it "to contain a collection of some, not very [?] decent, & heathen, fabulous accounts that I was afraid might tend to the hurt of young minds". Nevertheless, Bevan sometimes found his West Indian connections useful. Once he supplied books to a West Indian buyer, which he had obtained from his friend Dr. Fothergill; Bevan asked as a favour for Fothergill for "some of the many curious kinds of fern which your Island produces . . . They should be planted in a wooden box covered with hoops and the seamen should be desired to thro' a Tarpaulin over them on the appearance of what they call the white caps."

Undoubtedly, Bevan was not helped by the very high prices of his drugs, something for which he was not entirely responsible. Again and again he wrote to his customers apologising for his high prices. In 1776 he wrote to a buyer in Jamaica that snakeroot was very dear: "the cause is the stoppage of the American trade. Opium is also much higher than I have known it – The insurance is raised on account of the American privateers." A year later he wrote to another correspondent on that island: "You will be pleased to observe that the demand of many articles for the use of the navy has exceedingly raised the price – This is particularly the case with Turpentine and also the Oil; which are also dearer from the failure of the supply from America. I did intend to have increased the quantity of any important drug that might be cheap; but find very few in this predicament."[5] Manna, senna, opium and jalap were also inflated in price; many of these came from Italy and the frequent wartime disruption to the Mediterranean trade meant that Italian drugs were dearer than Bevan could remember.

However, as Bevan was to stress continually, his products should not be judged on price alone – quality must also be taken into account. For this reason he refused to circulate catalogues or publish price lists as did many of his competitors. He contented himself in the knowledge that, in his view: "honest and able apothecaries are not numerous & people in the long run will distinguish such from pretenders." Bevan hammered at this point so often that it becomes a kind of *leitmotif* in his letter-books. In 1777 he wrote: "The Castor Oil is much dearer than you have had it; but I think it is some of the best I ever saw, being pale in colour and very insipid. It is to be had much cheaper, but that has a hot, fiery taste & I think for my own part in medicine quality is always the first object." In 1783 he returned to this theme:

> There is one general observation will strike at first sight, which is that a comparison of prices *only* is not a fair way of estimating the dealings of different persons. Credit & quality of the things sold, must also be taken into account, as the former will considerably affect value, & the latter will affect in the greatest degree . . . On the whole I have to remark that taking my correspondence in general I believe none of my customers in Jamaica can fairly complain of me – For a seller of cheap medicines I never sett up; for a preparer of genuine ones I always did & while I continue in the trade always intend to do.

The high quality of Bevan's products, however, does not seem to have encouraged speedy payments from across the water. The problem of collecting his West Indian debts was to become Bevan's greatest headache. This partly reflected the state of the Caribbean economy. The prosperity of the planters was shaky and by 1776 the British West Indian Islands were in decline. Moreover, despite a seemingly excellent climate and situation, life on the islands was often precarious. Earthquakes and hurricanes were an occasional hazard and many of the settlers succumbed to fevers and other ailments, often by building their dwellings in the most unwholesome areas. For some the lifestyle and climate provided ample opportunity for idleness, dissipation and other pursuits that Bevan referred to, darkly, as the "vices of the West Indies". Bevan's belief that the environment of the West Indies was not conducive to hard work and steady habits was no doubt quickly confirmed by his business dealings. He was soon complaining that: "I am put to a considerable inconvenience by the tardiness of many of my [West Indian] friends in answering my demands, as I am not like a person who having long enjoyed a profitable business has many thousands to employ in it." In 1782 he wrote to Thomas Brown of Montego Bay: "I cannot help being fearful that part of thy inability to satisfy me arises from having entered more largely than was proper into extensive concerns of business, which has diverted into other channels that property which should have maintained our correspondence, occasioning an accumulation of debt to which I had no idea in the beginning of our connection."

Though American buyers were generally more prompt, some of them, too, occasionally disappointed Bevan's expectations. To William D. Smith in New York City, Bevan wrote in 1779:

> I am so well acquainted with the mode of correspondence with my father, & that from the time of its commencement to the present he never received a farthing remittance from thee –. It is probable that thou will urge the difficulties of the times, & the particular hardship to which thou has been subject, as occasion of thy inability to observe the regularity with [my father] which thou otherwise might, – but it must be remembered that when your connection began and for a considerable while after times were not so hard – I also could mention a druggist in America, who tho' the object of popular insult & at one time an exile from his business and situation yet has uniformly continued to make remittances.

Bevan's relationship with Dr. John Moodie of Jamaica typified his problems with the West Indian trade at this time. Moodie had originally run his affairs alongside Dr. James McIntyre and it was to this partnership that Bevan had dispatched in 1776 an order of medicines valued at over £1,000, a colossal sum for the time. Commented Bevan: "Amount of the invoice is so large my expressing my desire that you will use your exertions to make me as speedy remittances as the circumstances of your trade, and your prior engagements to my father, will so kindly allow." This fond hope, however, was not fulfilled, at least as regards payment; though Moodie & McIntyre were not slow to follow their order up with others, which raised their account to over £1,500. Apparently, Moodie was chiefly responsible for the accumulation of debt, which led to the dissolution of the partnership in about 1779. Bevan seems to have discovered this shortly afterwards, by which time McIntyre was writing with a fresh order for £400 of goods. This immediately put Bevan in a difficult position. McIntyre had made no mention of the dissolution in his previous letter and so, wrote Bevan: "I might therefore determine to decline [the order] wholly; but then the difficulty arises of depriving my friend of what he expects as the means of emolument". Eventually, he sent a third of the order, with promises of further consignments if payment followed. As to Moodie, Bevan was then forced to write to James Robertson, a business friend in the West Indies, and insist that Moodie make a will which made Robertson his executor, so that upon Moodie's death Bevan would have first claim on his property.

By 1780 Bevan was still grappling with "the tedious affair of McIntyre's and Moodie's debt". In March of that year Moodie had sent a paltry £52, which brought forth Bevan's caustic observation: "I had expected from the tenor of thy letter a larger remittance". Nevertheless, he sent out more goods to the value of £109. By now Moodie was "poorly" and was due to visit England in an attempt to recover his health. Any hope that Bevan had that he would be able to use his personal persuasion on his tardy client was soon dashed, since when he arrived in late 1790 he seemed to have lost all interest in living. Recorded Bevan: "His lodging is at a dirty Cabinet Makers in a dirty street in the Strand, which his friends cannot prevail on him to leave." He did manage to arrange an interview with him, after which he concluded: "Poor Dr. Moodie seems to me to be a Man by some means totally unqualified for business". After staying about six months he returned to the West Indies and died shortly afterwards, leaving accumulated debts to Bevan of over £1,000, which were presumably never collected.

It was hardly surprising that Joseph's requests for money became ever more pressing. "I really am in much need of money", he wrote to Dr. Ashton Warner, in June 1779, "& . . . I hope thou will be able to relieve me on thy arrival by a handsome remittance." Turnover in the pharmaceutical side of the business in 1776 was £4,762, yielding a profit of £625; in 1777 turnover was £6,778, bringing a profit of £1,250; a turnover of £6,527 in 1778 brought a profit of £1,477; in 1779 turnover was steady at £6,684, while profits remained at about the same level of £1,268.[6] This indicates a healthy return, but it must be balanced against unpaid debts, which at the end of 1776 totalled £2,603 and remained steady at about £2,000 until 1780.

If success as a businessman is rated by an enterprise's profitability, then clearly Bevan did not do very well. The failure is even more striking in view of the high profits that could be made on drugs in this period. Obituarists and memoirists, normally so reticent in such matters, put the state of affairs quite bluntly: they record that Bevan retired in 1794 "not, as is often the case, with an increase of property, but with some considerable diminution of it".[7] Why was this? Was it due to the unfavourable circumstances of the time, or due to Bevan's own business policies?

The clues can be found in the letter-books. Money could be made in the late eighteenth-century drugs trade, but usually by means that Bevan found distasteful. This was particularly true in the field of quack and patent medicines, where vast profits could be accrued, but upon which Bevan had very fixed views. When he was asked, as he often was, for

By his MAJESTY's Royal Letters Patent,

Dr. ROBERT WALKER's

Genuine and True Original Patent JESUITS DROPS,

And SPECIFIC PURGING REMEDY.

P epared and fold by JOSEPH WESSELS, Patentee and Succeffor to the late Dr. Walker, (as may be feen by his Will, a Copy of which has already been inferted in all the News Papers) at my Warehoufe, No. 45, the Corner of Fleet Lane, oppofite New Newgate, in the Old Bailey, where I prepared the *Patent Jefuits Drops, and Specific Purging Remedy* in Dr. Walker's Life Time, (who died in the Year 1761) and ever fince. All others fold in the Old Bailey under that Title are fpurious, and a bafe Impofition on the Public.

THE Virtue of the Patent Jefuits Drops being univerfally known, and the many thoufands that have experienced the happy Effeᵉs of them, let it fuffice to fay, they are a fovereign Remedy for Weakneffes and Obftructions in the Urinary Paffage, Gravel or Stranguary, incident to both Sexes ; likewife in fcorbutic or rheumatic Complaints for the Stone in the Bladder, and all Diforders in the Stomach, being void of all Mercurials, operating by Urine. Beware of Miftakes as feveral Compofitions are fold in the Old Bailey under that Title, which are fpurious.

Likewife *Dr. Walker's genuine Specific Purging Remedy*, which totally eradicates all Injuries in the Venereal Diforder, from the flighteft to the moft malignant Cafe, and purifies the Blood, with ample Directions. One Pot is fufficient in a flight Cafe.

At my Warehoufe as above, I continue (as in the Life Time of Dr. Walker) to give Advice *Gratis*, in all Cafes of Surgery and Phyfic, which I have practiced with Succefs Thirty-fix Years. The Bottles are fold at 5s. and 2s. 6d. each, and the Specific Purging Remedy, at 2s. 6d. the Pot.

Sold likewife by my Appointment, at Mr. Mackinder's, No. 5, Tottenham Court, and at Mr. Robinfon's, the King's Arms, Caftle Street, two Doors from Newman Street, Oxford Market ; at Bates's Printing Office, No. 16, Cumberland Street, near the Middlefex Hofpital ; Meffrs. Richardfon and Urquhart, Bookfellers, No. 91, next Door to the Print Shop, under the Royal Exchange; (all others fold about the Exchange are fpurious) Mr. Edmonds, at the Shoe makers, in Frying Pan Alley, oppofite St. Thomas's Hofpital, Southwark; Mr. Benjamin, Bleeder, Ship Yard, Temple Bar ; Mr. Stainford, at the White Hart, Greenwich ; at Mr. Byrn's Tin Shop, Spur Street, Leicefter Fields ; and at Mr. Lifter's, Grocer and Tobacconift, oppofite Shadwell Market, Ratcliff Highway. All others fold in Wapping, Saltpetre Bank, and in that Neighbourhood, are Counterfeits and Impofitions on the Public. Fer your Health's Sake, when you purchafe a Bottle, fee that my Name is wrote on the outfide, Jofeph Weffels, and that my Pots are fealed with my Cypher, J. W. without which it is a fpurious Compofition, and may be of the worft Confequences if taken.

☞ As feveral Perfons have lately been impofed on with a SPURIOUS Medicine, by thofe Impoftors in the Old Bailey, on the Directions of which the two initial Letters of my Name were forged, has determined me to write my Name in full Length on the outfide of each of my Bottles, and likewife on the firft Page of my Directions, given with my Bottles and Pots.

When a Medicine has raifed and fupported it's Reputation above Twenty Years, by the many thoufand Cures it has performed, Quacks and Empirics naturally endeavour (through their Incapacity to find an Equal) to imitate and impofe on the unhappy Patient fome Compofition no ways fimilar, and frequently dangerous to the Conftitution, and thus, by little mean and villainous Arts, deprive the Public of the Benefit from the Original, and rob the Patentee of his Property. This Villainy is now practifed in the Old Bailey by a Set of Impoftors, who have imitated my *Patent Jefuits Drops and Specific Purging Remedy*. There is no doubt but the Public will fhew fuch Refentment as fo bafe and infamous an Attempt deferves.

†‡† As a Proof of the Arts made Ufe of by thefe Impoftors, the following is fufficient : They have commenced Doctors, and in order the better to impofe on the Public, have copied in their Handbills and Advertifements Cures which were performed fo long ago as 1758, by my Predeceffor, Dr. Walker, and likewife Copies of Cures, which they inform the Public they have performed on Perfons who do not, nor ever did exift. Thefe Gentry are proper Perfons no doubt, to deal out Advice in Phyfical and Chirurgical Cafes !!

1770.

patent medicines, he replied: "Something of my reasons for not dealing in Patent Medicine Bottles and directions [are that] in general the directions abound with so many falsities & are calculated to make the purchasers believe that the medicine is prepared by the Inventor or his successor, that I have of late thought it inconsistent with my ideas of pure truth to meddle in them." Explained Bevan to another customer in the West Indies: "The directions in general, & the bottles in some cases profess that the medicine is made by the patentee or representatives of the patentee, & this when it is made by individuals appears scarcely consistent with that uprightness which our profession leads into – The directions are also stuffed with such extravagances that I am not easy to wrap about medicines of my preparing."

Bevan limited his custom to the City and transatlantic trade and mostly shunned the cut-throat "country" trade. To William Cowper in Chatham he wrote in 1784: "Thou will probably be able to buy from most of our Druggists who travel, at a much lower rate than I can sell . . . The competition for Country trade among them tempts them to beat each other down; but as I am not in the Country line I have not such an inducement & had I, I hope I should still keep an eye to fidelity in that trust which him who buys medicines ready-prepared reposes in him who is the compounder."

Bevan's Quaker beliefs also proved incompatible with profit-making on other occasions. He was uneasy, for example, at exporting saltpetre, a substance used in medicines at that time and also in gunpowder. Its export was prohibited during the American war and, in any case, the fact that it could be used in munitions conflicted with Bevan's strict pacifist ideals. "I wish another person than myself had the oversight of this business", he complained, "as it appears to be inconsistent for a person of my peaceable profession to be treating with the Board of Ordnance about ammunition." The American war brought other problems and Bevan often had to disappoint customers because "it is not permitted that anything shall yet be sent to New York in a mercantile way". Inevitably, Bevan's American customers devised a way to circumvent these restrictions by shipping goods to Canada, but Bevan would have none of it. In 1777 he wrote to William Stewart of New York: "My chief objection to send thy order by the ships which are now setting out for Halifax, and understood to carry goods for your place, is against the falsehood which is told in shipping them . . . [It is] too incompatible with my notions of truth for me to comply with." Bevan, in fact, would have little to do with smuggled goods of any description. In 1788 he wrote to a customer in Antigua that he was unable to send an ounce of musk. The India Company, who were responsible for its importation, had ceased doing so because it was adulterating their tea consignments. Any that did arrive (and in fact the Company's officers continued to bring it in, despite the restriction) was therefore strictly an illegal importation. Bevan decided that he would cease trading in it too, though in character-istic manner he sent some to a Barbadian customer "because you were not apprised of my scruple or intention".

In the West Indies the slave economy likewise troubled Bevan's

Broadsheet advertising Dr. Robert Walker's "Genuine and True Original Jesuit Drops", 1770. These were the kind of patent medicines Joseph Bevan avoided dealing in as far as possible. (Courtesy Royal Pharmaceutical Society of Great Britain)

conscience and his letters contain frequent references to his abhorrence of "the man-trade". He refused any kind of security that involved a mortgage on slaves. On one occasion when a Jamaican correspondent offered to meet his debt by selling slaves, Bevan quickly replied that he would prefer to wait longer for his money "than to be the means of obliging thee to sell thy negroes". He continued:

> The subject of slavery has at times, tho' not immediately concerned, engaged much of my attention; and, as I think it is an evil that wants removing, I wish every Man to look seriously about him & consider whether there is anything for him to do as an individual, to contribute towards its removal: as probably so great an affair will require the united effort of many; & if, as many think, it must be *gradually* abolished, let each of us deeply weigh what are the *steps* for us to take.

Bevan's kindly nature and attractive personality shines from his letter-books, but he lacked the ruthless streak of many of his contemporaries. He was not entirely to blame for the problems of the American war and the vicissitudes of the West Indian economy, but as the debts began to mount he scrupled to use the strong-arm tactics that might perhaps have brought him payment. As he himself admitted, he tended towards the "lenient side" in business. His stern little homilies ("The business, my friend, grows serious & I must treat it seriously") had no effect on men less honest than himself. The threat of debt-collectors and the courts were anathema to Bevan and he admitted that it was distasteful to him to detain "a fellow creature" in jail. As he came to the end of his business career in the 1790s, he remarked revealingly: "I got through business with as few disputes as most people; & now in the winding up, I had rather give up even a part of any due than contend."

The truth was perhaps that Bevan was not a businessman by inclination and he was only too pleased to relinquish his interest in the firm and turn to those pursuits which mattered most to him. Bevan's work within the Society of Friends was always his chief concern and "soon after his marriage, in the 24th year of his age, his usefulness in the Society became conspicuous, and his time was very much given up to its concerns".[8] Though no doubt Bevan was badly treated by some of his customers, he himself was not entirely blameless in his dealings. He often had to apologise for long delays in dealing with orders and sending medicines. On one occasion he wrote to a customer: "I ought to have paid more attention than I have done to thy wants & indeed to my own reputation for punctuality." On another, he pleaded that "I was taken up with some engagements that just then diverted my attention from business . . . [I] hope should we continue to have dealings that no such occurrence will again happen."

The reasons for these absences were inevitably to do with Quaker business. Increasingly in the 1790s the letter-books concern Bevan's dealings with Friends, rather than pharmacy. In 1786 Bevan's father, Timothy, died and financial transactions involving his estate and the substantial Bevan holdings of property in places such as South Wales occupied more and more of Joseph's time. His activities at Plough Court

The old Plough Court pharmacy, ideally situated for business off famous Lombard Street. The Bevans occupied the house in which the poet Alexander Pope was born in 1688.

had aged him and by the 1790s he was a tired man, able to walk only with the aid of a stick.

In July 1794 Bevan retired from the business and, as his health declined, devoted himself to writing. In fact, the *Dictionary of National Biography* describes him as a "Quaker writer", not a pharmacist. He had a reputation as a classical scholar and at the age of fifty began to learn Greek in order to read the New Testament. Henceforth, his literary output was considerable and included lives of Isaac Penington, Robert Barclay and other worthies.[9] He was also the editor of a small Quaker journal entitled *Piety Promoted*. After a long illness, met with characteristic fortitude and resignation, Joseph Bevan died at his home in Stoke Newington in 1814, his reputation secure as "the ablest of the Quaker apologists".

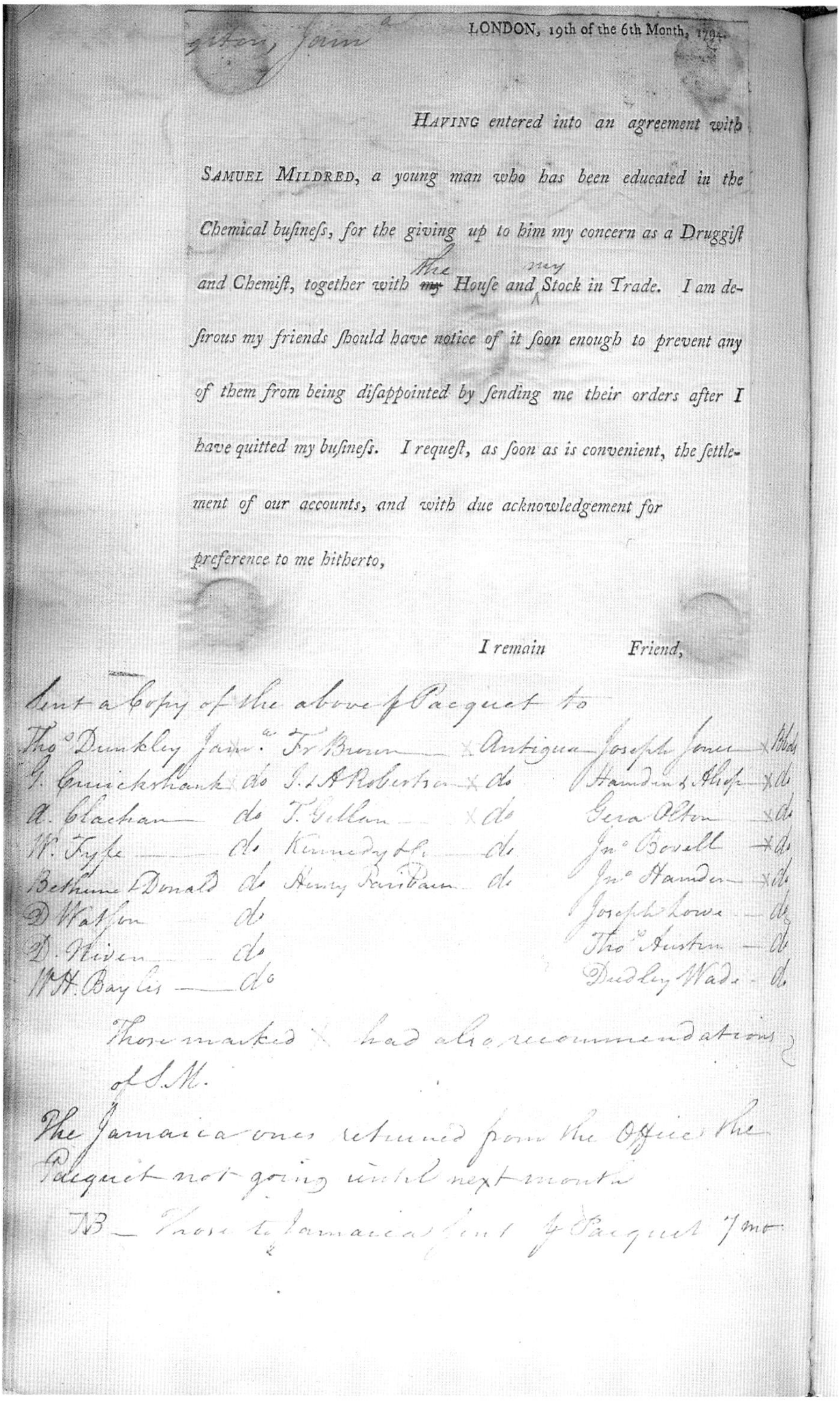

LONDON, 19th of the 6th Month, 1794.

HAVING entered into an agreement with SAMUEL MILDRED, a young man who has been educated in the Chemical business, for the giving up to him my concern as a Druggist and Chemist, together with the my House and Stock in Trade. I am desirous my friends should have notice of it soon enough to prevent any of them from being disappointed by sending me their orders after I have quitted my business. I request, as soon as is convenient, the settlement of our accounts, and with due acknowledgement for preference to me hitherto,

I remain   Friend,

Business card showing that in 1794 Joseph Bevan had given up the Plough Court pharmacy to Samuel Mildred, "a young man who has been educated in the chemical business".

32

Meanwhile, the business at Plough Court continued. In 1794 Bevan had given up the concern to Samuel Mildred, the son of one of the partners in the pharmaceutical firm of Mildred & Roberts. Commented Bevan: "[Mildred] is well qualified for carrying on the undertaking he is engaged in by his chemical knowledge & assiduity to sell a good article." Thus ended the Bevan connection with the pharmacy, since no other members of the family appeared willing to take over at Plough Court. (Was this because the other Bevans, such as Silvanus, the banker, no longer believed the business was a very sound one, or was Joseph, being a very strict Quaker, regarded as an uncongenial employer by the rest of the family?) By 1795 the firm was styled Mildred & Allen, since as Bevan explained: "[Mildred has] associated himself with William Allen Jr., who during the last two years of my remaining in business lived with me as Clerk; & I am by this means well acquainted with his merits, & am also much attached to him". By 1797 Allen had bought Mildred out with the sum of £525 and entered partnership with Luke Howard. A new era in the firm's history was beginning.

2

SCIENCE AND ENTERPRISE:
Plough Court under William Allen and
John T. Barry

[The extracts of opium] have been *boiled* down in *'vacuo'*, in an apparatus which J.T. Barry has lately introduced for the purpose of preventing the injurious effect of heat, and thereby not only increasing the strength of the Extract (as *2 or 3 to 1*) but giving more *uniform* efficacy to it. As the process has been much approved by several Physicians in London, it is likely that a paper on the subject will be handed to the Medical & Chirurgical Soc[iet]y.

Letter to Baron de Dupuy, 20 March 1819.

Joseph Gurney Bevan had firmly established Plough Court's reputation for quality products. But commercially he had been less than successful and it would have been obvious to his successors that the accumulation of bad debts could not be sustained if the business was to survive. The new partner William Allen must have watched the business drift in Bevan's last years with some misgivings, for it is evident that he had no intention of making the same mistakes when he took control.

William Allen was born in Spitalfields, London, on 29 August 1770, the eldest son of Job and Margaret Allen, who were members of the Society of Friends. Allen was educated privately and at a boarding school at Rochester, before joining the family's silk manufacturing business. At school, however, he had already demonstrated an aptitude for things scientific – at the age of fourteen he had constructed a telescope with which to observe the moons of Jupiter – and his interest in chemistry brought him to the attention of Joseph Bevan, who knew the young man's parents. Bevan offered William Allen a clerkship at Plough Court, which, to his parents' regret, was readily accepted in 1792.

Allen, as we have seen, soon took control of the firm. After 1797 he was in partnership with a friend Luke Howard (1772-1864), the business being styled as Allen & Howard. Howard, also a Quaker, had been a wholesale druggist in Bishopsgate before setting up as a retail chemist in Temple Bar. With his flair for devising apparatus for the making of heavy chemicals, Howard soon found himself in charge of the laboratory side of the Plough Court business, which was conducted at a separate location in Plaistow. Here Joseph Jewell was encouraged to begin manufacturing mercurials, which he did in a 12-foot square laboratory attached to his dwelling. Eventually the two businesses split and in 1806 the Allen-Howard partnership was dissolved, though as Allen explained to a customer, the separation was an amicable one and the two concerns "afford each other mutual support". Howard undertook to make certain heavy chemicals and process other articles, of which the subliming of camphor was one; while Allen concentrated on galenicals and on certain chemicals which were not required in bulk. Howard was henceforth free to build up a highly successful chemical manufacturing concern of his own,[1] leaving Allen in sole charge at Plough Court.

Eventually, William Allen's scientific and humanitarian interests were to make him one of the most famous Quakers of the nineteenth century. But on taking over the running of the firm, business matters inevitably occupied more of his time, and so it is Allen's hand we find in the company's letter-books. The style and content of his letters differ markedly from those of Joseph Bevan. A more business-like tone is evident, replies (unless they are to a close religious or scientific friend) are terser, and there are important changes in policy.

One policy, though, did remain unchanged – the commitment to quality goods, which had been Bevan's business motto. Indeed, some of Allen's comments to his customers precisely echo his old master. "I never profess to sell cheap", Allen stated in 1807, "but trust the quality of the articles will recommend them to those who are judges in our business."[2] Excusing his higher prices to another customer, Allen wrote that "it would have been easy to have forwarded inferior articles at a lower price". Allen was eager to please and the Plough Court correspondence still has a personal touch to it on occasions. In 1811 Allen wrote:

> I am sorry the articles did not answer thy purpose better. I make it a point to have everything of the best quality that is to be procured and am particularly at a loss to account for thy statement of procuring a better article than mine of magnesia . . . unless it were made from Epsom Salt which had not paid the Duty – I very much regret not having returned thy bill with prices annexed before the order was executed as it is extremely unpleasant to my feelings to do business in a manner not satisfactory to my correspondents.

The firm still stocked patent medicines and supplied their makers with raw material, though the amount of patent medicine sales at Plough Court was declining. Allen bought Dr James's Fever Powders from Francis Newbery, who supplied them in 1793 from the verbose address of "East end of St. Paul's on the coachway, five doors from Cheapside". He also did business with Hilton, Wray & Co, which supplied Turlington's Genuine and Original Balsam of Life. But like Bevan, Allen was keen to keep his dealings with such individuals to a minimum and also to differentiate his own business from that of mere "country" druggists dealing with the mass market. "I would sooner relinquish the business altogether", he told one correspondent in 1807, "than conduct it on the plan of other Wholesale Houses who lay themselves out for what is called the country trade." Allen was to underline this point some ten years later when some of his "esteemed friends" unfortunately provided him with an inappropriate order, which brought forth complaints about high prices. An affronted Allen replied:

Had I been aware that your correspondent was a mere dealer in the cheapest goods that he could procure I would never have executed the order at all. [And if he] expects to have selected Drugs & preparations made according to the London Pharmacopoeia on the same terms as the rubbish which I know to be sent out by some Houses for the American market, I must be permitted to say that it's perfectly unreasonable.

Allen was not a man to be trifled with. Unlike Bevan, he did not hesitate to claim his due from transactions. Credit was immediately tightened and Allen had no hesitation in refusing to extend it if payment was not forthcoming. On one occasion in 1807 he refused credit because of an unsatisfactory reference and communicated: "I am really concerned that any unnecessary delay shall take place, but having repeatedly suffered, and to no small amount by giving credit precisely in this way, I hope to be excused". Tardy payers were soon given a blunt reminder. A typical letter in 1808 begins: "W. Allen's respects to G.E. Hay and would thank him to request some of his friends in London to settle the above [account], which probably from its smallness has escaped his recollection." This even applied to such prominent figures as Humphry Davy, to whom Allen wrote in 1810:

It is not pleasant to me to say much about money matters, but on looking over my accounts I find that the last settlement with the Royal Institution was up to the end of the year 1806, and that beside the [account] for the Chemicals there is £105 due to me for 24 lectures begun near the close of 1806 and finished in 1807. If I were to charge interest, which I shall not there would be due to me £22.9.

If a gentle reminder failed, Allen, again unlike Bevan, had no hesitation in using other forms of persuasion. In his view, "treatment so base" as accumulating unpaid debts, would certainly "justify the application of those measures which the laws of our country enable us to employ". So he vigorously pursued debtors with the aid of his attorney. At times even the long arm of Allen's Quaker Friends was brought into play. In 1813 Allen wrote several letters concerning "the Itinerant Lecturer on Chemistry" Jackson, who had a longstanding £9 debt to Plough Court. Allen asked his correspondents to let him know when he appeared in their locality; and he was still pursuing the search as late as 1815. It is not clear from subsequent letters whether the debt was ever collected, but it is indicative of the lengths Allen was prepared to go in claiming payment. Quaker contacts were also used to scrutinise new customers. When a Mr. J. Atkinson of Pudsey, near Leeds, was setting up shop as a chemist and druggist with a stock of £200, an "esteemed friend" was asked: "What property of *his own* he has? His *character & habits* as a Man of Business? – And the probability of his success? also in *what place* it is proposed for him to set up?"

It was the winding down of the troublesome transatlantic trade, which had been the cause of so many of Plough Court's problems, that shows the greatest difference in Allen's and Bevan's handling of business. Allen decided at the outset that accounts would only be opened with the West Indies and America if solid security could be found. In 1807 Allen wrote:

Within the cartoon image:
RACING INTELLIGENCE—or MONEY, MAKES THE MARE TO GO.

Cartoon by Robert Cruikshank (1827), lampooning William Allen's third marriage to Grizell Birkbeck. (Courtesy Royal Pharmaceutical Society of Great Britain)

"I had not long ago determined against increasing a trade already extensive, by opening new accounts in Foreign Parts without a Guarantee on this side of the water." He added in 1811: "I am by no means inclined to extend my foreign business beyond its present limits"; and thereafter apologies to American and West Indian customers for refusing to open accounts become increasingly common.

Of course, other factors pushed Allen in this direction. The disruptions occasioned by the Napoleonic Wars made any transatlantic or Continental trading extremely difficult and risky. Allen wrote to Jesse Talbot in Baltimore in 1815:

> The World has of late years been so much agitated that I have been anxious to diminish rather than extend my Foreign correspondence and altho' I hope that the Governments of our respective Countries have concluded their arrangements in such a manner that we may reasonably expect a continuance of good understanding, yet I wish to avoid doing any Foreign Business upon long credit and have therefore invoiced the goods at very low prices, such as will enable thee to sell to advantage in the expectation that *thou will make thy Remittances within six months of the date of Invoice*. And I wish it to be clearly understood that on these terms only the Acct. is opened.

37

Thus Allen's policy was not entirely consistent. At this stage he was still finding his American contacts useful and Talbot was asked for "a plant called Pyrola Umbellata, which grows wild with you; and perhaps is well known", since Allen was "desirous of getting a little of it over, by way of trial". Allen also asked Talbot whether "*Baltimore* is a good place to purchase Sassafras *root*, Snakeroot, Indian Pink, & Seneka Root and what are the prices with you when plentiful and cheap". But in his dealings with Talbot he found himself prey to the same problems that had dogged Bevan, since the American proved to be yet another debtor. Allen's more robust tactics of dealing with such individuals proved inappropriate on this occasion. Allen later wrote somewhat contritely to Messrs Philip & Thomas, through whom he hoped to reclaim the debt: "we never desired to have harsh measures resorted to . . . [and] . . . if this unhappy catastrophe of [Talbot] giving way to the temptation of drunkenness could have been obviated by the loss of the whole claim, both my partner and myself would most cheerfully & thankfully have submitted to it."

No doubt such experiences rubbed in the lesson and hardened Allen's feeling that the American trade was not worth the trouble. In any case, circumstances were changing rapidly. Americans had less need of English drugs and other manufactured products. The foundations of America's own pharmaceutical industry were laid in the period 1818-22, when six enduring fine chemical manufacturers set up business in Philadelphia, and thereafter expansion was rapid.[3] By the 1820s and 1830s, therefore, it had ceased to be profitable to trade with the Americas and transatlantic orders gradually disappeared from the firm's order books. In 1844 a letter reports: "For many years past our attention has been confined to a home trade, having discontinued all our transatlantic correspondence." This was unlikely to have bothered Allen and his subsequent partners unduly. The English home trade was also expanding in the early nineteenth century. London's population, for example, doubled in the period 1800-40 (from one to two million) and a second wave of general hospitals was founded there in the early nineteenth century – Charing Cross, the Royal Free, University College, and King's College. In short, the firm had quite enough on its hands, without taking foreign orders, even from the Continent. "Our home trade is sufficient to satisfy us", was the reply to one foreign correspondent in 1819, and this situation was to remain unchanged until after 1850.

The truth was that, like many of his fellow Quakers, William Allen had far more on his mind than, as he once put it, "mere commerce". His outside interests in the humanitarian and scientific spheres occupied much of his time and were often intimately connected with his business. Christine Majolier (afterwards Alsop), his adopted daughter, wrote in her diary in about 1820 that Allen's "life was one of continual engagements; he rose early and lighted his own fire. The early hours were generally devoted to his correspondence, and during the time he was shaving, etc., his daughter used to read to him in Latin from Livy, and immediately after breakfast he would hear his sister, Anna Hanbury, read French . . . He seemed literally to have time for everything."[4]

Allen was a man of immense energy and great sensitivity, his passionate nature controlled (some might say repressed) by his rigid Quaker beliefs. Revealingly, the first entry in his diary – unhappily expurgated in its published form by zealous editors – reads: "Experienced some degree of comfort in striving against evil thoughts."[5] Other entries record Allen's efforts to lead a moral life. First month 2nd, 1794, he wrote: "I behaved foolishly in return for what I took to be disrespectful treatment from an ignorant and conceited person. I was favoured soon to perceive my error, and after a time went to him and confessed myself wrong, and in this I had peace. O self, self! how jealous thou art of thine honour!" Frequent bouts of low spirits, midnight fits of weeping and anxiety and, occasionally, the hasty expression of petulance or impatience were the visible signs of Allen's inward struggles.

Allen's vitality was apparent not only in his business, scientific, and humanitarian careers, but also in his full and varied family life. On 13 November 1796 he married Mary Hamilton of Redruth, who in the following September presented him with a daughter, Mary. The mother died a few days later and a grief-stricken Allen wrote: "O how I loved her – how we loved each other! I paid some attention to business today; but how heavily it went on!" In 1806, however, Allen married for a second time, taking as his wife Charlotte Hanbury of Stoke Newington. This time the marriage lasted ten years, before Charlotte Allen died on a visit to Geneva in 1816. Her husband, reported a partner at Plough Court, returned to London "under such heavy depression from the loss of his precious wife, that it is very doubtful when he may be able to resume his labours in the cause of humanity, if ever". The marriage, however, had linked together the Allen and Hanbury clans, a bond that was strengthened in 1822 when Mary, Allen's daughter, married Cornelius Hanbury. Their son, William Allen Hanbury, was born at Plough Court on 7 May 1823. William Allen clearly needed female companionship, for in 1827 he married for a third time, to Grizell, née Birkbeck, with whom he had been on friendly terms for several years. Even second marriages were not generally approved by Quakers, and Allen's third union at the age of fifty-seven to a rich widow of sixty-nine scandalised his fellow Quakers and was officially deeply frowned upon by the Society of Friends. It also brought the Society some bad publicity: the sight of a Quaker marrying for the third time was too good a target to miss, and Allen was mercilessly lampooned by the popular cartoonists of the day.[6]

Allen's humanitarian interests and his efforts, as he put it, "to promote the comfort and happiness of our species", were extensive and have been well documented.[7] Like Bevan, Allen abhorred the slave trade and was committed to its abolition. Thomas Clarkson became his friend in 1794, and he was on intimate terms with both Clarkson and William Wilberforce throughout his life. On the abolition of the slave trade he became an active member of the African Institution, which was formed to foster new trading links with Africa to replace the old slave trade, and also shared in the agitation for the world-wide abolition of slavery. In the educational sphere Allen was a member of the British and Foreign

*As a Quaker, William
Allen was firmly opposed
to the slave trade.* The
Anti-Slavery Convention
of 1840 *by B.R. Haydon
shows Thomas Clarkson,
President of the
Convention, addressing
the meeting, with Allen
sitting bottom left (in
gaiters). (Courtesy
National Portrait Gallery)*

41

School Society which was originally formed in 1808 for the support of Joseph Lancaster, a well-meaning but erratic Quaker educationalist, who pioneered schemes for teaching poor children. Educational topics featured in *The Philanthropist*, a quarterly journal, which Allen started in 1811 and maintained until 1817, and in which many other schemes of social improvement were discussed. James Mill was his chief contributor, and their friendly relations were undisturbed by radical religious differences. In 1814, Allen, with Jeremy Bentham, Robert Owen and four other partners, took over the New Lanark Mills near Glasgow (where Owen had built a model town) so that the industrial experiment might continue. It was not a happy partnership, since Owen and Allen proved incompatible as partners. Owen later characterised Allen as "active, bustling, ambitious, most desirous of doing good in his own way, (as a large majority of quakers are) . . . [who had] . . . returned from the continent of Europe, where he had come personally into communication with the Emperor Alexander of Russia and some other crowned heads, which turned his head".[8] Owen was unsympathetic to Allen's educational ideas and had little time for his Quaker "prejudices"; while Owen's contempt for the Lancastrian system and his partner's religious beliefs was hardly likely to endear him to Allen. Owen withdrew in 1829, with Allen retaining his interest until 1835.

Allen's renown brought him into contact with royalty. The Duke of Kent (the fourth son of George III and father of Queen Victoria) was interested in both Owen's and Lancaster's schemes; his affairs had become embarrassed, and Allen undertook to act as trustee for his estates, the Duke consenting to live on a fixed allowance until his debts had been discharged. When the allied sovereigns visited England in 1814, Allen was introduced to the Emperor Alexander as a model Quaker and a personal friendship arose between the two men. In August 1818 Allen left England, travelled through Sweden and Finland to Russia, saw Alexander at St. Petersburg, travelled to Moscow and Odessa, reached Constantinople in July 1819 and returned by the Greek islands, Italy and France to England in February 1820. In 1822 he went to Vienna to see Alexander again, chiefly in order to secure his influence in obtaining a declaration from the major powers that the slave trade should be outlawed. Allen made other journeys to the Continent in 1816, 1832 and 1833, examining schools, prisons and other institutions, and having interviews with statesmen and rulers, including the Crown Prince of Prussia, the King of Bavaria, and the King and Queen of Spain, to inculcate his views on reform. At home he took an interest in numerous philanthropic undertakings and his chief interest in later years was an "agricultural colony" with industrial schools, which he helped to found at Lindfield in Sussex.

In London Allen was also deeply involved with pharmaceutical politics. As one of the wealthiest and most prestigious chemists and druggists this was perhaps not surprising, especially in view of Allen's robust opinion of his profession's importance. He was an ideal spokesman for his fellow drug retailers and manufacturers at a time when their professional status was still to be defined and they faced attempts at control from both the government and other sectors of the medical profession, such as the apothecaries. In 1834 Allen opposed all

> interference on the part of the Government with the Trade & business of Chymist and Druggist under the specious pretence of increasing the respectability of the Profession, [since] experience has shown that all interference and meddling of Government in matters of Trade and Business does positive mischief. The corporation of the Apothecaries Company ought not to be permitted to exist in a country like England – and I hope never to see the day when monopolies shall be encouraged and Trade fettered in England as it is in some foreign countries.

In Allen's view, the chemists and druggists needed to organise themselves, otherwise they would be absorbed and controlled by outsiders. In 1812 the apothecaries had pressed for the establishment of a new medical body which would have wide powers over medicine, surgery and pharmacy. Opposition from the chemists and druggists began the following year, with Allen a member of a committee which ensured that the resulting Apothecaries' Act of 1815 did not affect the trade of the chemists and druggists. But the committee continued in being to keep a "watchful eye" on their interests, so that in 1841 when Benjamin Hawes's Medical Reform Bill proposed that chemists and druggists needed to be examined and licensed before they could practice medicine, it was ready once again to organise opposition. With William Allen heading the working committee, the proposals were once again successfully deflected (at least temporarily). But Jacob Bell (1810-59) of Oxford Street, another leading pharmacist, recognised that in the long term the chemists and druggists needed their own society to both educate their own membership and enhance their own prestige. Bell, like Allen, had been brought up as a Quaker, but this did not prevent him from lavishly entertaining leading artists, musicians and writers at his private residence in Langham Place, near Oxford Circus. It was there in March 1841 that Bell organised for interested members of the committee a "pharmaceutical tea-party". This led to a historic meeting at the Crown & Anchor Tavern in the Strand on 15 April 1841, where, under the chairmanship of Allen, the following resolution was seconded by Bell: "That for the purpose of protecting the permanent interests, and increasing the respectability of Chemists and Druggists, an Association be now formed under the title of the 'PHARMACEUTICAL SOCIETY OF GREAT BRITAIN'".[9]

The chemist and druggist could now join the ranks of the "professional men" – a fact possibly of greater importance to the more wealthy and prestigious houses than the country druggist. The Society had 2,000 members by the following year, by which time its School of Pharmacy had opened at 17 Bloomsbury Square, London. Allen became the first president of the Society and it may have been his connections in high places which secured the Royal Charter for the Society in 1843.

Allen's outside activities undoubtedly raised the prestige of the business. They may also have helped business directly. Allen was closely associated with the foundation of a colony for emancipated slaves in

William Allen's membership certificate for the Pharmaceutical Society, of which he was the first president. (Courtesy Royal Pharmaceutical Society of Great Britain)

44

Sierra Leone and on occasions sent medicines there. His links with scientific societies, such as the Royal Institution, also resulted in a few orders. But there was a price to be paid – his frequent absences from day-to-day business. He had relinquished his share in the laboratory to Howard, so that he could be "more disencumbered from business", but even so by 1816 he had to admit that he was "almost overwhelmed with a variety of engagements". Indeed, in the same year he had to reassure one customer that "the reports of my having withdrawn from the business is a mistake". Nevertheless, Allen was having to delegate more and more of the routine business to his confidential clerk, John T. Barry. Wrote the latter to one customer in 1813: "Our friend Wm. Allen this morning departed for Norfolk with his family, intending to stay six weeks, leaving myself (as usual) in charge of his trade affairs." Gradually, Allen relied upon Barry increasingly, as his diary documents:

> 1 January 1813: Business, John Barry took stock without me; this is the first time for nineteen years that I have not been actively engaged in it.

> 29 January 1813: This month has been a very busy one, but John T. Barry has taken almost the whole weight of the business off me.

> October 1813: On returning from Cromer: found my friend JTB has taken especial care of the business during my absence, and had things in excellent order.[10]

By the 1820s Allen's reliance upon Barry had become so great that certain aspects of the business, especially the practical side, entirely depended upon him. Thus, in 1822, Allen had to apologise for the delays in dealing with certain chemicals because Barry was absent from London. Appropriately, by that date Barry was a partner.

John Thomas Barry (1789-1864) was well qualified to direct the business. Although his education had been delayed by the need to care for his parents' large family, he had studied various aspects of medical science at Guy's Hospital in London, and had soon distinguished himself in practical chemistry. Joining the Plough Court business in 1804 as a clerk, he had soon reorganised the retail side of the business, devoting particular attention to the dispensing department. Before long Barry was in charge of the manufacturing laboratory and in 1818 he was admitted as partner, the firm henceforth being styled as William Allen & Co.

As Quakers, Allen and Barry shared similar interests. Barry laboured tirelessly for the abolition of the death penalty (before his death he is said to have stated that he had spent at least £500 in cab fares to the Home Secretary in endeavours to lift the death sentence for individual minor offenders) and was a liberal contributor to philanthropic organisations. But, unlike Allen, he was not a committee man and avoided publicity. Self-reliant, individualistic, and apparently something of a martinet in business discipline, he instead preferred to exercise his considerable talents behind the scenes. As such, he was a perfect foil for his famous partner.

Both men possessed a passion for science, especially chemistry, so reflecting the growing nineteenth-century development of the subject.

Better laboratory techniques and more accurate analysis helped in the identification of new substances from plants. Two particularly important figures were François Magendie (1783-1855) and Pierre-Joseph Pelletier (1788-1842). In 1809 Magendie conducted a series of ingenious animal experiments to study the toxic action of several vegetable drugs, such as *upas* and *nux vomica* (strychnine). Magendie held that the toxic or medicinal action of natural drugs depends on the chemical substances they contain, and that it should be possible to obtain these substances in a pure state. This idea was vindicated in the hands of Pelletier, whose investigation of drugs at the Ecole de Pharmacie in Paris founded the science of the isolation and identification of the large group of active principles or alkaloids. By pioneering the use of mild solvents, Pelletier (assisted by a student, Joseph Caventou) from 1817 successfully isolated a whole range of important biologically active compounds from plants – these included emetine, brucine, caffeine, cinchonine, colchicine, narceine, strychnine, veratrine, and, most important of all, quinine. Well over thirty alkaloids were discovered in the early nineteenth century by Pelletier and other chemists and many of these were soon introduced into medical practice.

Pelletier and Caventou urged medical practitioners to study the therapeutic properties of the pure cinchona alkaloids. This plea, which was soon acted upon, marked a new departure: until then the active principles of plants had been isolated for scientific rather than therapeutic purposes. Magendie was one of the first to experiment with quinine. Having first evaluated it in dogs, he then went on to treat patients. By including it in his revolutionary therapeutic manual, *Formulaire Pour La Préparation et L'Emploi de Plusieurs Nouveaux Medicaments* (1821), he ensured that knowledge of quinine spread quickly around the world. Magendie's small volume, the first of many subsequent editions, listed single chemicals rather than the usual standard mixtures and plants, so allowing his successors to build their knowledge of experimental medicine on a firm base. In Paris quinine was soon confirmed as a successful fever drug, which could be used instead of the nauseating powdered cinchona bark. Pelletier and Caventou began manufacturing it themselves in France, so gradually establishing the pharmaceutical industry. Quinine was also exported. In England in 1821, Thomas N.R. Morson (1800-74), who had studied alkaloidal chemistry in Paris, founded a successful London pharmacy, which specialised in quinine imports and the production of other alkaloids. By the 1830s Luke Howard was also a supplier of quinine and Luke's son, John Elliott Howard, became a world authority on the drug.

Another great influence in this period was Justus Liebig (1803-73), whose work involved the isolation, analysis and synthesis of new compounds, and included investigations on ethyl and benzoyl radicals, on the hydrogen theory of acids, and in agricultural chemistry. Liebig greatly advanced the development of practical chemistry by pioneering the use of his chemical laboratory at the University of Giessen as a teaching instrument. His transformation of animal and vegetable chemistry into organic chemistry and biochemistry guaranteed the emergence of pharmacy into the front rank of those disciplines engaged in the fight against diseases. Gone, it seemed, were the days of crude drugs of variable and unknown composition, to be replaced by pure compounds administered in accurate dosages. With the entry into medicine of such drugs, pharmacists needed to be skilled practitioners, whose technical skill and knowledge of science and chemistry could be guaranteed.

After taking up residence at Plough Court, William Allen devoted all his leisure time to the study of chemistry and other scientific subjects, attending lectures at Guy's and St. Thomas's Hospitals and the meetings of scientific societies. In a review in his diary of the year 1793, he wrote: "I have attended some of [Bryan] Higgins's lectures [a chemist and physician in Soho] – learnt something of shorthand and the new system of chemistry and instituted a plan for my future studies."[11]

In April 1794, he was elected a Fellow of the Chemical Society and on 3 July 1795 he noted in his diary that he was entered "physician's pupil at Thomas's Hospital". In October 1795, he was elected member of the Physical Society at Guy's Hospital. In January 1796 there are several notices in his diary of his working all night to prepare for lectures and making experiments, and on the 28th of the month he wrote: "Gave my second lecture this evening on 'Attraction'." On 28 March 1796 he recorded: "Our little Philosophical Society met the second time at Plough Court – confirmed the rules." This little gathering was the Askesian Society, founded with the idea of elucidating the latest advances in experimental science, a group which later included, besides Allen, Richard Phillips, Luke Howard, Joseph Fox, Henry Lawson, Arthur Arch, Astley Cooper, Dr. William Babington, A. Tilloch, Joseph Woods Jr., W.H. Pepys and Samuel Woods, the last of whom was president. It included a significant number of Quakers (such as Pepys and Phillips).[12] Favourite topics usually involved mineralogy and chemistry and amongst the Society's activities in 1800 was an experiment with laughing gas (nitrous oxide), which, related Allen: "took a surprising effect on me, abolishing completely, at first all sensation: then I had the idea of being carried violently upward in a dark cavern, with only a few glimmering lights." (Interestingly, despite the presence in the proceedings of an eminent surgeon from Guy's, Astley Cooper, the possibility of using the gas for surgery appears never to have been considered – a comment perhaps on the primitive state of surgery and antisepsis techniques at that time.)

In 1801 Allen became a Fellow of the Linnaean Society. He also appears to have taken an active part in the formation of the Royal Jennerian Institution; Allen met Jenner in 1802 and in the following year recorded that he was involved in establishing an institution for cow-pox inoculation. On 25 March 1801, Davy is first mentioned in Allen's diary: "Went to the Royal Institution with W.H. Pepys and R. Phillips to hear Davy's first lecture on 'Galvanism'. A most capital one. He bids fair to rise high in the philosophical world." In 1803 Davy suggested that Allen should deliver at the Royal Institution the course on natural philosophy he had given at Guy's. Allen, after some initial hesitation, accepted and began lecturing in the following year. In 1807, with Humphry Davy, Dr.

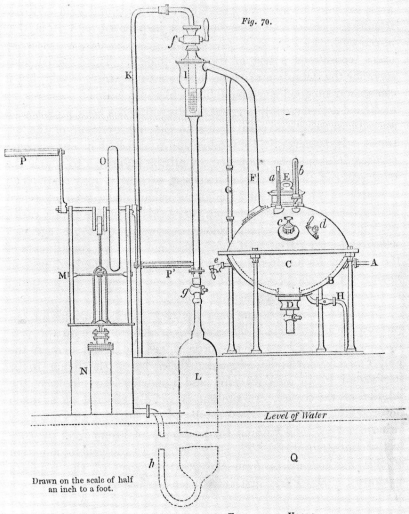

Fig. 70.

APPARATUS FOR PREPARING EXTRACTS IN VACUO.

Drawn on the scale of half
an inch to a foot.

A. Pipe for conveying steam to the steam-chamber.
B. Steam-chamber for heating the pan.
C. Body of the pan.
D. Aperture for the discharge of the contents of the pan. This aperture is fitted with a plug, which is removed on taking out extracts, and has a stop-cock for the discharge of liquids.
E. "Man-hole" for charging the pan, having a cap which fits on air-tight.
F. Neck for conveying the steam from the body of the pan.
G. Glass tube for indicating the boiling up of the contents of the pan.
H. Pipe for conveying the waste steam from the steam-chamber.
I. Perforated copper funnel for supplying a shower of cold water to the descending steam-pipe and condensing cylinder.
K. Pipe for conveying water from the cistern underneath the apparatus, to supply the perforated funnel.
L. Condensing cylinder, partly immersed in cold water, for receiving the steam from the pan, and the condensing water from I.
M. The frame of the air-pump.
N. The barrel of the pump, connected by the pipe h with the cylinder L, and standing in a cistern of water.
O. The fly-wheel of the pump.
P, P. Handles of ditto.
Q. Cistern of cold water underneath the floor.
a. Thermometer inserted in the pan.
b. Barometer, for indicating the exhaustion of the interior of the pan.
c. "Proof-stick," for taking out small quantities of the contents of the pan, to observe the state of inspissation, without destroying the vacuum.
d. Stop-cock for admitting air into the pan.
e. Valve for letting out the air on the admission of steam into the steam-chamber.
f. Stop-cock for regulating the supply of condensing water to the perforated funnel.
g. Stop-cock for shutting off the communication between the pump and the pan.

In vacuo *apparatus for boiling fluids at low temperatures to produce extracts, similar in design and principle to that used by J. T. Barry. Illustration from F. Mohr and T. Redwood,* Practical Pharmacy *(1849). (Courtesy Royal Pharmaceutical Society of Great Britain)*

Babington and several others, he assisted in the foundation of the Geological Society.

Also in 1807 Allen was elected to the Fellowship of the Royal Society, having refused the honour seven years before, probably because he felt it was undeserved or premature. Along with William Hasledine Pepys (another Quaker chemist and director of the Imperial Continental Gas Association), he had undertaken chemical experiments using the Eudiometer, a simple device designed by Pepys, which could measure gas absorption during a chemical reaction. In 1807 an important paper was delivered to the Royal Society, in which they proved that diamond was pure carbon, like charcoal, and that the materials did not contain hydrogen as was previously thought. They also proposed that diamond and all carbonaceous substances differed from each other only in the state of aggregation of their particles. Following on from this research the two men delivered papers on respiration in 1808 and 1809, describing the changes produced in atmospheric air and oxygen by respiration.

According to one historian, "Plough Court had by that time become one of the centres of scientific research in London."[13] Allen's laboratory became known as a repository of chemical reagents, a collection of which, from Plough Court, was exhibited to the National Institute of Paris by Professor Pictet in 1801. Allen was also very friendly with the eminent Swedish chemist, Baron Jons Jakob Berzelius (1779-1848), whose English manuscript on *A View of the Progress and Present State of Animal Chemistry* (1810) he had revised. In 1820 Berzelius had sent to Plough Court a quantity of the metal selenium which he had isolated in 1817.

John T. Barry's involvement with science can be seen in his family roots – two brothers had been Fellows of the Royal Society, one the youngest Fellow ever – his early medical training at Guy's Hospital, and his growing reputation as a keen and exact chemical experimentalist at Plough Court. His chemical activities were directed towards the business and he seems to have been particularly concerned with improving the standards of drug production. This manifested itself in about 1819 when Barry attempted to overcome the variability in drug preparation by evaporation *in vacuo*. In a patented apparatus of his own devising, Barry boiled fluids at a low temperature to produce extracts. According to Barry, "the *prices* of *these* Extracts are higher than those of the common; but their increased efficacy and uniformity will more than compensate." Clearly Barry envisaged some kind of mass production of such extracts, since in 1821 he wrote to a customer that the firm had "erected Apparatus for the purpose upon a large scale".

Yet, although the influence of science in industry was clearly growing at this time, it would be a mistake to stress this too much. Modern eyes would regard activities at Plough Court under Allen and Barry as shockingly "unscientific". Few technological breakthroughs occurred in pharmaceutical manufacture before the 1850s; alongside Barry's *in vacuo* method, only perhaps Joseph Bramah's invention of the hydraulic press in 1795 was of major significance. Barry's invention, though it was efficient and worked successfully, never came into general use – for some reason it never proved entirely practicable and the apparatus was expensive.

In drug preparation the rule of thumb still held sway. Indeed, Allen himself admitted that this was the problem with adulteration, which:

> is sometimes so artfully done as to escape the notice of the experienced and can only be traced by the effect when used medicinally, or by the tests which chemistry in *some* (but unfortunately *not all*) instances affords. This especially applies to vegetable powders . . . [and in fact] . . . wherever a substitute can be found without great danger of detection by the senses.

In such a situation, Allen often recommended drugs of which he clearly only had a vague idea of the effects. This produces some comic passages in the company's letters. Concerning a popular specific for gout, Allen communicated to one customer in 1812: "The Eau Medicinal . . . is a medicine not to be trifled with, but I certainly know that within the circle of my friends & acquaintances it has produced most beneficial effects – Sir Joseph Banks has taken it repeatedly – but I could by no means advise a full dose to be taken in the first instance." This was prudent: the saffron root from which Eau Medicinale was derived contained both colchicine (a mainstay of gout therapy until the 1960s) and veratrine, a cardiac poison. On another occasion, an applicant was advised that the firm found "kreosote" a "very valuable" remedy in some cases. More seriously, in such circumstances, the element of chance and error was introduced into the dispensing of drugs. "My dear Friend", begins a letter from Allen in 1822:

> I read thy letter on the subject of Sarsaparilla Extract with much pain – it is obvious that the extract returned is not Extract of Sarsaparilla. It smells like Extract of Stramonium, but it is impossible to say; and I am equally at a loss to say how the thing could have happened – Our Warehousem[an] Wm. Booz has been with us Six Years – he is a remarkably exemplary and steady character and very careful and competent in his business . . . I sympathise with thee very much under the feelings thou must have experienced on this trying occasion & I shall be anxious to hear that the parties are restored to health.

On an even more alarming occasion, the "dreadful poison" mercury was sent out to a buyer in an unlabelled bottle – a mistake in the dispensing department, which Allen quickly assured would not happen again. Dispatch and storage were obviously major problems at that time. Even the procurement of a regular supply of good-quality glass bottles proved difficult. In the 1820s, Allen tried the products of T. & R. Hawkes of Dudley but found their vials "defective in form", with necks either too narrow or too wide, their bodies too long, and told the firm that "there is another improvement necessary – *uniformity in size* – some of your 8 oz. hold little more than 6 oz.". But not until mid-century was a satisfactory supplier found. Once bottled, medicines had a disconcerting habit of deliquescing or becoming desiccated; often only a thick layer of wax across the top of the medicine prevented this – a practice which obviously would have done little to enhance its appearance to the consumer.

A page from William Allen's Plough Court Laboratory Calculation Book, 1795-8. (Courtesy Royal Pharmaceutical Society of Great Britain)

Emp. Pic. Burg. C

Pic Burgund	1/.	lb1..2	1..3
Ladani	17/.	℥9	9..6¾
Cera flav	2/1	℥3	5..
Resin	2d.	¼ ℥3	..½
Ol Macis p Expr	24/.	℥1	1..7½
Carbon,			3
Attend.ᵉ		3 hours	1..6
lb2	@ 7/3¾	..14..7½	..14..7¾

Sp Ammon

Ammon ppt	2/4	lb2 T	..3..¾
Sp Vin Rect	17/	2 Gals	1..14..
Coals		½ Bush.ˡ	9
Attend.ᵉ		½ a day	3..
16 Pints	2/6	£2....	2....9¾

Crystalli Tartari Pulveratæ

Crystalli Tart	£5.10	2 Cwt	11..
Attend.ᵉ		2 days	..12..
lb223	@ ½	£11..12..3½	£11..12..

Senna Pulv

Fol Sennæ	4/10	lb1½ ∧	7..3
Attend.ᵉ		4 hours	2..
lb1¼	@ 7/6	£ 9..4½	9..3

Pulv Asari Comp
Pharm. Edin.

Asarum	℥3½	1..6
Majoran	℥1½	3
Flor Lavend	℥1½	5
Attend.ᵉ	at 1½ hours	9
℥4½ @ 8d.	£..3..	2..11

Elect. Scammon

Gum Scammon	2/6	℥6 T (half Aleppo & half Smyrna)	8..9
Caryoph	12/.	℥3	2..6
Zinzib	4/6	℥3.	..4
Ol Carui	7/6	ʒ2	2
Syr Rosæ	1/8	lb1..6	2..3½
Attend.ᵉ		4 hours	..2..
lb2..2.	@ 7/6	..15..11¼	£ ..16..½

Sp Lavend

Ol Lavend	32/.	℥4 ∧	..8..
Sp Vin Rect	17/	4½ Gal	3..16..6
Coals	1/6	½ bush.ˡ	9
Attend.ᵉ		4 hours	2..
5 Gals or 40 Pts	@ 2/2¼	£4.7.6	£4..7..3

Lin Sapon

Sapon Hisp	½	lb4 T	3..10¼
Camphor	5/.	℥16.	5..7½
Ol Rorismarin	3/.	℥2.	..5..
Sp Vin Rect	17/.	1¾ Gal.	1..9..9
Attend.ᵉ		½ a day	3..
16 Pts	@ 2/8	£2..2..8	£ 2..2..7¾

Sp Nuc. Mosch

Nux mosch	32/.	℥12 T	1..6..6
Sp Vin Rect	17/.	3 Gals	2..11..
Coals	1/6	½ bush.ˡ	9
Attend.ᵉ		4 hours	2
48 Pints	@ 1/8	£4......	4....3

Magnes Ust.

Magnes	2/8	lb6..10 ∧	17..8
Charcoal			1..6
Attend.ᵉ		½ a day	3..
lb3	@ 8/4	£ 1..5..	£ 1..5..2

Sp Æther Vit

Sp Vin Rect	17/.	3 Gals	2..11..
Acid Vitriol	5d.	lb10 ∧	4..2
Coals	1/6	¾ bush.ˡ	1..1
Attend.ᵉ		1 day	6..
lb17	@ 3/8	£3..2..4	£ 3..2..3

Ung Picis

Tar	lb1	3
Tallow	lb1	10½
Charcoal		2
Attend.ᵉ	1 hour	6
lb1¾	@ 1/. £..1..9	£ 1..9

Hydrarg. Mur.
made at twice — viz. 8 of 11 mo & 12 of 12 mo 1796

Natron muriat.	12/.	cwt qr lb 2..1..27	1..9..10½
Hydrarg	4/9	lb240	57....
Acid Vitriol	4½	lb279	5..4..7
Coals	1/6	29 bush.ˡ	2..3..6
Glass			3..
Attend.ᵉ		12 days	3..12..
Carry to & from Plaistow in 8 Jars 7½			..10..
			£73....
lb307	@ 4/9	£72..18..3	

Allen's methods, as shown in his "Laboratory Calculation Book" for the period 1795-8 (now in the Library of the Royal Pharmaceutical Society of Great Britain), were relatively unsophisticated. As each prescription was made up, Allen simply recorded it in chronological sequence, referencing the name and page number at the beginning of the book. The laboratory calculation itself included such information as the name of the medicine (and occasionally its source, such as a particular Pharmacopoeia), the date, the ingredients, the quantity and their price. Allen totalled the costs, including a charge for "attendance" – the cost of labour.

Direct information on the size of manufacturing operations at Plough Court is scanty. An unpublished study of Allen & Hanburys describes the layout of what was perhaps London's biggest medicine and drug manufacturer at that time, the Society of Apothecaries at Apothecaries Hall.[14] The Society had established its laboratory in 1623 and by the early nineteenth century had developed it into what appears to have been an efficient factory and warehouse for the manufacture and supply of drugs to the apothecaries of London. The largest room was the "chemical laboratory", which housed more than a dozen furnaces; and there was also a "chemical warehouse", alongside various rooms for the preparation of specialisms – a magnesia room, a gas room, a saline room – and a still house. Steam boilers provided heat for the chemical operations. Although this description conveys the impression that a large factory was in operation at the Apothecaries Hall, by modern standards it was a modest undertaking (the laboratory measured only fifty feet by thirty!).

As regards Allen's concern, illustrations of the premises and a copy of the lease of 1725 provide some means of assessing the scale of operations.[15] From the time of Silvanus Bevan, the firm had occupied two buildings in Plough Court, Nos. 2 and 3. The larger building was No. 2. It consisted of a fore and back garret; a fore room and a back room and a "room backwards"; a lower room, middle room, kitchen and a yard; a cellar and a back cellar – four storeys in all, excluding the cellar. The next-door building also had four storeys and a cellar: it included a fore garret, a back garret and a little room; a middle room, front room, dining room and back room; and a parlour, kitchen and yard. These premises served not only as a factory, warehouse and retail shop, but also as the living quarters for Bevan and, later, for Allen, before he acquired a more spacious dwelling in Stoke Newington. The firm must have possessed "the essential fittings" for a pharmaceutical laboratory, as described in a contemporary manual. These included:

> the furnaces, stills, steam apparatus, refrigerators, and presses . . . a capacious sink, with water laid on, and perforated shelves fixed over it, for draining bottles; a fixed side table, for performing the smaller operations upon, and, above this, a set of tests, test glasses, funnels, glass measures, and a perforated shelf, for supporting funnels . . . ; a strong moveable table, which may be placed in any part of the laboratory; a druggist's root cutting or slicing knife; a large marble mortar, and an iron or bell-metal mortar. There should also be a desk, on which to keep the journal of the operations of the laboratory, and, above it, a glass-case, containing the Pharmacopoeias and a few other books.[16]

Views of the Plough Court laboratory in about the mid-nineteenth century.

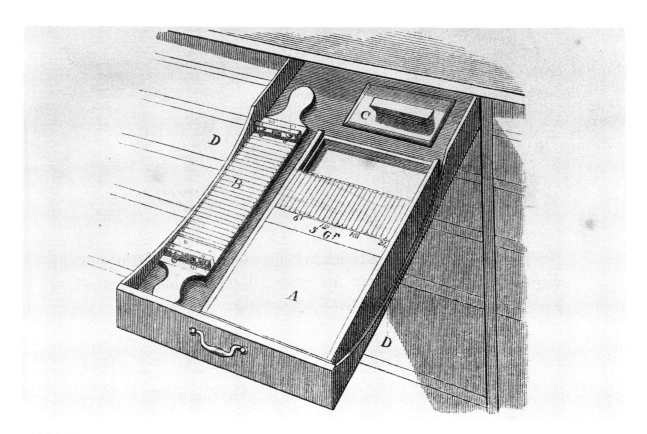

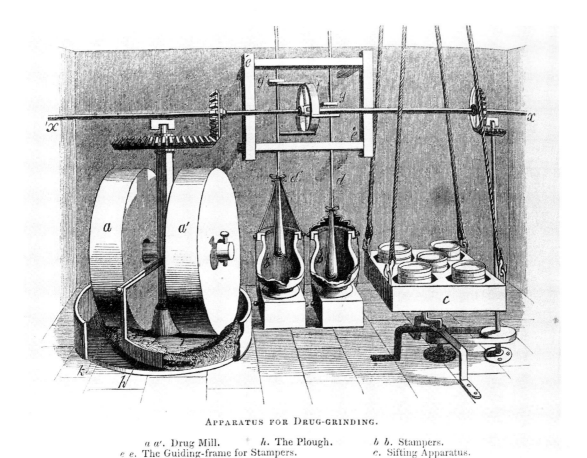

APPARATUS FOR DRUG-GRINDING.

a a'. Drug Mill.   *h*. The Plough.   *b b*. Stampers.
e e. The Guiding-frame for Stampers.   *c*. Sifting Apparatus.

Apparatus for drug-grinding. From Mohr & Redwood, Practical Pharmacy *(1849).*

(above left) Drugs were mostly prepared manually at this time, with the occasional use of gadgets, such as this pill machine. From Mohr & Redwood, Practical Pharmacy *(1849).*

(opposite) A few of the requisites of the nineteenth century pharmacist. From Mohr & Redwood, Practical Pharmacy *(1849).*

All of these could have been easily accommodated at Plough Court. In short, the business probably compared favourably with the Apothecaries Hall in size, and, like its competitor, it was not a large-scale undertaking.

Probably Plough Court was somewhat cramped. In the Bevan period there appears to have been one shopman (perhaps two), who was concerned with the retail trade; one or two "warehousemen" were responsible for dispatching goods; probably assistants were employed on the manufacturing side; and the whole was administered by Bevan and a clerk. By the 1830s the retail business had expanded enormously and there are frequent references to Allen looking for new staff. In 1815 Barry had written that "we are about to entirely new model our shop" and that a new assistant would be needed at £40 a year:

The situation is behind the Counter, where the attention from 9 in the morning till 9 at night is required unremittingly in the compounding of Prescriptions. The Assistant must be *well acquainted* with the business, and very *capable* & *assiduous* that it may be conducted with *dispatch*, while exceedingly careful to do it *correctly* & *neatly*. It is of much consequence to us that his manners of address be good, such as to keep and promote the attachment of our customers: and that he *appear* a person of *responsibility*, one in whom strangers can readily place *confidence* from his very look. The being middle-aged is a step toward this, & if his person, as to size, be certainly not below mediocrity, it would be another step towards a *responsible appearance. Cleanliness* & *neatness in his person* is another point of essential importance [and he should be] just the reverse of what we mean by dull.[17]

By 1829 the firm was writing to William Hoyland of Sheffield that the shop business "now employs five assistants, there being no Apprentices", besides needing nearly the full-time attention of two partners. There was also expansion on the management side, stemming from the family links between Allen and the Hanburys, which resulted in the admission into the business of two Hanbury brothers (Allen's nephews by his second marriage to Charlotte Hanbury). Daniel Bell Hanbury had joined the firm early in 1808; his brother, Cornelius, two years his junior, joined the firm five or six years later. Both became partners in 1824, when the firm was styled Allen, Hanburys & Barry.

The increasing size of the staff gives some idea of Allen's and Barry's success in building up the firm's trade after the lean years of Bevan's involvement. The turnover figures for the enterprise show how solid the business was in the period 1815-45. Turnover reached £14,500 in about 1816, and thereafter it never fell below that total, nor rose above £18,000, except in 1844-5.[18] Total retail sales, including the dispensing of prescriptions, remained constant at about forty percent of the total. By the time of Allen's death (he died in 1843 at Lindfield), the business was indeed securely established and the "tight time" that had occurred in the early years of the nineteenth century was firmly in the past.

It should be stressed, however, that the pharmaceutical industry scarcely existed at that time; there were no really large-scale manufacturing units; and Plough Court was by no means unique. It shared in the technological backwardness of the industry at that time, which was partly due to the inadequate nature of chemical theory. Medicines were still compounded according to the recipes in the pharmacopoeias, and their inclusion of ingredients such as vipers and toads still gave such books a medieval air. The firm prospered, but in an era of expanding demand and healthy prices, when profits of a hundred percent could be made on retail medicines, this should not be surprising. Indeed, with its established reputation for fine products, which ensured that the business never needed to advertise, it would have only been surprising if the firm had not done well. Commercially, though, the pharmacy at Plough Court lacked dynamism and avoided efforts at expansion, preferring to remain uneasily placed between manufacturing and retailing. This was partly due to the Quaker philosophy of its partners, for whom business was never an end in itself. Plough Court became stronger under Allen and Barry and, through Allen's indefatigable scientific and humanitarian activities, much more widely known; but it was still recognisably the pharmacy of the Bevans.

3

EXPANSION UNDER THE HANBURYS, 1850s-1893

I had always desired to develop the wholesale and manufacturing possibilities of the business . . . & with this object in view acquired the lease
of premises at Bethnal Green. Various specialities were . . . very carefully
produced and made known to the Medical Profession and Trade. Thus
grew up the Company's manufacturing business at home and abroad.

Cornelius Hanbury, unpublished "Recollections" (1914).

While it remained tied to its limited product line – proprietaries and
galenicals – and its relatively modest clientele – chiefly, retail buyers and
selected druggists – Allen, Hanburys & Barry's had few opportunities for
real growth. The restricted site at Plough Court did not help either. Its
reputation was tidy enough, but there is little doubt that it would have
been soon submerged by economic developments in the late nineteenth
century, which offered pharmaceutical firms so many greater chances of
expansion.

These opportunities did not arise from brilliant new advances in
chemistry or medicine. Pharmacy remained a relatively simple calling.
The physician still depended for the treatment of disease almost entirely
upon vegetable drugs and a few chemicals, mainly inorganic. There were
some advances in the late nineteenth century. By the 1880s physicians
were becoming more precise in the use of drugs, which were now prepared according to the *British Pharmacopoeia* (first issued in 1864, under
the direction of the General Council of Medical Education), which drew
on the experience of the newly established pharmaceutical associations,
schools and journals. The significance of bacteria was becoming better
appreciated after the 1860s following Pasteur's work; in 1882 the
organism causing tuberculosis was discovered; and this was followed in
1883 by the finding of the cholera vibrio. These developments coincided
with the rise of immunotherapy, which promised to provide an effective
remedy for all infectious diseases. In the 1880s Robert Koch, the
eminent German bacteriologist and discoverer of the tuberculosis
bacillus, successfully isolated and cultured pathogenic organisms, which
enabled the rational search for chemotherapeutic agents to begin. But all
these developments made little difference to the trade of the chemist and
druggist. Of far more importance was the development of the economy.

The country's national product was growing most rapidly in the second half of the nineteenth century and it was also this period that saw a marked advance in the standard of living; this was despite a relative slowing down of growth and increasing competition from overseas suppliers. Consumption of what had until then been considered luxury items – sugar, tea, tobacco and beer – increased dramatically. Annual average consumption of sugar, for example, more than doubled in the period 1850-1900 (from 30lbs. to 78 lbs.).[1] Increasingly, the public was indulging itself in all the delights of an emerging consumer society – Pears' Soap, Cadbury's Cocoa, Wills' Cigarettes, and cheap railway excursions to the seaside. This society was an increasingly urban one. In 1850 England was evenly split between town (defined as communities above 5,000) and country; but by 1900, three-quarters of the nation lived in towns. Inevitably, the attendant social problems and diseases meant new markets for medicines.

The amount of their incomes that ordinary people were spending on health preparations was also growing dramatically. According to the stamp duty figures, sales of such medicines more than doubled between 1852 and 1870, while real wages rose by only 18 percent, and trebled again by 1890, real wages having risen by another 43 percent. It was at this time that some famous household names appeared on the scene. Thomas Beecham was advertising his "Beecham's Pills" as worth "a guinea a box" in St. Helens; James Crossley Eno, a Tyneside druggist, had launched upon the world his famous "Fruit Salt"; and Thomas Holloway, in London, was drumming up business for "Holloway's Pills". Jesse Boot, in Nottingham, was busy selling a whole range of proprietary medicines and had embarked on the building up of a vast retail empire.[2]

The compounding for most of these medicines was a simple procedure; the claims were usually extravagant (Eno claimed that his Fruit Salt had helped win the Afghan War); and the profits handsome, to say the least (Holloway may have earned over £50,000 a year from his patent medicines). Invariably, the products were marketed with flamboyant and costly advertising campaigns. By 1884 Beecham's was spending £22,000 a year on advertising; some firms, such as Holloway, spent more. Holloway's success grew as he increased his investments in printed advertisements from £5,000 in 1842 to £50,000 in 1883. Of course, the Plough Court pharmacy never spent anything like as much on advertising; in fact, the firm's advertising bill was negligible before about the 1880s. And the company would never have stooped to the vulgar level of Holloway's advertisements, one of which combined the images of Britannia, Queen Victoria, a sailor and a guardsman, surrounded by a Red Indian, a Zulu, a turbaned Oriental, and veiled Muslim ladies along with traditionally dressed Chinese women.[3] Nevertheless, Allen, Hanburys & Barry was not immune from these developments and after the 1850s the tempo of the business began to quicken.

At Plough Court the old order was changing. By the 1850s John T. Barry's health was failing and increasingly the responsibility for business affairs fell upon the Hanburys, a family as ancient, widespread and influential as any of the leading Quaker families. The Hanburys traced

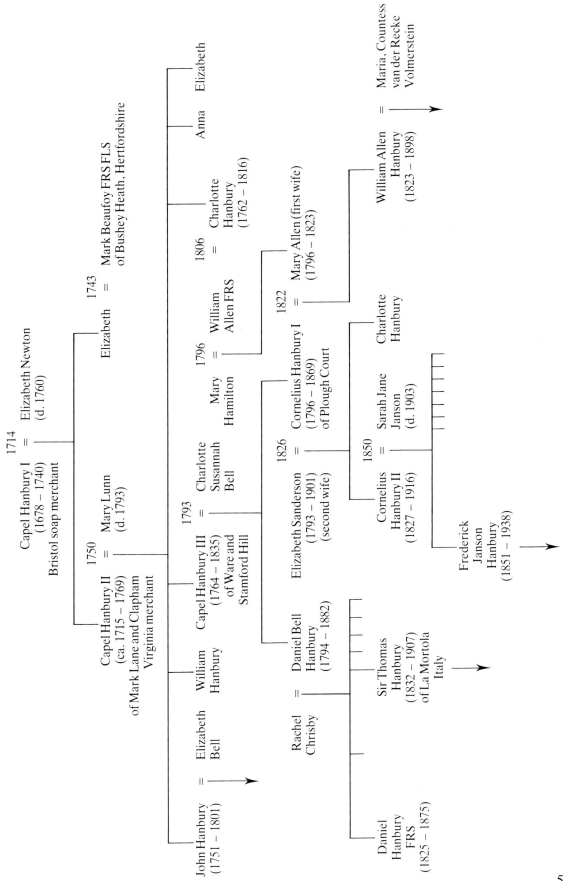

The botanic garden at La Mortola, near the town of Ventimiglia, on the Franco-Italian frontier, was designed by Sir Thomas Hanbury in the nineteenth century. It has now fallen into disrepair.

their lineage to Hanbury in Worcestershire, where a namesake had held land in the neighbourhood as far back as the twelfth century.[4] In subsequent generations the family was to achieve distinction in the Church, the services, diplomacy, Parliament, the professions and commerce. At the end of the seventeenth century John Hanbury took an active part in the development of an iron works at Pontypool, where he pioneered the rolling of iron plates. Another descendant, Capel Hanbury, achieved prominence as a Bristol soap merchant at the beginning of the eighteenth century and from this line the family infiltrated the business life of the capital. A second Capel Hanbury became a Virginia merchant and from his issue the family linked itself by marriage to William Allen. (The complicated genealogy of the Hanbury family and its relationship to Allen is illustrated on p. 59.) A key figure was a third Capel Hanbury, who in the early nineteenth century became established at Ware as a corn merchant and later as a dealer in malt. It was his sons, Daniel Bell Hanbury (1794-1882) and Cornelius Hanbury (1796-1869), nephews of William Allen, who had joined the Plough Court business.

Daniel Bell Hanbury had been recruited in 1808, two years after his father's younger sister, Charlotte Hanbury, had married William Allen. As far as is known, he was never formally apprenticed. Throughout his long business life (he retired in 1868) he spent much of his time in the dispensing department, which was said to have had a peculiar fascination for him. Close association with William Allen brought him into the great man's orbit. He accompanied Allen on two of his Continental trips; and he also became a founder member of the Pharmaceutical Society and held the office of treasurer to the Society from 1852 to 1857.

Cornelius Hanbury had joined the business at the age of eighteen in 1814, being apprenticed for a period of seven years to William Allen "to learn the Art of chemist and druggist". Eight years later the Hanbury's linkage with the Allen family was further cemented when Cornelius married Mary, the only daughter of William Allen. By 1824 both Daniel Bell and Cornelius were partners. As Barry increasingly took charge of the business during Allen's absences, the Hanburys concerned themselves with the routine running of the shop. Daniel Bell spent much of his time dispensing, while Cornelius worked in the counting-house and was the partner to whom Allen wrote when away from Plough Court.

By the 1850s this management team was growing old. In 1856, Barry retired; two years later so too did Cornelius. At this point, the firm was re-styled under its present name – Allen & Hanburys – and two new members of the Hanbury family were admitted as partners.

The first new partner, Daniel Hanbury (1825-75), the eldest son of Daniel Bell Hanbury, had joined the business in 1841. Like most of the Hanburys he had been groomed for a career at Plough Court; and indeed Daniel had qualified as a pharmaceutical chemist in 1857. By then, however, he had already come under the influence of some of the leading pharmacists and botanists of the day: men such as Jonathan Pereira, John E. Howard, Jacob Bell, Theophilus Redwood, and Henry

Mitchell

London 15 Decr 1857.

Dear Sir

It has afforded me great pleasure to receive
your letter of Nov. 14.

If during the journey which you have in
contemplation, you should come across any forests of
Liquidambar trees, such as are to be found in the
Extreme S. W. of Asia Minor, I should be Ex-
= ~~tremely~~ glad if you would Endeavorer to obtain
for me some of the solid resin which I have reason to
believe may be found on the wounded trunks.

If the trees are in flower (and I suppose they
blossom quite Early in the spring) it would be well
to press and ~~dry~~ (in a book or some sheets of
paper) a few flowering twigs.

Any additional information as to the Extraction
of the Butchus Yaghy or Liquid Storax would be
valuable & interesting.

With regard to Zeal Storax, it is as you
~~know~~ are aware, utterly unknown as an article
of trade in modern times. If it could be
obtained at Even 2/ ℔ ounce, I think a little of
it could be sold. At all Events I place Five

=cedingly

£b. 11°.

62

Deane, who had awakened his interests in scientific matters. Botany quickly became something of a passion with him, as it was with many other members of the Hanbury family. (Daniel's younger brother, (Sir) Thomas Hanbury, laid out a famous botanic garden at La Mortola, near the town of Ventimiglia, close to the frontier between Italy and France; and Frederick Janson Hanbury, the grandson of Cornelius, was the editor of a standard work on British plants.[5]) Daniel's interest in the subject was even more obsessional. In particular, he became devoted to the study of pharmocognosy, or the knowledge of drugs, especially in their natural or imperfect state. At this time knowledge of drugs was still superficial and the botanical and geographical sources of many of them were still unknown. It was this situation that Daniel Hanbury, inspired by his teacher and close friend, Jonathan Pereira, Professor of Materia Medica at the Pharmaceutical Society, set out to change.

Daniel Hanbury's numerous notebooks, which are extant in the Allen & Hanburys' archive, show the immense care with which he approached the study of the sources of drugs: he wrote to botanists, pharmacists, travellers, government officials and anyone who could supply him with information and materials; he familiarised himself not only with the classical and contemporary literature, but also foreign languages, such as Chinese and Arabic; and, on occasions, travelled abroad to collect specimens himself. His dispassionate, scientific approach can be seen to best effect in his comprehensive researches into the origins of liquid storax, which were published after 1857. In a series of careful studies, Daniel Hanbury showed that, while the original and classical storax was obtained from *Stryax officinale*, the liquid storax of commerce derived from *Liquidamber orientale*. But this was only a small part of his investigations, which were eventually published in a series of over eighty articles.

Seen through modern eyes, Daniel Hanbury's labours and his compulsive investigations into the minutiae of plants and drugs can seem rather dated and antiquarian. It must be remembered, however, that his work had a tremendous impact upon all those associated with the use and study of crude drugs, who lacked a definitive textbook. Hanbury was to provide such an authoritative account when he collaborated with Professor F.A. Fluckiger, a teacher of pharmocognosy in Berne, in the publication of *Pharmacographia* (1874).[6] The aim of this book was to investigate anew the field of vegetable materia medica in order, as far as possible, to clear up doubtful points and to remove some of the uncertainties by which the subject was surrounded. This surpassed all previous publications in the field, such as Pereira's *The Elements of Materia Medica* (1839) and Guibourt's *Histoire Naturelle des Drogues Simples* (published in numerous editions after 1820), and for the first time gave facts about drugs which had been thoroughly checked beforehand and could be verified. This required a tremendous effort by both authors, but Daniel Hanbury is usually regarded as the major contributor.

A page from one of Daniel Hanbury's science notebooks, 1857. He was a prolific correspondent.

Such endeavours proved incompatible with a business career and in 1870 Daniel Hanbury wrote to a friend: "I don't know if I told you that I am about to quit business. It is a step I have had in view for the last two

63

Styrax officinale, *the subject of one of Daniel Hanbury's most thorough investigations. From W. Woodville,* Medical Botany *(1832). (Courtesy Royal Pharmaceutical Society of Great Britain)*

years and I look forward with great pleasure to freedom from a great deal of weary but not too disagreeable occupation."[7] Thus, Daniel's direct influence on the business ceased; though his indirect influence was important, not only in advancing the science of pharmacy, but also in immeasurably raising the prestige of the family firm. Daniel's passion for scholarship, coupled with his reclusive and abstemious lifestyle – he disliked tobacco and alcohol, avoided meat and never married – and his tragically early death from typhoid fever before he reached fifty, made a profound impression on his contemporaries. They regarded him in almost romantic terms, a feeling that is well caught in some of Daniel's portraits, one of which shows him in Byronic pose – a contrast with the more aged figure in the oil portrait presented by his brother to the Pharmaceutical Society. They also presented him with a string of honours, which included election to the Fellowship of the Royal Society in 1869;

and his work was commemorated after his death by the Hanbury Memorial Medal, awarded biennially by the Pharmaceutical Society.

Of even greater importance for the fortunes of the firm was the second new partner admitted in 1856 – this was Cornelius Hanbury (1827-1916), the son (confusingly) of the aforementioned Cornelius the elder, who had married again after the death of his first wife. (Henceforth, the second Cornelius is referred to simply as Cornelius; his father as the elder.) It was Cornelius who was to be the dominant influence on the firm during the next fifty years, setting the pattern for much of its development as far ahead as the twentieth century.

Cornelius received a training as a surgeon and apothecary: it was thought to be a useful insurance in case druggists were prohibited from prescribing. At the age of eighteen he was apprenticed to Henry

Daniel Hanbury (1825-75). Oil portrait presented to the Pharmaceutical Society by his brother, Thomas, in 1875. (Courtesy Royal Pharmaceutical Society of Great Britain)

Yours very faithfully

Dan. Hanbury

Callaway, a young surgeon-apothecary, for the required period of five years; he also later enrolled as a student at St. Bartholomew's Hospital. He became clinical clerk under Dr. (Sir) George Burrows, passing the examination for membership of the College of Surgeons in 1849, and that of Licentiate of the Society of Apothecaries the following year. He also attended classes at the Birkbeck Laboratory, University of London, and became a Fellow of the (Royal) Institute of Chemistry. By 1850 he had joined the family pharmacy, of which he has left a record in his unpublished "Recollections":

> I now [1849] began to attend daily to the business in Plough Court . . . & became intimately associated with my Cousin Daniel. We each took part in the daily routine of the business, including some amount of Counting-house work, & as had been the custom for a generation previously gave personal attention to the Dispensing & other details of the business. The Firm had in this way and with careful attention to all other details acquired a great reputation.

Apparently, though, Cornelius found the drudgery of routine office work "far from congenial & agreeable to [his] tastes",[8] and initially he hankered for his medical studies. But gradually, the Plough Court business came to dominate his life. When Daniel Bell Hanbury retired in 1868, Cornelius became the sole partner; a position that remained until Cornelius's elder and only surviving son, Frederick Janson Hanbury (1851-1938), was able to join as partner in 1874. Even then, it was Cornelius who supplied the directing hand, firmly pushing the company into more ambitious wholesaling and manufacturing activities.

Initially, the plans for expansion had been checked by the firm's old guard, particularly John T. Barry. In his private diary (1847-68) Cornelius had recorded that Barry had "distinctly refused to enter into partnership with any fresh persons or to open a branch establishment so long as he remained in the firm and yet to withdraw he asked a sum about double the maximum value of the goodwill of his share". But in 1856, as soon as Barry had been forced to accept a more reasonable price and had retired, Cornelius and Daniel Hanbury made extensive alterations at No. 2 Plough Court. This was necessitated by the rapid growth of the dispensing side of the business. Although the majority of London merchants and businessmen no longer lived in the City, they continued to attend there daily; for convenience they often left their prescriptions at Plough Court in the morning, as well as orders for other requisites, calling for them in the afternoon or evening. Before Harley Street became the domain of the medical men, the fashionable abode for specialists was Finsbury Square; and a study of Allen & Hanburys' prescription books of the period reveals the large number of prescriptions from residents in the area dispensed at Plough Court. The type of prescription was also changing. The six or twelve draughts which were once ordered, each in a separate bottle, were being superseded by one bottle containing six or twelve doses – a great saving of bottles and labour. Usually, one or two dozen pills were ordered with the mixtures and these were made up freshly on each occasion. Pill making was a laborious job,

Daniel Hanbury, from Science Papers, Chiefly Pharmacological and Botanical. *Edited with a Memoir by J. Ince (London, 1876).*

67

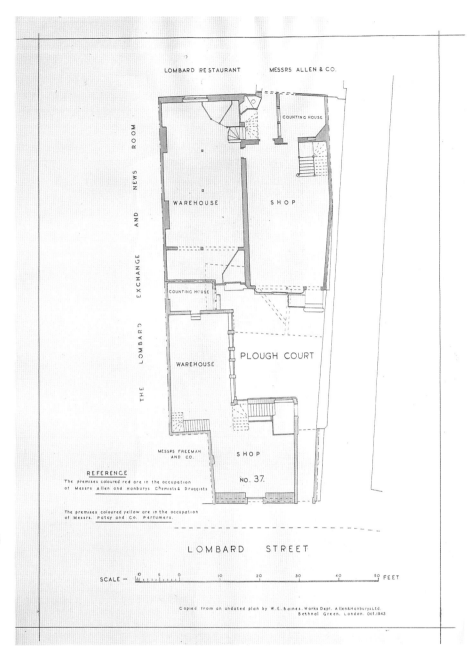

Cornelius Hanbury (1827-1916), the main driving force behind Allen & Hanburys Ltd in the second half of the nineteenth century, who greatly expanded the scope of its activities.

Plan of Plough Court.

since each pill was virtually hand-made with a pestle, mortar and pill-machine. They were coated with shellac pill varnish, though often wealthier Plough Court customers ordered silvered pills, which were thought to look more elegant. Five dispensers were employed, and there were also two shopmen who dealt with miscellaneous orders.

In expanding this dispensing side of the pharmacy, the firm spent £400 on structural alterations. The shop was enlarged by the addition, on the ground floor, of the assistants' dining-room, and a bigger shop window to admit more light. A new counter was also fitted, which was divided into separate stations for each dispenser. Argand burners were used to throw the maximum amount of light on the compounding. Possibly, numbered discs were given to those customers who were unwilling to wait for their prescription and wished to return later. All dispensing was done in full view of the public. Other alterations and improvements made were a speaking-tube from the shop to the dining-room on the first floor, improved ventilation, the repainting of the interior and the relabelling of the bottles. Special attention was given to the display of ships' medicine chests and travelling medicine cases.

These alterations coincided with a reorganisation of other departments of the firm: new business was anticipated as different sections of the community became interested in the practical application of chemical advances to scientific and commercial purposes. This involved the preparation of circulars for apothecaries, merchants, and firework makers; and the manufacture of fluoric acid for glass stainers, ships' chests for seafarers, mineral waters for physicians, essential oils for confectioners, chemicals for laboratories and professors, and photographic chemicals for professional and amateur alike. There is evidence that firework making was conducted at Plough Court by one of the Hanburys, but no details have been discovered. Certainly, though, the firm provided photographic chemicals from a very early date – probably for the "wet plate" process, which dates from 1851.

The issue of circulars, with an appeal wider than that made to personal callers, marked the beginning of the domestic wholesale side of the business. The firm was gaining a reputation for preparations made at Plough Court outside the circumscribed limits of the retail dispensing and sale of medicines. Orders began to come in from chemists for drugs and galenicals.[9] Some of those ordering them had been assistants at Plough Court and appreciated the quality of the articles supplied; others acquired the habit of sending for small emergency supplies. In a few years this side of the business assumed considerable proportions, orders coming in regularly from all parts of London, from the south coast as far as Cornwall, and from as far north as Edinburgh and Belfast.

In 1856 changes were also planned to the manufacturing laboratory at Plough Court. Until then much of the work of making galenicals had been done in the basement of Nos. 2 and 3. During 1867, premises at the back of No. 1 were taken and into these were fitted some of William Allen's old plant, as well as a new still and other apparatus. The preparations made were galenicals such as tinctures, extracts, confections, and various ointments. There was no room for drug grinding, for which there was no great demand apart from the firm's limited needs, and the work was therefore contracted out to local grinders.

The year 1872 saw the final structural alteration of the Plough Court premises, necessitated by major building changes in Lombard Street itself. Cornelius Hanbury was offered the chance to purchase the freehold of Plough Court at this time, but, to his eternal regret, he declined. He did, however, secure a building lease for a term of eighty years and the old premises were reluctantly demolished. A new building was erected, which gave the firm a new aspect. Henceforth, the two houses leased by Allen & Hanburys (Nos. 2 and 3 Plough Court) looked out over the open court direct to Lombard Street; the retail pharmacy

The Plough Court pharmacy. From Old and New London *(London: Petter & Galpin, n.d.).*

being No. 2. Stretching away at the back of No. 1, with an entrance into Three King's Court, later Lombard Court, were the firm's laboratories. The leasing arrangements meant that these laboratories occupied only the third floor of this building.

The greater part of the ground floor was occupied by the pharmacy, which, as surviving photographs show, was an impressive sight. An ample counter of old mahogany extended round the horseshoe-shaped interior, behind which an armoury of drugs was arranged on shelves. The public floor space was occupied by a double settee in mahogany, and there were six fine old Georgian oak chairs, relics of the old pharmacy (which are now at the Royal Pharmaceutical Society). Customers could watch the dispensing and all prescriptions were meticulously noted down in the record book. The basement was used as a general store and for packing and despatch. Drugs, bottles and stationery were stored in a sub-basement.

The staff was still a small one. A manager recalled that: "In 1868 there were Mr. Cornelius Hanbury, the clerk, three men in the laboratory, two in the warehouse, a shop-porter with two boys, and an outside porter; seven or eight dispensers. The dispensers lived on the premises, so did the shop-porter; he slept in the warehouse, and by day his bed was tucked under the warehouse counter."[10] By the time the new building was opened the staff numbered thirty, including the shop assistants.

The scale of the third-floor laboratory can be judged from the recollections of a retired veteran of the firm:

> The laboratory . . . was rather on the crowded side – with three stills, an extraction tank . . . 5 steam pans (one solid tin tilting), a mash tun, vacuum pump and vacuum pan, furnace and fume cover for distilling prussic acid, hydrobromic acid, sweet spirits of nitre, etc., copper and earthenware percolators, marble mortars, and in an adjoining room, edge runners, stampers, and a huge bell metal mortar, the steel pestle suspended on a long springy branch, which helped the operator considerably, and he wanted it – when he was told to 'bruise 64 lbs. of Jamaica ginger thro' a No. 11 sieve *and make no dust*': that was always the strict order! Then of course there was an hydraulic press with press box – and a supply of horse hair bags for pressing fresh dandelion roots, green (fresh) henbane, belladonna, etc., etc.[11]

Cornelius Hanbury's appreciation of the technological advances in drug manufacture and the growing demand for new products led inevitably to the establishment of separate manufacturing facilities. In April 1874, part of an old match factory called Letchford's Buildings was leased at Bethnal Green, in the borough of Tower Hamlets, east London.

At that time Bethnal Green was still semi-rural in character. The future Allen & Hanburys' site, situated in Three Colts Lane, was flanked with poplars and a picturesque caretaker's lodge stood at one of the entrances. Almost across the road was Bethnal Green Library, erected on the site of Bethnal or Bednal House, where, in the garden on 26 June 1663, Samuel Pepys dined on the "greatest Quantity of Strawberrys I ever saw, and good". Nevertheless, by the late nineteenth century that area of the East End of London was rapidly developing into a major centre of industrial activity. A remarkably diverse range of industries – bread (Allinson's), furniture and timber (Mallinson's), matches (Bryant & May), brewing (Charrington's) - had moved into Tower Hamlets. Letchford's Buildings mirrored this diversity, since it comprised a number of small businesses where the bottling of mineral waters, cane-splitting, the manufacture of disinfectant and the making of matches had been conducted.

Cornelius was not infallible as a businessman – his "Recollections" document a number of costly speculative blunders in his career, including the loss of £20,000 in a fraudulent silver manufacturing venture in about 1897. For a time it seemed as if the Bethnal Green factory

Men unpacking outside Plough Court, c. 1886.

would be another folly, since at first Cornelius found it "almost superfluous". The move, however, was a shrewd one, especially as the cost of land in the City soared, forever ruling out the possibility of further developments at Plough Court. Gradually, the whole of Letchford's Buildings was acquired by Allen & Hanburys by the end of the nineteenth century (though a small section was occupied by the Sanitas Co until 1907, when that too fell into the firm's hands): eventually, they provided crucial space for offices, warehouses, laboratories, and a whole range of specialities.

Cornelius appears to have continued to make Plough Court his base, so that from the outset Frederick Janson Hanbury had charge of the new and continuously growing factory at Bethnal Green. Shortly after the move there the firm had the good fortune to recruit a pharmaceutical chemist, William Ralph Dodd (1856-1917), who in 1878 began nearly forty years' service with the firm as a dispensing assistant at Plough Court. Educated under Sylvanus Thompson at University College, Bristol (as it then was), Dodd's career began at a druggist's in Market Drayton, at an establishment of "miscellaneous description – a departmental store . . . described as a chemist and druggists, grocery, tea dealers, Italian warehouseman, dealers in china and glass, wine and

A view of Allen & Hanburys' Bethnal Green factory in the late nineteenth century.

spirits, fruit, vegetables, tobacco and cigars. There was very little drug-trade done excepting of the crudest kind, involved in very hard work in grinding and powdering, and in making horse-balls, sheep-dips and wheat dressing."[12] More rewarding for Dodd was a spell with the old pharmaceutical house of Giles & Son of Clifton, which led to him passing the examinations of the Pharmaceutical Society. He studied at the City of London Guilds, where he won many prizes, and gained pharmaceutical experience in the West End of London. On joining Allen & Hanburys his talents were soon recognised by his transfer to Bethnal Green as head of the manufacturing laboratory. He brought with him George Wessendorff, his assistant at Plough Court.

The work of converting the somewhat scattered buildings at Bethnal Green into an efficient factory had not been easy. Fortunately, Dodd had a mechanical turn of mind and proved helpful to Frederick Janson in adapting old machinery and plant from Plough Court to more modern uses, as well as devising new machinery for novel processes. A still capable of producing 50 gallons per day was installed, which utilised an American idea of speeding evaporation with revolving jack towels. Machinery for pharmaceutical manufacture could not yet be bought off the shelf and, judging by the surviving illustrations of Dodd's plant and machinery, there was a good deal of Heath Robinson-style improvisation at Bethnal Green. Nevertheless, the plant did work, if not always in the quickest time or with the minimum of labour.

Dodd and his crew worked well together and the laboratories progressed smoothly. A retired workman remembered Dodd

pacing through the departments apparently deep in thought, and wearing in all weathers a straw hat worn well down over his face. Punctually at eleven o'clock he would send out to the nearest public house for a pint of beer, then costing threepence. His method of rewarding those members of his staff, who to his knowledge had worked specially well in routine work or had shown initiative and ingenuity in other ways over a period, was to give each a sovereign or, in special cases, even a five-pound note as a bonus. He extracted this from his pocket and gave it on the spot and not in the wage-packet.[13]

Expanding demand and the development of new products allowed Allen & Hanburys greater freedom to develop a line of specialities. Amongst the first was the making of refined cod-liver oil. This oil (rich in vitamin D), extracted from fish livers, was an old folk remedy which had been used for hundreds of years in the fishing villages along the northern European coastline. It was regarded as a particularly efficacious treatment for rickets and bone disorders, the oil being rubbed into the affected limbs and sometimes swallowed.

The oil was gradually adopted as a medicant in British hospitals in the late eighteenth century. The first recorded clinical trial of cod-liver oil in England was conducted at the Manchester Infirmary by Drs Samuel Kay and Robert Darbey in the 1770s. Apparently, the doctors were so pleased with the result that no less than fifty or sixty gallons were prescribed annually. It was "given in obstinate chronic rheumatisms, sciatica of long standing, and in those cases of premature decrepitude, which originate from immoderate labour, repeated strains and bruises; or exposure to continual dampness and cold".[14] Cod-liver oil was publicised in the nineteenth century by Dr. John Hughes Bennett, an English medical man of note, whose *Treatise on the Oluem Jecoris Aselli, or Cod-Liver Oil, as a Therapeutic Agent in Certain Forms of Gout, Rheumatism, and Scrofula* (1841) effectively awakened the medical profession to the virtues of the new agent. Another advocate for its use at this time was a London physician, Dr. Theophilus Thompson, who was, significantly, a friend of John T. Barry.

Barry, perhaps having had his interest in the subject aroused by Thompson, began experimenting with the production of cod-liver oil in the 1840s, so setting the company along the road to over a hundred years of involvement with the product. A major drawback with cod-liver oil was that the smell and taste were so repulsive. A doctor at a London hospital, for example, complained that patients would take the brown, fishy-flavoured substance home and burn it in their lamps, rather than drink it. By 1841 some progress had been made towards making the oil more palatable and hygienic by boiling and filtering, but only in a laboratory. Barry decided to take the idea up commercially and by 1845 he was offering cod-liver oil "of a very pale straw colour" made by his own process. He was thus a pioneer in cod-liver oil's commercial production in this country, though manufacturing techniques at Plough Court were somewhat crude:

> The livers were bought at Billingsgate market and were boiled down during the night in copper pans over charcoal fires. Two of the staff would spend most of the night over the preparation, the livers being stirred till pulped and the oil strained out through flannel. The method of storing the oil was in large earthen Florence jars; an ordinary dinner plate covered the mouth and was secured to it by plaster of Paris.[15]

(right) William Ralph
Dodd (1856-1917), who
organised the technical
operations at the Bethnal
Green factory and
eventually became a
director of Allen &
Hanburys.

(left) Views of the drug
laboratory and pill room
at Allen & Hanburys,
c. 1886. Manufacturing
was still modest in scale.

Nevertheless, the firm was soon regularly supplying surgeons and hospitals with small consignments of a few pounds at a time; in 1851 ten gallons were shipped to an Australian customer at 17/- per gallon; in the same year the firm sold ninety-two gallons of what was described as Newfoundland oil to a wholesale London firm. Other companies were also selling the oil. Duncan, Flockhart (a name we shall come across again), druggists in Edinburgh, had scarcely sold a gallon of cod-liver oil in 1841, but by 1847 they were dispensing 600 gallons. Also at about this time a Hull firm, founded by T. J. Smith in 1856, was building its fortune on sales of the product – it later achieved fame as Smith & Nephew.[16]

Allen & Hanburys held its own with the competition by the quality of its product (at the 1876 Centennial Exhibition in Philadelphia the firm won a medal for its cod-liver oil exhibit) and by keeping up with the latest processing methods. The most important of these was a filtering method for removing the solid stearin or fats in the oil, so improving the product's appearance (though also, unfortunately, removing some of its goodness). The company also established factories abroad – a logical step in view of the nature of the raw material and of the limited space available at Plough Court for what must have been an offensive operation. In 1860 Cornelius sent a trusted laboratory assistant, John Tuttle, out to Newfoundland to make cod-liver oil at Quidi Vidia. The venture was short-lived, because in 1864 medical opinion pronounced the oil from cod caught in Norwegian waters as superior. Thereupon, early in that year, Allen & Hanburys set up the first British cod-liver oil factory in Norway (one or two French factories had led the way in Newfoundland). It was a processing plant for producing the oil, which was then shipped to England and refined at Plough Court (and later at Bethnal Green). Cod-liver oil production was a fickle business: demand remained steady, but the cod was an elusive creature and occasionally fisheries failed. The first factory was situated at Langved on the island of Scholarn, but it was soon followed by a string of other Allen & Hanbury processing plants in Norway, most of them replacements for factories which had been taken out of production. By 1897 the firm was opening its fourth plant at Henningsvar, and this was to be followed by yet another at Finmarken in 1914; this was besides factories at Aberdeen and Hull, built in the early years of the twentieth century as a response to supply problems from the Norwegian cod fisheries.

Another Allen & Hanbury speciality that soon proved to have a wide demand was malted extract. Before 1880, this was a far from attractive product. The manufacturing process began when malted grain (usually barley) was mixed with water and allowed to stand until the starch was converted to sugar: the resulting "wort" was then evaporated to a thick treacle. If too much heat was employed or if the process was too prolonged, "caramelisation", or the burning of the sugars, occurred, and the extract became dark brown, or even black. In 1879 the Pharmaceutical Society investigated fourteen specimens of malt extract by various makers: they varied in colour from yellow to dark brown; the amount of moisture ranged from 19 to 61 percent, with a maltose content of from 5 to 67 percent, with one sample containing 4 percent of alcohol, presumably due to fermentation! Only three samples contained diastase (a group of enzymes that hydrolyse starch to maltose) and that of low starch conversion value.[17]

By 1879 John Fordred, who had joined Allen & Hanburys as "technical chemist" and already had a patent for purifying cod-liver oil to his name, began experiments to produce a malted food for infants in a more soluble form than was available at that time. The malted foods on the market were either crude evaporated extracts or only roughly refined ground malt, which contained impurities from the malt grain that were apt to produce intestinal irritation when given to youngsters. Fordred's solution was to use a vacuum apparatus in which the "wort" was evaporated under a low temperature, so producing a malt extract rich in diastase with the maltose uncaramelised. In October 1879 he secured a patent for "Improvements in the Manufacture of Nutritive Foods and Confectionery", thus becoming the first person in England to produce commercially a malt extract by using a vacuum pan. Although the new extract was first used in making malted farinaceous food, it was soon found to be ideal for mixing with such products as cod-liver oil, and, in a more liquid form, with a whole range of medicaments. This led to the marketing of such Allen & Hanbury staples as "Bynin Amara". The manufacture of foodstuffs was, in fact, to become a major line. In 1892 Dodd had patented "An Improved Form of Food Suitable for Infants", which was to launch the company into the milk food business. Fordred's method of low temperature evaporation had proved readily adaptable for dried milk production: after evaporating the liquid milk into a thick paste, it was a simple step to dry it in an oven. The result was a product which won immediate approval from the trade press. Reported the *Chemist and Druggist*:

> [Allen & Hanburys'] 'Mothers' Milk Food' . . . [is] . . . for feeding infants on true scientific principles. The principle adopted – and, we may add, patented – is a sound one, and when it is considered that half the children who die under one year old die through improper feeding, further, that medical men are beginning to see that deficiency of fat in food induces rickets and tuberculous complaints in children, the importance of these compounds requires no emphasis.[18]

Throat pastilles were also added to the line of Allen & Hanbury products at this time. Medicated throat jujubes, as they were then called, date from 1850, when small batches of various kinds were first made at Plough Court. Manufactured from a mixture of gum, sugar and water with the medicant added, jujubes were more palatable than the harder lozenges, but they did not keep too well. But while visiting his cousin Thomas Hanbury at La Mortola on the Italian Riviera in the early 1870s, Cornelius had become acquainted with French methods of manufacture which resulted in a more attractive product. The services of Monsieur Charles Benet, who had previously been employed by a firm in Lyons, were acquired to initiate Allen & Hanburys into the art of making the

Manufactured Drugs, Chemicals and Pharmaceuticals

Prepared by the best and most modern methods.

Including Cachous, Gelatin Capsules, Effervescent Preparations, Fluid Extracts, Jujubes, "Kapsol," Lozenges, Pastilles, Pills (soluble), Resinoids, Suppositories, Aqueous and Concentrated Tinctures, Compressed Tablets, etc.

ALLEN & HANBURYS' COD-LIVER OIL FACTORY AT HENNINGSVAER, IN LOFOTEN ISLANDS

For prices of The "Allenburys" and "A. & H." Specialities, see Section III., page 189. For Sectional Index, Section II., see page 88.

Allen & Hanburys Ltd.

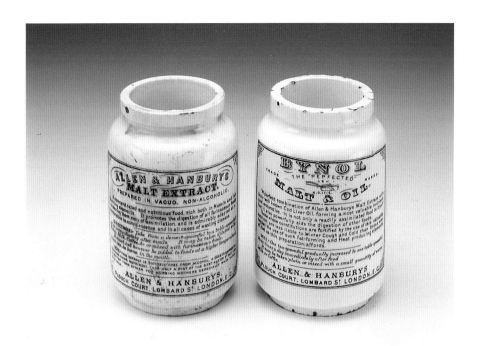

*(left) Allen & Hanburys'
cod-liver oil factory at
Lofoten, Norway,
illustrated in an early
trade catalogue.*

*(right) Allen &
Hanburys' malt products
were established as a
major line after the 1880s.*

pâte de jujube, or sheet mass from which the jujubes were cut. Cornelius set up a small factory at Nimes, which in 1876 was transferred to Lewisham in Kent, and then to Bethnal Green. Two improvements in jujube manufacture were made. At the Lewisham factory a new patented coating process was used which ensured that the jujubes were impervious to moisture and kept their shape for long periods. Originally, jujubes were cut or punched out by hand from a sheet mass, but by 1878 Benet had introduced a method by which the liquid was poured into starch moulds. A selection of these improved jujubes was shown at the Paris Exhibition of 1878, where the pharmaceutical press was favourably impressed by jujubes which did not lose their edge or brightness, despite the summer heat. From 1880 onwards, as a result of a paper read that year by Dr. James Prosser to the meeting of the British Medical Association at Cambridge, at which Allen & Hanburys exhibited a range of medicated jujubes made to a formula prescribed by him, this type of preparation became known as "pastilles". The universal popularity of pastilles resulted in an enormous business for the firm in the twentieth century.

Frederick Janson Hanbury, after his visit to the Centennial Exhibition in Philadelphia in 1876, ordered the first machine the firm used for making compressed tablets: six or so more were soon added. By 1903 Allen & Hanburys had designed its own high-speed automatic machine, apparently the first of its kind to be made in the UK, which was capable of compressing 800 tablets per minute.[19] In five minutes such machines could produce more tablets than a worker could make in a day with a hand-machine. The firm not only used these new machines for its own products, but also produced them for other wholesale firms.

The "Express" Rotary
Tablet Machine

(Patented)

Cornelius Hanbury, as a surgeon, also took a great interest in the development of surgical instruments. Since the Bevan days, the firm had often received requests for instruments, but had never manufactured them. In the early 1880s, however, Cornelius installed a small forge and workshop at Bethnal Green. Skilled workmen from Sheffield were recruited to launch the firm into this new business.

In the 1880s, with the manufacturing facilities at Bethnal Green well established, Allen & Hanburys also expanded westwards in London. The lack of space had always been a problem at Plough Court and one can never read accounts of the pharmacy without feeling an acute sense of claustrophobia. Even in William Allen's day the growing need for office accommodation in the City meant that families who once lived in the many courts and squares adjacent to Plough Court were gradually moving over the River Thames to south-eastern or south-western districts, so beginning a life of "commuting" to work. In addition, districts west of Marble Arch were being developed and many of the wealthier merchants took the opportunity to move from the grimy City to leafier, suburban localities. The medical and surgical community inevitably followed them, vacating fashionable Finsbury Square for fresh residences in the area west of Tottenham Court Road.

Cornelius had early in his career appreciated the importance of this westwards migration. Enthusiastically supported by his cousin Daniel, Cornelius had pressed for the opening of a branch in the West End of London, but had been stymied by John Barry. In June 1884, however, Cornelius's long-cherished dream became a reality when he was able to secure premises for the firm at No. 7 Vere Street, near Cavendish Square, where an Allen & Hanbury retail pharmacy was established.

Nationally, Allen & Hanburys was becoming a name to be reckoned with. In 1880 the firm's expansion attracted the admiring comment of the leading trade journal, the *Chemist and Druggist*, whose reporters treated its readers to a tour of the Bethnal Green factory, where more than fifty workers were employed. They commented on the changing character of the business:

> Twenty years ago Allen & Hanburys' prominence in the advertisement sections of the general newspapers would have surprised their fellow-pharmacists as much as Saul's appearance among the prophets astonished his contemporaries. Hidden in Plough Court, cut off from the public thorough-fare, their selected seclusion seemed to the highly-respectable druggists of the last generation symbolical of the system in which pharmacy should be conducted.[20]

In contrast, Cornelius had developed a modest apothecary's shop, with its cramped laboratory, into a much larger concern, with major retailing and manufacturing divisions and interests overseas.

The emerging pharmaceutical industry could now more clearly be discerned. On the one hand were the marketing companies (such as Boots, Taylors, and The London Drug Cooperative), which were coming to dominate retail pharmacy, having developed the concept of multi-outlet chains with standardisation of products and prices. The

Allen & Hanburys' rotary tablet-making machine.

Forging surgical instruments at Allen & Hanburys. This became a major product line for the firm, largely due to the initiative of Cornelius Hanbury, who had once trained as a surgeon.

growth of many of these firms was spectacular, far more rapid than that of Allen & Hanburys. However, Plough Court belonged more to the "traditional" sector of companies. This sector (which included Morson, Whiffen, Howard and May & Baker[21]) dealt with a more specialised market, dealing with some alkaloids such as quinine, metal salts such as those of mercury and bismuth, and proprietaries and galenicals. Many of these firms, such as Howard and Allen & Hanburys, had strong links with the Quaker community with its great emphasis on botany; others, such as Morson, were influenced by the Paris school of the 1820s which specialised in the isolation of alkaloids from natural products. There were also the Edinburgh alkaloid companies (Macfarlan; T. & H. Smith;

and Duncan, Flockhart) dealing with morphine extraction and the preparation of chloroform and ether – a consequence of the link with the pioneering Edinburgh medical school. Within this sector of firms Allen & Hanburys rated very highly. Moreover, in the early 1890s the firm was still expanding: in 1893, to exploit fully its opportunities, the company embraced limited liability – henceforth it would be known as Allen & Hanburys Ltd.

4

ALLEN & HANBURYS LIMITED:
The Universal Provider

> The Directors after considering & visiting a great number of sites at length decided to take an old flour mill on the Lea at Ware, known as "Ware Mills". The situation, the water power & the land around, about five acres, seem to present special advantages for the purposes of the Company & operations to adapt the building to the requirements of the special manufacture are now in progress.
>
> Allen & Hanburys Ltd, Minute Book, 21 January 1897.

The period 1893-1918 saw Allen & Hanburys blossom fully as a pharmaceutical manufacturing company, engaged in both wholesaling and retailing, and also adopt a shape that was to stay unchanged until well after the Second World War. It was a period of spectacular growth for the firm, with a rate of expansion that was not to be bettered until after the 1960s.

The period began with the company's adoption of limited liability status in 1893. Limited liability avoided one of the pitfalls of an ordinary business partnership, which, if it failed, saddled the partners with personal responsibility for the firm's debts. For companies enjoying a period of sustained growth there was the further attraction of being able to increase the number of partners and secure future funding. Allen & Hanburys was one of several thousand limited liability companies which were registered in the period 1880-1914. They should not be thought of as public companies, with their shares quoted on the Stock Exchange: the bulk of them were "private" concerns, with the controlling ordinary share capital held by the family.

Allen & Hanburys Ltd, too, remained a private concern. It was incorporated on 29 December 1893, with an authorised capital of £75,000, consisting of 750 shares of £100 each. The purchase consideration was £60,000, which was satisfied by an allotment to the vendors of £20,000 in ordinary shares and £40,000 in preference shares. The shares were held by the directors – Cornelius Hanbury and his son, Frederick Janson Hanbury – and although further shares were issued as the company expanded, its private character was (at least in this period) carefully maintained. The annual meetings of the ordinary shareholders were confidential – in effect, they were no more than a discussion amongst the directors in the presence of their private secretary, from which the preference shareholders were excluded. Preference shares themselves were only issued to relatives, members of the medical profession and chemists, or to those with a close connection with the company.

Cornelius took the chair at the first meeting of Allen & Hanburys Ltd. He was now well into his sixth decade, still in excellent health and very much the captain of the firm, though he had long since shared leadership with his son, Frederick Janson. Cornelius had once said that from the retirement of his cousin Daniel in 1870 until Frederick came into the business in 1875, he had never been away from the office for more than three consecutive days at a time. Gradually, however, Cornelius withdrew from the routine running of the business, especially after 1900, though he retained the chairmanship until his death. In his "Recollections" he remarked: "At first I used to go up to the City four times in the week, but gradually reduced this & finally gave it up altogether." Now he could rely on other members of the Hanbury family to continue his business policies. The second and third sons of Frederick Janson Hanbury, Reginald Janson Hanbury (1877-1935) and Frederick Capel Hanbury (1879-1957), became junior directors in 1904. William Ralph Dodd also enjoyed the distinction of being elected to the board in 1894 as a director.

It was soon evident that the resources of the factory at Bethnal Green were insufficient for the company's burgeoning business, especially the production of milk foods. This was to be the most profitable and successful of all the firm's specialities in these years. Seen from the vantage point of the 1990s, the manufacture of dried milk seems neither very technologically sophisticated nor important. However, in the early twentieth century milk was invariably contaminated with bacteria, especially the tuberculosis bacillus. In 1910 it was estimated that 20 percent of British milk contained "living tubercule": drawn from infected cows (which for political reasons it was impossible to quarantine or destroy), sold by tuberculous milk vendors, and distributed in open cans and unsterile containers, it could hardly be otherwise. The consequences were disastrous, particularly for infants. In contrast, dried milk was near sterile, it could be stored, contained a high nutritive value, and its use encouraged mothers to boil the water in which it was mixed. The purity of dried milk was soon noted by medical authorities and infant welfare centres, who increasingly began to recommend it, especially after a severe outbreak of summer diarrhoea amongst infants in 1911.

But Allen & Hanburys could obviously produce dried milk at a far more appropriate site than Bethnal Green. The need for unpolluted air, an unlimited water supply and an abundant supply of fresh milk, all dictated a rural location for the milk food business. Such a site, being well outside the city, would also have the advantage of cheaper labour, rent and rates.

In the autumn of 1896, Dodd, in an endeavour to locate such a pastoral setting, explored the banks of the River Lea and eventually found what he wanted at the little malting town of Ware in Hertfordshire. The River Lea, which was to play an important part in the working of the future Allen & Hanbury factory at Ware, had always been of importance

(left) Frederick Janson Hanbury (1851-1938), the son of Cornelius.

(above) View of Old Ware Mill in the late nineteenth century, before the arrival of Allen & Hanburys.

in the history of the town as the chief means of communication between the eastern side of Hertfordshire and London, some twenty miles or so distant. Alongside its banks the red-roofed maltings and oast-houses, reminiscent of a scene from a Dutch landscape painting, were a visible sign that for many centuries Ware had been the chief malting town in the east of England. Thus, besides its attractions for milk products, the location also gave access to the best barley available. Dodd's eyes alighted on some old picturesque flour mills, mentioned in Domesday Book, that were situated to the west of the town and close to the track of the old Roman road, Ermine Street, where it crossed the Lea Valley. The flour mills stood in a river meadow, described in old maps as Mill Mead, on an arm of the Lea and close to Ware Lock. The meadow, surrounded by the mill-stream and the river, was a complete island (see map). The owners were the New River Company, from which Allen & Hanburys leased the old mills for £200 a year, together with five acres of meadow surrounding the site.

By 1897 work was well in hand to convert the mills to the company's use. The intense activity this entailed is well documented in the Allen & Hanburys' directors' minute books.[1] The old wooden mill was

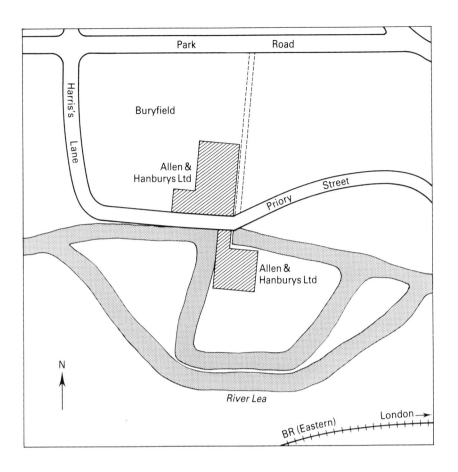

immediately demolished and replaced with a brick building. Two water turbines were installed, supplying over 30 horsepower, together with a boiler and generator; and a low pressure steam engine already on the premises was repaired and brought into service. The original staff was six and manufactured goods were sent to Bethnal Green in a one-horse van. At first, the finishing processes for the milk foods continued at Bethnal Green; but as soon as the new building was completed the whole milk department was transferred to Ware, to be swiftly followed by malt extract production.

This was only the beginning. In 1898 a freehold of eleven acres of meadow known as Buryfield was acquired, an area which faced the old mills on the other side of the stream and of Priory Street. Here a large, simply planned warehouse was erected connected by a footbridge to the new mill building. Essentially it was laid out to provide packing facilities for Allen & Hanburys' milk foods, the speciality where the directors admitted "the business of the Company has made by far the most important strides". Here the filling and soldering of the infant food tins, their labelling, packaging and storing were all conducted on separate levels. But business was also expanding in London. In 1895 the directors reported that: "The Bethnal Green Department shows a considerable increase in sales and a still more remarkable increase in net profit. This appears to be due to larger sales of most of the 'specialities'." The jujube and lozenge department and malted foods all showed considerable expansion and it was logical to transfer their production to Ware.

Malted food production began at Ware soon after that of milk and in 1900 the pastille and capsule departments followed. The new warehouse was expanded at the rear by a large area of workrooms and a new power plant; and the Buryfield frontage was doubled. Three large Galloway boilers were installed, with horizontal and beam engines; jujube manufacture was mechanised with the introduction of new machinery for moulding, pouring and sifting; there was a new building for milk products, together with a larger milk-evaporating pan; and a new air pump for the malt vacuum pan and an enlarged mash tun were added. From 1900 to 1910 the growth of the various manufactures and the need for such plant as engineering and woodworking shops, with timber yards and saw mills, caused almost constant activity at Ware. This demanded building rather than pharmaceutical skills. These were provided by William Radford, who had joined Allen & Hanburys in 1878 as a laboratory worker. Radford had served his apprenticeship to a builder, a training that proved useful at Bethnal Green, and even more so when it was necessary to organise manufacturing operations at Ware. The directors were so impressed by Radford's efforts in overcoming the teething problems in installing new plant that they made him the Ware factory manager, a post he occupied until his retirement in 1926.

In 1905 the directors had decided on yet more additions to the Ware plant:

> Grinding Mills, Disintegrators, Rollers, Roller Mills, Sifting machines, Stills, Electric Motors, Refrigerating Machy, & the like, involving in all a Capital Expenditure of about £8,000 at Ware alone, but we hope to turn all this to good account in the near future, and we believe that we are approaching the end of extensive Capital outlay, at least for some years to come.

Nevertheless, the need for fresh capital for these developments became pressing. In 1899, when each £100 share was subdivided into 100 £1 shares, the capital of the firm was increased from £75,000 to £125,000 by the issue of 50,000 new preference shares of £1 each. In 1906 75,000 new preference shares of £1 each raised the capital of Allen & Hanburys Ltd to £200,000.

There was further capital expenditure at Ware of £8,500 in 1910, when more premises were provided for the milk and malt departments. This appears to have been the last of the major additions to the site until after the First World War. The Ware factory, in not much more than a decade, had become, like Bethnal Green, a major manufacturing centre with a diverse product line. The correspondents of the *Chemist and Druggist* visited the Ware factory at this time and reported their impressions on 28 July 1906 in an article entitled "Allenburys on the Lea". It highlighted the wide range of specialities: milk and malted foods, jujubes, pastilles and capsules, toilet-soap, and the production of certain bulk galenicals, such as cascara sagrada and liquorice. The meadow allowed some curious experiments in self-sufficiency. In 1907 the directors reported that 500 lavender bushes had been planted and had produced 8 ounces of oil. They estimated that £300-worth of oil could be obtained from this

source if all the available land was planted, to say nothing of the black-currant bushes which had produced several tons of fruit. (Sadly, in the following year, the Allen & Hanbury fruit crop was hit by blackcurrant blight!)

The growth of the Ware factory eased the pressure on space at Bethnal Green, but so fast was Allen & Hanburys expanding at the turn of the century (the Bethnal Green operations alone reported an increase of 26 percent in 1901) that any spare capacity was soon filled by the firm's other lines. In 1897 bottle-washing at Bethnal Green had been moved into arches beneath the Great Western Railway, so allowing plenty of space for returned empties, and giving the cramped capsule department room to expand. However, in 1905 the firm admitted that the premises at Bethnal Green were inadequate "owing to the large quantity of goods now put up ready for sale by numerous customers, some of whom take large quantities". A fresh lease was negotiated and two years later the premises of the Sanitas Co, which occupied part of Letchford's Buildings, were acquired to provide ground floor warehouses for the packing of Allen & Hanbury products.

Building workers at the Allen & Hanburys' factory at Ware, c. 1900. Work entailed the demolition and replacement of the old mill and the construction of a new building on Priory Street.

Despite the transfer of milk, malt and pastille products to Ware, the activities at Bethnal Green continued to be varied. The main surgical instrument workshops of the firm were located there; a printing department was established in 1894 to produce the company's advertising and office materials; a pill department produced another Allen & Hanbury speciality; and the oil refinery processed castor oil and liquid paraffin and also cod-liver oil (although the main refining of the latter was conducted at Hull). In particular, the Bethnal Green factory was the nerve centre for Allen & Hanburys' extensive packing and dis-tribution department, where myriads of drugs, hospital requisites, and pharmaceutical specialities were individually packed for dispatch throughout the UK and the world. (A description of the workings of all of these departments is contained in the next chapter.) Here, too, was the administrative heart of Allen & Hanburys. In 1901 the directors stated that at Bethnal Green:

> a new three-storey building has been provided for office purposes . . . the top floor being used for typewriting letters, and the filing of all letters on a new American system, by which the whole of the correspondence, including orders from a particular customer, is kept in a separate cover which can be found at a moment's notice. Carbon copies are taken of all letters written, & are filed with the customer's letter, so that no letters have to be press-copied in the books as heretofore.

Another American invention, the "Addressograph", was used to speed up the distribution of circulars and leaflets to members of the medical profession.

In short, Bethnal Green appears to have been a mixture of the old and the new at the turn of the century. An old worker at the factory gave the following description of the scene in 1910:

View of Allen & Hanburys' Ware factory, looking east, c. 1910.

> On entering the yard, one faces direct north so as to pass down the centre roadway . . . Firstly there are the warehouses and transport section of Allen &

(above) Bethnal Green remained the administrative and distributive heart of Allen & Hanburys at the beginning of the twentieth century. This is a packing department.

(left) Evaporating pan at Ware, c. 1900, used for the manufacture of malt extract.

Hanburys on the left with the offices and interviewing room on the right, consisting of a ground floor with two storeys above. Further along on the left there is a 'Cane and Walking Stick' maker. Returning to the right are some ground floor premises occupied by the makers of "Butterine" – the equivalent of present day margarine! On the second floor is a cycle maker who claims that he introduced the first 'free wheel'. Turning sharp left, with buildings only on the right, there is the remaining part of the "Allenburys" plant – the surgical manufacturing department, the hospital furniture and sterilizing departments, the unit for producing the fine steel surgical instruments and, at the top, the "sheet metal work" shop. On the ground floor – where I spent the best part of 50 years – there is a pair of large wooden doors clearly marked on the reverse side: "Allen & Hanburys Ltd, Surgical Instrument Makers – 48 Wigmore Street W. to which all enquiries should be addressed". Then there are the departments for the processing and refining of the cod and halibut oils and, right at the end of this 'cul de sac', the entrance to the boiler house. And now the manufacturing laboratories with the pill and tablet rooms. For the "staff" – mainly recruited through recommendation or church clubs – there is a tiny chapel in which short services are held during the lunch break by the resident deaconess. There is also a 'Glee Club' manned by the staff. Wages are paid in hard cash, gold, silver or copper. So as to prevent loss in transit from the bank to the factory the money is placed in strong linen bags which in turn are buried in fine silver sand in tall tapered milk churns.[2]

Increasingly, Bethnal Green was regarded as the company's headquarters, though before 1914 the board continued to meet at the registered offices at Plough Court. Allen & Hanburys continued to prescribe and

(above) Allen & Hanburys' steam motors. The firm's first steam traction vehicle took five hours for the journey from Ware to Bethnal Green at four miles per hour!

(right) Malt extract with cod-liver oil was an important speciality in the early nineteenth century.

dispense medicines there, but commercially this pharmacy in the City had become moribund by 1900. Nevertheless, the firm was unable to countenance selling Plough Court because it added "much in prestige, historical continuity and advertisement". It also served as a bridge between the firm's Bethnal Green and West End activities. Here, too, Allen & Hanburys had ambitious plans for expansion after 1893, though initially things did not go as smoothly as at Ware.

Considerable efforts were expended in making surgical instruments a major product-line. This was no easy task, since surgical instrument production was one of the most skilled of all handcrafts. Forging, grinding, tempering and fitting-up were skills only learned after an apprenticeship of at least eight years. In 1894 the workshop at Bethnal Green was enlarged under the advice of the manager of that department, Mr. Longmate. The result was a "very serious loss", which meant that the directors soon "found it necessary to part" with Longmate's services. However, in the autumn of 1894 a large, recently built house was taken at 48 Wigmore Street in the West End, and the firm announced: "For convenience of Medical Men these premises have now been equipped with a Suite of Fitting Rooms, suitable for every class of patient; also with an aseptic Operation Theatre and Sterilising Room. A visit will be appreciated." Within walking distance of Harley Street, this location was ideal for keeping in close touch with surgeons and specialists in the area. (Those familiar with the Wigmore Street area will know that it is still home to the surgical instrument trade.) Soon the workshop at Bethnal Green was transferred to the West End, too, at a building in nearby

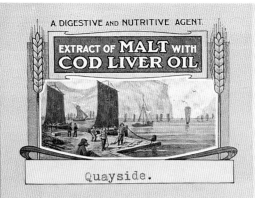

Quayside.

Waggon.

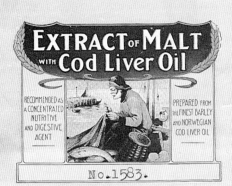

No. 1583.

Reaper.

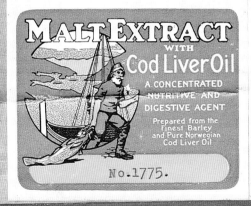

No. 1775.

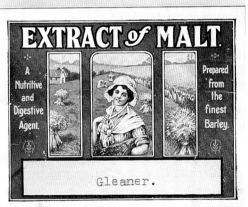

Gleaner.

Extract of Malt
— AND —
Cod=Liver Oil

This preparation contains 15 per cent. (by volume) of pure Cod-Liver Oil, which is guaranteed to possess full activity in regard to both the growth-promoting or anti-infective vitamin A and the anti-rachitic Vitamin D of which it is the best and natural source.

DOSE—A teaspoonful, gradually increased to a tablespoonful, three times a day, immediately after food.
It may be taken plain, or mixed with milk or coffee.

White & gold.

Extract of Malt
— and —
Cod-Liver Oil
A CONCENTRATED NUTRITIVE AND DIGESTIVE AGENT.

This valuable and perfect combination of the purest Cod-Liver Oil, with Extract of Malt, contains in a palatable and easily digested form the well-known properties of Cod-Liver Oil, in conjunction with the digestive principles of the finest Malted Barley.

DOSE.—A tea-spoonful gradually increased to a table-spoonful, three times a day, immediately after meals.

Red reverse.

Wesley Street. A lavish and expensive 900-page surgical instrument catalogue, with over 10,000 illustrations, was also completed in 1901.

The losses in surgical instrument making continued, however, and these were not helped by a disastrous attempt to produce "Skiagraphs", or "pictures taken by means of the Rontgen Rays". But the sales (if not the profits) of Allen & Hanburys' instruments were increasing and in about 1904 a new manager was appointed, Mr. Lewis, who energetically began enlarging the business. The reports of the surgical instrument department in the directors' minute books at this time, which sometimes occupy as much space as those of the Ware factory, show that Lewis was a persuasive and expansive talker, with grandiose plans for surgical instrument manufacture. In 1904 the Wesley Street factory was expanded for the making of aseptic hospital furniture, which provided profitable work for twelve men, and brought in orders for the fitting out of operating theatres from St. Mary's Hospital, Manchester, the General Hospital in Nottingham, and St. Thomas's Hospital, London. The front of the Wigmore Street shop was also enlarged. In 1904 Lewis told his directors, somewhat immodestly:

> My improved registered pattern of Ward Dressing Table is considered by everyone who has used it to be the most perfect Aseptic table in use. My new Patent Foot & Head rest for operation tables is being well received, and is also considered to be the most perfect in the market. My new Patent Operation Table, which was patented about 2 years ago, is still selling well, and we must have sold about 15 of these altogether at an average price of £35.

It was true, though, that Allen & Hanburys was a leader and pioneer in the production of operating tables at this time – a position it was to maintain until it relinquished this branch of manufacture. The firm's operating theatre furniture reflected the advances in surgical technique at this time – especially the ideas of a German surgeon Friedrich Trendelenburg, who demonstrated the advantage of elevating the pelvis in certain operations. The Allen & Hanbury operating table of 1900 was the first British design to incorporate the so-called Trendelenburg position.[3]

At this point it was decided to construct a new workshop for surgical instruments at Bethnal Green, on the north-east side of the factory, and to re-start production there. To add to the problems caused by these disruptions, which obviously affected the department's profitability, there were difficulties in finding skilled staff and in 1906 a fire at Bethnal Green destroyed over £1,500 of stock. On the other hand, Lewis continued to push up output and sales and progress was being made in selling the firm's products abroad in India, Egypt and Canada. Allen & Hanburys relished the honour of dealing with surgeons and the major institutions. In 1911 the directors reported that: "During the past twelve months we have secured the account of University College Hospital and several other important Hospitals & Institutions on which our special representatives call regularly. And this gratifying mark of the Profession's appreciation of the Company's instruments, is the fact that we have been requested to supply the instruments for use at the various examinations of the Royal College of Surgeons." Allen & Hanburys often produced custom-made instruments after consultation with leading surgeons. This did not mean, however, that the business was making money. As we shall see, surgical instruments made steady losses in these years and probably accounted for Lewis's departure from the company on the eve of the Great War.

More successful was Allen & Hanburys' other West End outpost, Vere Street, though even here bad management was a problem in its early days. Matters improved with the appointment of Frederic William Gamble (1872-1948) as manager in 1900. Gamble had joined the Plough Court pharmacy in 1896 and was transferred to Vere Street in the following year. A respected pharmacist, with a distinguished record as a student (he was awarded the Pharmaceutical Society's Bronze Medal in 1894), Gamble epitomised the increasing professionalisation of pharmacy at this time. He was a hard-working member of the original committee appointed to compile and produce the first *British Pharmaceutical Codex* in 1907; later he established himself as an authority on serums and vaccines and was a frequent contributor to the meetings of the London Pharmaceutical Society. His success in building up the Vere Street pharmacy was eventually recognised by his election to the Allen & Hanbury board in 1913, when he was also rewarded with 500 ordinary shares.

Gamble had "a genius for friendly relations with the medical consultants of the neighbourhood",[4] an invaluable asset for the Vere Street pharmacy. This became Allen & Hanburys' main "shop window", now that the centre of the medical and dispensing trade had shifted westwards, making the old Plough Court Pharmacy increasingly irrelevant. Originally, Vere Street had only been involved with retailing, but after 1900 it was decided to add a wholesaling side. The growth of the manufacturing side of the business at Bethnal Green, particularly of galenicals, and the increasing number of medical men and retail chemists who were drawing their supplies of these goods from the company, made it necessary to open a depot in the West End. Small supplies, as well as the Allen & Hanbury specialities, could now be swiftly obtained by those in the western suburbs of London, far from Plough Court and Bethnal Green. As Gamble noted in 1907: "The outstanding feature of the wholesale department is the large & increasing number of small urgent orders to be delivered by hand at very short notice over a large area." Vere Street, handily situated near the major railway stations, was well placed to facilitate this. The pharmacy also offered a constant service day and night, not only dispensing prescriptions, but also offering advice in difficult cases.

The firm prided itself on being able to give information on the latest treatments, the details of which were often not known outside the West End. Allen & Hanburys saw itself as being actively involved in the treatment of the patient, something which was also of benefit to the "medical man . . . [whose] . . . suggestions on the clinical treatment of some new disease or modification of the treatment of an old one can be elaborated and perfected in a practical manner, so combining the skill of the pharmacist with the knowledge of the physician".[5] This link was fostered by the publication of small booklets exclusively "for members of

*(left) Allen & Hanburys'
surgical instrument
branch at 48 Wigmore
Street was ideally situated
for close contact with
consultants in Harley
Street.*

*(above right) Intestinal
instruments. Such
products were all hand-
made by highly skilled
Allen & Hanbury
craftsmen.*

*(below right) One of
Allen & Hanburys' first
operating tables, for
which the firm was to
acquire a world-wide
reputation. One of about
15 operating tables in a
c. 1910 catalogue of
surgical instruments.
Associated text indicates
"made for His Majesty the
King".*

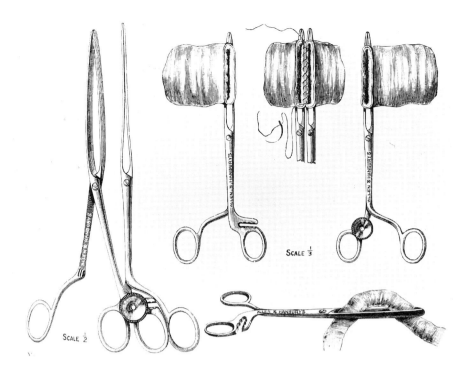

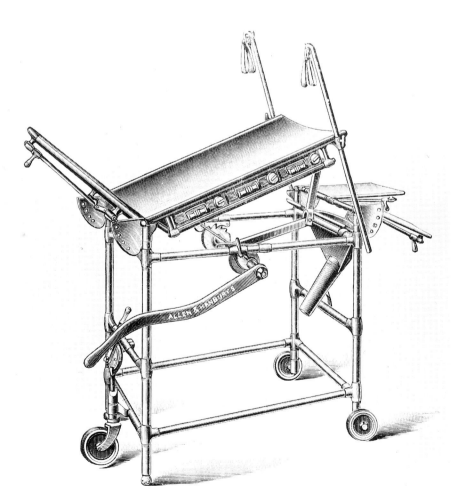

the medical profession", which listed Allen & Hanbury products and advised on their use. In 1892, for example, the firm published *Notes on Some New Remedies and Pharmaceutical Products with Lists of Soluble Coated Pills, Soluble & Disintegrating Tabellae of Compressed Drugs, also of "Hypoderms" or Easily Soluble Tabellae for the Immediate Production of Hypodermic Injections . . . [and] . . . General Posological Table.*

Treatments were changing rapidly at this time. The introduction of coated pills, of compressed tablets, of capsules and of cachets, soon began to affect the habits of the drug-buying public. Increasing use was being made of preparations from animal glands. The growing scope and complexity of surgery created a demand for anaesthetics, both general and local, which were no longer based on chloroform and ether. Hypodermic therapy was becoming increasingly popular with the medical profession, demanding sterile instruments and solutions. The first of the major synthetic drugs appeared, known as antipyrin (or phenazone), a type of early pain and fever reliever, which was marketed in the 1890s and for a time became the world's best selling drug.[6] New elixirs were compounded, sometimes using many of the older tried and trusted ingredients, but in a concentrated and reduced dosage and with more attractive packaging.

These developments gave Allen & Hanburys the chance to market new specialities at Vere Street. One of them was the anti-tuberculosis vaccine (tuberculin) developed by Robert Koch in the 1890s. Gamble noted that "our preparations of Tuberculin for use in the treatment of all forms of Tuberculosis have come into increased demand, and have brought us into close contact with a large number of medical men. The same method of preparing hypodermic syringes is being applied further." Gamble was one of the first to develop in a West End pharmacy the hypodermic method of injecting drugs, for use with vaccines, Salvarsan (the first effective anti-syphilitic remedy, discovered by Paul Ehrlich in 1909), and therapeutic serums. Large numbers of ampoules of these injections were prepared from a wide range of drugs, many of which had previously only been administered by mouth.

The firm's close contact with the medical community enabled it to respond quickly to new trends and treatments. When liquid paraffin was first introduced, "Chrismol" was placed upon the market and enjoyed a ready sale. When Pasteur's protégé, Elie Metchnikoff, began recommending sour milk as a method of combating the supposed absorption into the body of bacteria from the intestines (a controversial idea that was readily accepted by a Victorian public obsessed with the idea that purgatives and antiseptics were necessary to rid the system of foul contaminants), Vere Street marketed "Sauerin", which had a tremendous sale while the vogue lasted. Another successful liquid preparation, made from the thyroid gland, was prepared at the suggestion of the late Sir Victor Horsley and was used to treat sufferers of myxoedema, a disorder of the thyroid gland which produced mental degeneration.

Plough Court, Bethnal Green, Ware, Vere Street and Wigmore Street – such was the Allen & Hanbury "empire" in Britain on the eve of the First World War. A bald description of the history and activities of all these branches, however, cannot hope to catch fully the scope of the firm's output at this time. A better flavour of Allen & Hanburys' huge range of products can be found in some of the company's trade catalogues at this time. There is hardly a pharmaceutical product which does not appear somewhere in these publications: Allen & Hanburys was indeed the Universal Provider![7]

Such catalogues were not produced as part of a massive publicity campaign. Indeed, the firm complimented itself at this time on keeping its advertising costs to a minimum by confining its announcements, samples and circulars to the medical profession and the chemists and druggists. These were also the people for whom the catalogues were designed: hence their lavish format and extensive layout.

Allen & Hanburys' *Catalogue of Surgical Instruments and Appliances, Ward Requisites, [and] Aseptic Hospital Furniture*, is perhaps the most extraordinary of these documents. Indeed, with nearly 1,500 pages, thousands of illustrations, and tipping the scales at about five pounds, it is an extraordinary trade catalogue by any standards and surely must be one of the largest ever produced by a British firm at this time. The range of products is equally astonishing. It is no exaggeration to suggest that it would have been possible to equip a complete hospital by consulting and ordering from the catalogue. Displayed in its pages are needles, syringes, retractors, instruments for anaesthesia and every conceivable operation and gynaecological procedure; besides splints, artificial limbs, and wheelchairs; and ward and theatre requisites, including operation tables and even hospital sinks and cutlery. If all this failed to save the patient, then a set of post-mortem and dissecting instruments could be ordered! Sets of surgical instruments – all individually made in hand-crafted boxes – were an Allen & Hanbury speciality. For £50 one could choose a Field Medical Pannier: it contained about a hundred items and had *everything* a field surgeon would need, including instruments, basins, bandages, screwdrivers and even paper and ink. It would be surprising if Allen & Hanburys manufactured everything in this catalogue – and surely many of the items, such as the sinks, uniforms and cutlery (to name only a few) must have been contracted out – but even if the firm only manufactured the surgical instruments, the range is impressive.

Equally comprehensive was Allen & Hanburys' *General List of Drugs, Pharmaceuticals, and the "Allenbury" Specialities*, published in February 1911. Again it was lavishly produced, with high-quality illustrations of all the firm's most successful lines, such as its capsules and jujubes. Much space was given to an extensive selection of "Bynin Preparations" – the malt food products. Everything that could be mixed with malt and then ingested seems to have formed a "Bynin" preparation. A typical specific was "Bynin" Emulsion, a "palatable" combination of the firm's cod-liver oil and liquid malt. Most of these mixtures were described as tonics and aids to digestion. Occasionally, the claims were more ambitious and there are echoes of some of the older medieval remedies amongst the mumbo-jumbo. A 2/6d bottle of "Byno" Hypophosphites consisted of a "neutral solution of the Hypophosphites of Iron, Manganese, Calcium and Potassium, with the alkaloids of Cinchona and Nux Vomica, in

(above) A selection of Allen & Hanburys' medicine bottles.

(right) Field Surgical Pannier from the Allen & Hanburys' Catalogue of Surgical Instruments *(c. 1910).*

combination with 'Bynin', Liquid Malt" and was described as a "popular tonic, which stimulates the appetite and also aids the digestion. It strengthens and invigorates the nervous system, restores tone to the muscles of the arteries and heart, and acts both as a blood-producing agent and as a concentrated nutrient." It was no doubt a bracing combination, especially since nux vomica contained strychnine and other poisonous substances (though it had long been used as a heart stimulant). Another ancient "tonic" appeared in Allenbury's "Cokay" wine for invalids: this was made by macerating coca leaves, a plant that had been used by the Incas to allay fatigue, which contained cocaine.

Most of the products, however, were more innocuous and beneficial – notably, the cod-liver oil and the baby milk foods. The firm devoted particular attention to the presentation of its "Allenburys" Milk Foods, which were specially mixed for various stages of a baby's life. The separately packed "Allenburys" Milk Foods Nos. 1 and 2 were designed for the first six months of the infant's life. This was followed by the more nutritious "Allenburys" Malted Food No. 3 and the "Allenburys" Malted Rusks. Powder gauges, food measures and thermometers, and various baby-bottles and sterilisers completed the range of baby food products.

Also in this *General List* was a huge selection of "Druggist Sundries" –

Field Surgical Panniers

LATEST ARMY REGULATION PATTERN.

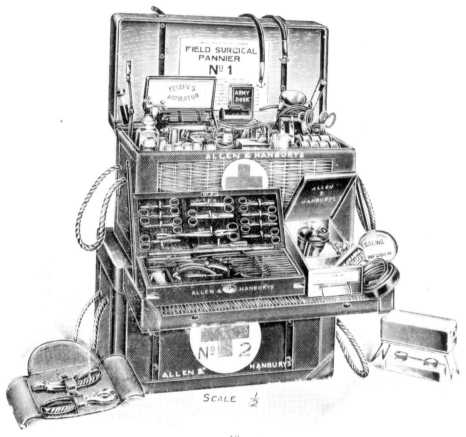

SCALE ½

10

Contents of No. 1 Field Surgical Pannier.

Top of Pannier.

Aspirator, Potain's, in leather-covered case	No.	1
Apparatus, Saline, Infusion, Horrock's, in japanned tin case ...	,,	1
Book, Specification, tally (A.B. 166), with pencil	,,	1
Bottles, Drop, for chloroform ...	,,	2
Carbolic Acid	lb.	1

Cases, Hypodermic, containing —

Syringe, Hypodermic, all metal	No.	1
Needles, Platino-Iridium ...	,,	2
Strychnine, Hydrochloride, ¹⁄₁₀ gr. tablets	tube	1
Morphine Tartrate, ¼ gr. tablets	,,	2
Digitalin, ¹⁄₁₀₀ gr. tablets ...	,,	1
Cases, metal, to contain above	No	1

Catgut, sterile, 30 in. lengths, twelve glass tubes in metal case	cases	6
Chloroform, in 2 oz. tubes ...	lb.	3
Corrosive Sublimate, tablets, in roughened red cylinder ...	No.	250
Forceps, Lion, } in waterproof canvas roll	pair	1
,, Hoffmann's }		
Gouge }	,,	1
Iodoform, in vulcanite dredgers (2)	oz.	6
Lantern, Candle	No.	1
Pins, Safety	tins	4
Plaster, Rubber, adhesive, 1 in. × 10 yds.	spools	3
Potassium Permanganate, 2 gr. tablets	No.	300
Razors, Axillary, metal handles	,,	2
Scissors, in sheath	pairs	2

Allen & Hanburys Ltd., London.

12

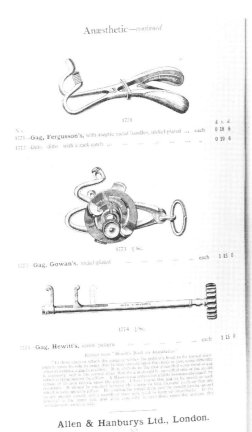

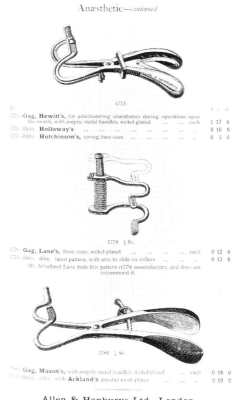

Examples of the extremely wide range of surgical products available from the firm in the 1900s. Illustrated are anaesthetic equipment and ambulances.

(above right) The malt food products – the "Bynin Preparations".

(below right) The famous "Allenburys" Milk Foods, designed for each stage of an infant's life.

"Byno" Glycerophosphates
(Trade Mark)

"Byno" Glycerophosphates contains the Glycerophosphates of Iron, Potash, Magnesia, and Soda in combination with "Bynin," Liquid Malt.

Therapeutics—"Byno" Glycerophosphates is a digestive nerve tonic and concentrated food of the highest therapeutic value. The Glycerophosphates contain Phosphorus in an easily assimilable form, and they are reputed to enrich brain and nerve tissue in this important element. They are valuable agents in restoring strength and vigour to the thin and emaciated. The employment of "Bynin," Liquid Malt, as the vehicle for the solution of the Glycerophosphates, provides an active digestive agent which promotes the assimilation of all farinaceous or starchy foods.

Dose—A dessert-spoonful to a table-spoonful, in a little water, three times daily, immediately after meals.

Prices—Retail 2/6 and 4/6 each ; Wholesale 24/- and 41/- per doz.

"Byno" Hæmoglobin
(Trade Mark)

"Byno" Hæmoglobin is a combination of Hæmoglobin with "Bynin," Liquid Malt. It contains only the natural organic compound of Iron, and in as large proportion as the digestive organs can readily assimilate.

Therapeutics—A blood-forming digestive tonic and nutrient. Useful in all cases of convalescence from acute diseases, where an iron tonic is often indicated, but where, owing to the weakened and impaired digestive powers of the patient, the ordinary preparations of iron are frequently harmful.

Dose—One table-spoonful, with meals, three times daily.

Prices—Retail 2/6 and 4/6 each ; Wholesale 24/- and 41/- per doz.

"Byno" Pancreatin
(Trade Mark)

"Byno" Pancreatin is a solution containing the active digestive ferments of the Pancreatic Juice and "Bynin," Liquid Malt. It is specially adapted for use in preparing peptonized foods. By its aid milk, farinaceous foods, jellies, etc., can all be treated so as to be partially predigested before being taken by the patient. The food is thus rendered easy of assimilation, a condition very necessary in the case of persons who are greatly reduced in strength, or for those who, like weakly children, cannot digest ordinary food.

Dose—One or two tea-spoonfuls, in a wine glass of water, with meals.

Prices—Retail 2/6 and 4/6 each ; Wholesale 24/- and 41/- per doz. 30 oz., for dispensing, 72/- per doz.

"Byno" Hypophosphites
(Trade Mark)

"Byno" Hypophosphites consists of a neutral solution of the Hypophosphites of Iron, Manganese, Calcium, and Potassium, with the alkaloids of Cinchona and Nux Vomica, in combination with "Bynin," Liquid Malt. The replacement of the sugar of the ordinary preparations by the active Malt Extract, "Bynin," greatly increases the value of the Hypophosphites, for they are more easily assimilated in "Byno" Hypophosphites than in any other preparation.

Therapeutics—A popular tonic, which stimulates the appetite and also aids digestion. It strengthens and invigorates the nervous system, restores tone to the muscles of the arteries and heart, and acts both as a blood-producing agent and as a concentrated nutrient.

Dose—A dessert-spoonful to a table-spoonful, in a little water, three times daily.

Prices—Retail 2/6 and 4/6 each ; Wholesale 24/- and 41/- per doz. 40 oz., for dispensing, 72/- per doz.

The "Allenburys" Milk Food No. 1
(Trade Mark)

Specially adapted to the first two months of Infant Life.

A reliable substitute for the Mother's Milk.

A Dried Humanised Milk which contains no uncooked starch.

The "Allenburys" Milk Food No. 1 is the result of a very careful study of the requirements of young infants and the capabilities of their digestive organs, and will be found the best substitute for the mother's milk when this is wanting or deficient, being much more readily digested and assimilated than cow's milk. It is made up and prepared from the cow's milk, the excess of curd being rendered more easily digestible, the albumen and milk sugar added, so that the constituents and proportions are in harmony with those of human milk. The resulting food is then prepared and is preserved in hermetically sealed tins. It is made by simply adding boiling water only.

Prices—Retail 1/6 and 3/- each ; Wholesale 15/- and 30/- per doz.

The "Allenburys" Milk Food No. 2
(Trade Mark)

Specially adapted to the second 3 months of Infant Life.

Contains no uncooked starch.

The "Allenburys" Milk Food No. 2 contains all the elements of human milk in their true natural proportions, with the addition of readily soluble albuminoids and other products resulting from the malting of wheat meal with a malt store. This food thus prepared contains a small proportion of soluble starch, helpful at this stage of the infant's development for the gastric digestive organs and nervous system. Due to the ideal food requirements it adds to the prolonged nourishment so that the child can digest and assimilate the food during the day-time. The child can with advantage continue this for more infants up to 3 to 6 months. It is made by simply adding the addition of boiling water only.

Prices—Retail 1/6 and 3/- each ; Wholesale 15/- and 30/- per doz.

The "Allenburys" Malted Food No. 3
(Trade Mark)

Specially adapted to Infants of 6 months of age and upwards.

A Malted Farinaceous Food.

The "Allenburys" Malted Food No. 3 is a partially digested food composed chiefly of a carefully cooked wheaten flour, specially selected on account of the large amount of gluten contained in it. To this the active and nutritive constituents of pure malt are added in soluble form, thus excluding the irritating particles usually found in the common varieties of malted foods, and which are prone to cause diarrhœa. This Food is not so completely digested as to leave no work for the infant's stomach to perform, as, however, readily assimilated by the most feeble digestions, the starch grains being thoroughly broken up in the process of cooking, and rendered partially soluble by the subsequent admixture with the soluble constituents of the malt.

The "Allenburys" Malted Food No. 3 forms an excellent evening meal for a growing child taking other food during the day-time. The child can with advantage continue this nutrient after three years.

Prices—Retail 1/-, 2/-, 5/-, and 10/- each ; Wholesale 9/3, 18/-, 42/6, and 85/- per doz.

The "Allenburys" Rusks (Malted)
(Trade Mark)

An invaluable addition to the dietary of babies ten months old and after.

The "Allenburys" Rusks are baked from specially selected flour rich in protein muscle-forming constituents. Eaten plain, they have a pleasant sweet flavour.

Added to hot milk and water, with sugar, the "Allenburys" Rusks is a very nourishing and easily assimilable food for young children.

Adults equally appreciate the "Allenburys" Rusks, which may be eaten plain, buttered, or with cheese, wine, etc.

Prices—Supplied in tins. Retail 1/6 and 2/9 each ; Wholesale 15/- and 28/- per doz.

107

abdominal belts, bandages, crutches, catheters, scales, tablet machines, printed labels (which could be produced with the druggist's name), and even sealing wax and string. If the Allen & Hanbury surgical instrument catalogue enabled the buyer to equip a complete hospital, then the general list enabled him to set up as a druggist. Nothing appears to have been left out of the catalogue. A reference section at the end thoughtfully included the addresses of the main crematoria!

There was also a *Wholesale List of Packed Drugs, Toilet Preparations, Perfumes and Toilet Soaps, Including Household Requisites* (December 1912). This catalogue included sunburn and freckle cream, dandruff lotion and sulphur hair restorer, alongside some formidable-looking veterinarian "Horse Balls" and "Horse Powders".

This vast range of products was not only available in the UK, for it was in this period that Allen & Hanburys began expanding overseas by establishing foreign branches and factories. They joined a number of British firms, such as Lever Bros (soap) and J. & P. Coats (cotton thread), which were already active in overseas markets before 1914. Allen & Hanburys, however, were far smaller than these giants and so were perhaps less typical of firms which decided to begin overseas operations (it is tempting to use the word "multinational" here, but the word did not come into vogue until the 1960s). Why did Allen & Hanburys invest abroad? The motives were never stated explicitly and can only be guessed at. The firm had, of course, been heavily involved in transatlantic trading in the eighteenth century and the successful cod-liver oil business and the opening of an Australian agency had given it a further taste of overseas business. Undoubtedly, many markets, such as those in the colonies and in America, would have been attractive because of their sheer size. Allen & Hanburys' dominance of the domestic milk food market might prove temporary and foreign countries offered a huge alternative outlet. There was the further advantage of being able to exploit patented technology and also to avoid the high tariff barriers that protected such countries as the USA. The business outlook of the Allen & Hanbury directors must also not be ignored. The urge to carry the "Allenburys" name to the far corners of the globe fitted in with Cornelius's and his co-directors' vision of the future. After all, why should a country that had built up such a vast political Empire, not similarly dominate the international business world? It was a view that was to lead Allen & Hanburys, as it was other British firms, seriously to underestimate the difficulties of operating overseas.

Allen & Hanburys Ltd Overseas Subsidiaries

Country	Company	Incorporation	Capital
Canada	A & H Co Ltd	1902	£50,000
Australia	A & H (Australasia) Ltd	1904	£20,000
South Africa	A & H (Africa) Ltd	1904	£5,000
South America	A & H (S. America) Ltd	1909	£20,000
Russia	A & H (Russia) Ltd	1913	£20,000

Dodd had visited the USA in 1897 and had "returned much impressed with the belief that there was a large opening for some of the Goods

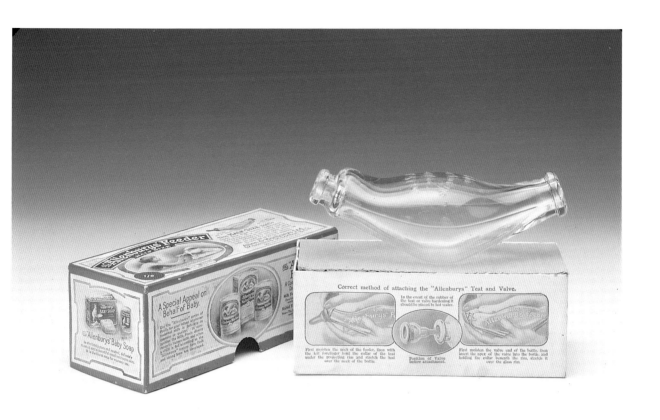

Besides baby food, Allen & Hanburys sold a full range of accessories, such as feeders.

Horse Balls

FIG. 414.

Veterinary preparation from the firm's wholesale catalogue.

manufactured by our Company, both in the States and in Canada". In the following year F.J. Hanbury followed up this visit and arranged for an agency in Canada and a branch office in New York. The American branch did not do well. In 1900 it was causing the directors "some anxiety . . . [since] . . . considerable outlay has been incurred, and large quantities of free samples have been distributed, but hitherto the sales have been quite small". The activities of the US branch were curtailed, after writing off a £4,634 loss, and it was decided to run the North

American operations from Canada. In 1902 F.J. Hanbury and his son Capel visited the USA and decided to open a subsidiary company in Canada.

The Allen & Hanburys Co Ltd was incorporated in Toronto in 1902 with a capital of $250,000, of which $100,000 (£20,000) was issued. The British parent held $20,000 (£4,000) and the remaining shares were held by the Toronto manager Lloyd Wood and his associate, A.R. Deacon, "an English gentleman well known in America for his remarkable success in the development of the trade in Listerine". The American trade was continued by a branch in Niagara Falls, but Allen & Hanburys soon found that the country was a far different proposition than the UK. A loss was immediately incurred in advertising "Allenburys" Foods and the American directors advised the firm that "great caution be observed in increasing the general advertising to the public in America, trade conditions being so different there from what they are in Great Britain owing to the enormous extent of the territory, and the great difficulty of the economical distribution of the goods". The Canadian branch was performing well, but the steady American losses before 1914 swallowed its profits. In 1913 total North American sales were $165,000, which were at last sufficient to pay a small dividend of 5 percent. Profits and dividends remained feeble during the War, when it was decided to open a small factory for "Allenburys" Foods at Lindsay, Ontario. This was in the centre of a rich farming district, producing large quantities of good milk, and the area also had excellent transport facilities. The chief engineer and head of the food department at Allen & Hanburys, P.S. King, was sent out to superintend operations in 1918, but the finance for building the factory was provided by Lloyd Wood. Allen & Hanburys must have had enough of the North American market by then, since they allowed control of the Lindsay factory to pass to the Canadian company.

South America, too, occupied Allen & Hanburys' attentions. At the turn of the century the firm had an agency in Buenos Aires, which covered the Argentine, Mexico, Bolivia, Peru, Chile and Brazil. This proved inefficient and in 1909 this branch was also converted into a separate company capitalised at £5,000. Mr. Hall, an Allen & Hanbury office manager, was sent out to secure suitable premises and register the company, "a process which", as the directors stated, "the courts there deal with in a very leisurely fashion". It made consistent losses, totalling over £10,000 by 1917, and was crippled by economic and political disturbances, particularly in the Argentine.

The Australian business was more satisfactory. This was where Allen & Hanburys had established its first important overseas agency, when in 1884 it appointed Messrs. Forrest & Co, of Melbourne, as their sole agents for infant foods and other articles. From the first this agency showed satisfactory signs of progress, so much so that in 1894 Mr. A.J. Firkins, who had already been in Australia, returned to assist it as direct representative. Ten years later the business had increased to such an extent that a private company was formed under the title of Allen & Hanburys (Australasia) Ltd, with a depot, showrooms and distributing centre at Smith Street, Sydney, under Firkins' direction. In 1910 it was necessary to acquire additional premises for the special development of the surgical instrument business, which had become an important section of the activities of the branch company. It enjoyed exceptional prosperity at this time and paid good dividends to the firm, which owned all the shares. In 1914, for example, the dividends earned the company £10,000. Turnover of the branch had reached £60,000 in 1916, but in that year the branch incurred its first loss of £1,286. During the War the "Allenburys" Foods, which had been exported under licence, could no longer be sent there and the Australian business came to a standstill.

Also in 1904 the company incorporated Allen & Hanburys (Africa) Ltd, with a depot in Cape Town. According to the directors, an earlier agency at Durban had proved "very inefficient", and it was decided to switch operations to Cape Town, under Thomas William Tullett, an Allen & Hanbury salesman. The depot proved short-lived: expenses were heavy and the directors complained that "the policy of Mr. Tullett is scarcely in accord with our views". Within two years the subsidiary was once again based in Durban and Tullett had returned home, leaving his brother John Samuel Tullett in charge. By 1908 the company was able to pay its first dividends of about 2/- per share. Trade expanded further under another new manager, Thomas Robert Walton, who joined in 1912. Under his direction a small beginning was made in local manufacture, and laboratory and printing equipment was brought from England for that purpose. Surgical instruments sold well and a sales office was opened in Johannesburg. Walton soon undertook a comprehensive tour of South Africa, advertising the company's products amongst medical men, hospitals and chemists, rapidly building up Allen & Hanburys' reputation and laying a basis for a prosperous business in South Africa. Fortunately, the War did not damage the profitability of the South African trade.

The firm made energetic efforts to open up the Far Eastern trade. In 1894 a branch business was established in India under George Reddick, an East India merchant. This was a shrewd choice. Reddick was widely travelled in India and the Far East and possessed the tact and energy necessary to sell Allen & Hanbury products in scattered areas that had never heard of the firm's goods. In 1910 the directors reported that: "This sphere of the Company's operations is becoming increasingly important. Mr. George Reddick is systematically visiting India and the sale of the Company's products shows a steady increase." Total sales in India had reached £16,365 by 1914 (a 24 percent increase on the previous year), and ambitious attempts were being made to break into the Chinese market, where sales from the Shanghai office had topped £10,000, and where the firm believed that "on the successful termination of the war, this Agency will open additional avenues of trading which will give great opportunities for further progress".

Closer to home the firm maintained a presence in some European countries, such as France and Germany. But competition from other European firms here made any business hardly worth the effort; thus the firm's attentions were always directed further afield.

Running these operations was expensive, despite the predicted gains

Allen & Hanburys overseas. This is the site of the Allen & Hanbury surgical showroom in Sydney, New South Wales, in about 1918.

113

(which were, of course, by no means certain). By the end of the First World War only the South African subsidiary was making a significant profit and, on balance, it seems that Allen & Hanburys' overseas ventures before 1918 were only just in the black – a situation not helped by the fact that the parent was supplying them with products at cost price. This was very similar to the experiences of other British firms at this time, many of whose foreign subsidiaries performed well below expectations.[8] Investing heavily in such ventures also involved significant risks, as Allen & Hanburys was to discover in Russia.

Here branch trading had begun in Moscow in about 1910 under the direction of S.S. Selitrenny, a local chemist and druggist, and three years later a subsidiary was formed. Despite initial losses, Allen & Hanburys was particularly struck with the possibilities of this territory and as trade began to flourish invested heavily in a factory in Moscow for the manufacture of various chemicals. No sooner had the company moved into profitability, however, than the First World War brought disaster. At first this locked up the firm's capital in Russia, some £288,849 in 1918 (at a time when the total capital employed in all the subsidiaries was £332,674). Optimistically, the company declared that it did not "regard the Russian situation as involving the Company in any large permanent loss, and not necessarily in any loss at all". It was wrong. During the Russian Revolution the company's assets were seized, greatly reducing Allen & Hanburys' working capital and causing the company to pass the dividend on its ordinary shares for the first time in its history.

At this point it is perhaps appropriate to provide some assessment of Allen & Hanburys' performance in the period 1893-1918. More so, because towards the end of this period two of the central architects of the business, Cornelius Hanbury and his fellow director, William Ralph Dodd, both died. Shortly before his death in 1916, Cornelius wrote:

> I have greatly enjoyed the quiet life [at Little Berkhampstead] and am now entirely unfit for action; sight, hearing, and memory for recent things having failed. This is scarcely surprising as I have now entered my eighty-seventh year, but still enjoy boundless causes for thankfulness in my daily life and bright hopes beyond.[9]

He had, however, lived to celebrate the bi-centenary of the company in 1915, which was marked in appropriate fashion by the presentation of an oil portrait to Cornelius's son, Frederick Janson (Cornelius had received such a gift some years earlier), soon to become chairman of the firm. Dodd was also honoured at the celebration, though sadly he was to succumb to typhoid fever in 1917.

These men had achieved spectacular success after the formation of the limited company. The firm had now burst through the chrysalis of its Quaker origins and its old religious linkages were fading as the firm became more "worldly".[10] The number of Allen & Hanburys' workers had grown from less than a score in 1850 to some 500 in 1915. Unfortunately, no data is available for Allen & Hanburys' turnover and profits between 1893 and 1910; but the growth of the company's reserves, which grew from £3,200 to £32,500 in this period, gives some indication. So, too, do the

(above) *The rewards of industry. Cornelius Hanbury's residence, the Manor House, at Little Berkhampstead.*

(right) *This remarkable photograph taken in 1913 shows four generations of the Hanbury family. Seated, right, the bearded and stately Cornelius Hanbury (aged 86) and, in descending order of age, Frederick Janson Hanbury, Frederick Capel Hanbury and John Capel Hanbury.*

dividend payments. These, to say the least, were very satisfying for the Hanburys and the few lucky holders of the firm's ordinary shares. Yearly dividends had reached 50 percent by 1902, and between 1904 and 1910 the payments were never less than 20/- per share. After that date more figures are available and the firm's progress can be more accurately plotted (see p. 125). Particularly noteworthy is the huge rise in turnover from below £500,000 in 1912 to nearly £1 million at the end of the First World War. The firm continued to pay excellent dividends – never less than 15/- on the ordinary shares – and adopted a conservative policy, with the setting aside of ample reserves (see p. 118). As can be seen, the War entailed no interruption to Allen & Hanburys' growth. The firm found, as did other British enterprises, that conflict was by no means detrimental to profits. Certain aspects of the business were disrupted: some of the branches suffered staff shortages as men enlisted for the colours and in May 1918 a German bomb wrecked the south-western part of the Bethnal Green factory. But, as would be expected, other Allen & Hanbury products were much in demand in the War. Government orders for operating theatre equipment kept the surgical instrument department very busy.

Allen & Hanburys Ltd Annual Financial Statistics, 1911-18.

(£)	Turnover	Net Profit	Dividend	Reserve
1911	383,211	57,500	30/-	36,505
1912	434,000	61,000	32/-	40,350
1913	476,000	76,000	22/-	44,060
1914	508,000	?	28/-	50,000
1915	544,000	?	30/-	77,415
1916	597,000	?	30/-	82,416
1917	650,000	?	25/-	92,416
1918	766,700	87,054	6/-	67,000

Capital issues:

1911 capital £300,000; 100,000 £1 cumulative preference shares issued.

1912 capital £475,000; issue of 175,000 £1 "C" preference shares.

1915 capital £480,000; issue of 5,000 new ordinary shares.

1918 capital £550,000 (£369,150 paid up); issue of 70,000 new deferred ordinary shares of £1 each.

Source: Allen & Hanburys Ltd, Minute Books.

The firm had every reason to be pleased with its record. Looking over the results for 1915 the directors commented:

> there is great cause for present thankfulness and future encouragement in the fact that, in this, the bi-centenary year of the Company's existence, the business is more diversified, vigorous and prosperous than at any previous period . . . Such a result goes far to prove that contrary to general opinion, a diversity of departments can prove of advantage to a Company if efficiently and economically managed.

In retrospect, however, Allen & Hanburys' strategy was not without its weaknesses. That strategy was the opposite of Allen & Hanburys' present-day policy which "adheres to the principle of a unitary theme in business, and has doubts about the advantages of synergy between different activities, particularly between the pharmaceutical business and others".[11] These doubts would be supported by the record of the firm's numerous departments in this period, which as the directors admitted "show wide differences in the profitableness or otherwise of their trading".

The patchy performance of the overseas subsidiaries has already been highlighted. A similar picture is presented by other departments of the UK business, many of which proved far from profitable. This accounted for a key feature of Allen & Hanburys' financial performance: although turnover rose spectacularly, this was not matched by a proportionate rise in net profit which, as can be seen in the graph on p. 125, remained remarkably static before 1940.

The London branches of the firm – Plough Court, Vere Street and Wigmore Street – seem to have cultivated more prestige than money. Plough Court was knowingly retained simply as a showpiece, and usually hardly covered its running costs. Vere Street made a good profit once Gamble had reorganised it, but this was offset by poor trading at Wigmore Street. By 1909 Lewis had tripled the annual sales of this department to £30,000, but not until two years later was the *first* profit for the surgical instrument business reported, a paltry £1,756. This was perhaps not surprising: virtually all the instruments were hand-forged by highly skilled craftsmen and the market was a small one. Made to last a lifetime, there was little obsolescence built into Allen & Hanbury products. The firm admitted in 1909: "The manufacture of Aseptic Hospital furniture is not a profitable branch of business. The demand is limited and there are now very few institutions which are not already fitted out with Aseptic furniture." However, in its role as a Universal Provider of medical equipment the company seems to have felt obliged to persevere.

Other branches did consistently poorly. Soap manufacture did not return any satisfactory results until 1918, and the cod-liver oil and pastille departments had a fluctuating performance. Some of these manufacturing operations were small scale and did not affect Allen & Hanburys' overall results unduly. On the other hand, they were a distraction from the company's main business and dissipated its energies.

Above all, it was the milk and malted food section of the business which underpinned the firm's success. In 1900, for example, the firm had noted that it was in infant foods that "the business of the Company has made by far the most important strides". Two years later there was another "*large increase* in sales and output of Foods and other specialities, and it is from these sources that the profits from the year's trading are principally derived". By the end of the War the turnover from the food department had passed the £500,000 mark, some fifty percent of the firm's total business. Besides the profits, the firm had the satisfaction of knowing that its bacteria-free dried infant foods had probably saved as many childrens' lives as all the other vaunted vaccines, antitoxins and surgical procedures combined. Nevertheless, this reliance on a single product obviously had its dangers.

Some misgivings can also be expressed when Allen & Hanburys and the other British pharmaceutical firms are compared with their international competitors. In pharmaceutical manufacture Allen & Hanburys remained characterised by its traditional business practices of importing and refining basic raw materials and packaging them for distribution to chemists and druggists. Its laboratory was essentially a quality control centre for the testing and analysis of imported products and its own manufactures, and not a place, as it is today, where the latest scientific methods were systematically applied in the search for new drugs. This was typical of British drug companies before the First World War. Burroughs Wellcome, it is true, had established its Physiological and Chemical Research Laboratories at Herne Hill and London in the 1890s and was committed to large-scale research.[12] (Significantly, the major influence on this firm was Sir Henry Wellcome (1853-1936), who was American born and trained.) But only Evans Sons Lescher & Webb Ltd, which had forged links with Liverpool University Medical School, had followed this lead.

This was in marked contrast to America and, especially, Germany. In these countries by the 1890s many of the leading pharmaceutical companies were adopting a new scientific image: they began employing medical men and establishing laboratories, which by the First World War had evolved into significant research institutions. It was these laboratories which spearheaded the major pharmaceutical breakthroughs in the 1890s and early 1900s, which transformed the industry. At Bayer, for example, a new, centralised laboratory was opened in 1891, which by the end of the century had a chemical staff of over 130. Within a decade this laboratory was involved in the discovery of a historic money-spinner – aspirin. Also in the 1890s, after several years of painstaking work German pharmacists announced a clinically effective antitoxin for diphtheria. Thus the products that Allen & Hanburys listed in its 1898 catalogue under the heading "The Treatment of Diphtheria and Other Diseases by Anti-Toxic Serums" were due to German and not British development work. (Allen & Hanburys distributed these products as agent for the Lister Institute, as a result of an agreement made in 1895.)

The German scientific approach scored one of its greatest successes in 1910 with the discovery of Salvarsan, an effective treatment for syphilis. This was the work of Paul Ehrlich who, actively supported by the German chemical firm, Hoechst, believed it was possible to develop

"Allenburys" baby soap and the soap packing department at Allen & Hanburys. The soap department, like some other parts of the business, was never very profitable, though it enabled the firm to offer a vast product-line.

drugs that would act like "magic bullets" – chemical missiles that would attack the disease and not the patient. Despite early setbacks in its use because of its toxicity, Salvarsan represented the first major chemotherapeutic agent and secured Ehrlich's reputation as the founder of modern chemotherapy.

In America the development of scientific pharmacy was fostered by corporate reorganisation which expanded opportunities for the exploitation of national markets. Here firms such as Merck, which had 2,000 employees by 1913 (a figure not equalled by Allen & Hanburys until about 1930), were far larger than their British counterparts. In Germany the growth of the dyestuffs industry financed research and development in fine chemicals on a scale unknown in the UK and allowed German firms – Badische, Bayer, Cassella and Hoechst – to dominate the world pharmaceutical industry on the eve of the First World War. It was then that the British lag in pharmaceutical manufacture became apparent when it was found that Britain had become heavily dependent upon German dyestuffs and synthetic drugs, such as Salvarsan.[13]

Judging by the directors' reports, this competition does not seem to have been a major concern of Allen & Hanburys. They did not see themselves as competing in the same field as some foreign manufacturers. Synthetic drug manufacture did not yet play a significant part in its output and the firm did not seem to feel it should. Indeed, Cornelius Hanbury had been quoted as regarding German synthetic drugs as a "passing phase".[14] In pharmaceutical manufacture its position was essentially reactive – it would make money where it could, adapting its product-line as events unfolded, rather than setting the pace with new innovations. Nevertheless, this policy could hardly succeed in the long term. The milk food business would not last for ever – indeed competition was already apparent before the War – and how it might be replaced set the agenda for Allen & Hanburys in the inter-war years.

5

THE FIRM BETWEEN THE WARS

The Company is financially stronger today than at any time in its long history.

Allen & Hanburys Ltd, Minute Book, 32nd Annual Report 1924.

At the end of the First World War Allen & Hanburys faced the major task of adjusting itself to peace-time conditions. Like all British companies it had to contend with the problems of labour shortages, the increasing cost of raw materials, and a rise in overheads; whilst around the corner, unknown to the directors, was a severe post-war slump.

In some ways Allen & Hanburys had escaped lightly from the conflict. Its turnover was unimpaired – indeed it had continued its steady expansion – and the firm's direction had not been distorted, as had some of the engineering industries, by wartime demands for products outside the normal run of business. The Hanbury family remained in control of the company, ensuring stability and continuity in management. Frederick Janson Hanbury was now chairman, with his sons as senior directors. F. Capel Hanbury, a qualified pharmacist, had assumed responsibility for the production of foods and pharmaceutical products at Ware. Reginald Hanbury, who like his grandfather, Cornelius, had qualified as a surgeon at St. Bartholomew's Hospital, developed the surgical division of the company. These men were assisted by John Netherway (1871-1951), the former company secretary, who had joined Allen & Hanburys in 1894 and had been made a director in 1916.

Despite these advantages, the sequestration of the Russian subsidiary was a major blow: it gave the firm its first "outstanding difficulty . . . a shortage of capital".[1] In 1919, for the first time in its history, Allen & Hanburys passed both the ordinary and preference share dividends and the annual profit of £93,129 was applied to reducing the Russian debt of nearly £300,000.

Another immediate consideration was the repair of bomb damage to the Bethnal Green factory. No lives had been lost during the raid on Whit Sunday 1918, but the destruction, which was viewed by King George V and Queen Mary on the following day, was considerable. A good idea of the damage sustained by the buildings can be obtained if the illustration of the Bethnal Green factory prior to 1918 (reproduced on p. 74) is studied. The two- and three-storey buildings in the foreground, housing the drug department, were so badly damaged that they were pulled down. The square building in the centre with "Allen &

F. Capel Hanbury (1879-1957), who assumed control at Ware in the inter-war period.

Hanburys" along the top, in which lozenges were made, besides the two-storeyed building on the right of it, which housed the directors' offices and the analytical laboratory, were wrecked; and the connecting-bridge from the directors' rooms to the advertising department had to be removed.

Accommodation for the drug department was swiftly found in the undamaged sections of the factory; the analytical laboratory was transferred to nearby Hague Street; and the opportunity was taken to remove the lozenge department to Ware. Rebuilding began at once: it was to occupy the firm until the end of 1922 and, together with the purchase of the freehold at Bethnal Green, was to cost £133,000.

Fresh capital was needed for these developments. In 1918 the ordinary share capital was increased from £30,000 to £100,000, thus increasing the company's authorised capital from £480,000 to £550,000, of which £369,150 was issued and paid up. In 1920 the capital was further increased to £850,000 (of which £535,000 was paid up) by the issue of 300,000 £1 cumulative "A" preferred ordinary shares. This made Allen & Hanburys only a moderately sized company, when compared with its largest competitors. Imperial Chemical Industries Ltd was capitalised in 1926 at over £50 million; and in Germany IG Farbenindustrie had been formed at this time with an initial capital, soon increased, of over £20 million.

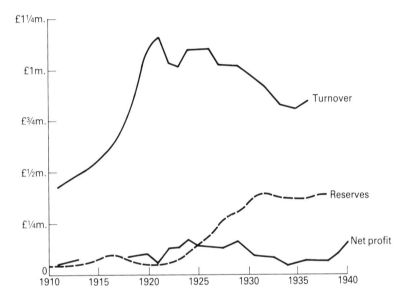

Nevertheless, Allen & Hanburys' trading remained good. In 1920 turnover passed the £1 million mark (see above) and caused the directors to reflect on the firm's remarkable record since 1893. As they pointed out, sales had virtually tripled since 1911, an impressive figure, even allowing for some rise in prices. On the converse side, net profits had been 14 percent in 1914, and by 1920 were "only a shade over 9%, though on the greatly increased turnover this lower rate results in total net profits well in advance of any previous years".

The milk and food business was still highly profitable. Although there was at least one bad year, the First World War had stimulated the demand for baby food and also Government demand for dried milk. The available statistics are rudimentary, but one authority has highlighted a dramatic rise in the consumption of powdered milk (among infants) from about one pound per head in 1913 to about 18 pounds per head in 1934-8.[2] In 1918 Allen & Hanburys' infant food sales were up by £38,000 and contributed £35,000 in profits to the business. Other branches of trading were doing nowhere near as well. Some idea of the respective positions of the various departments can be seen from the directors' annual report for 1920, which shows the following:

	(£) Turnover	(£) Net Profit
Branches		
Plough Court	18,906	2,027
Vere Street	45,000	48 (loss)
Wigmore Street	87,898	under 1,000
Departments		
Wholesale drugs	207,772	12,100
Packed drugs	105,220	6,000
Oil	44,500	2,019
Pastilles	60,000	19,070
Malt	94,700	28,252
Infant foods	500,000 approx.	30,000 approx.

Allen & Hanburys' dependence on milk and malted food products is striking. It contributed over half the turnover and well over half the net profits at this time; though it must be said that the net profit on the massive turnover of infant food was also strikingly low. (As will be described below, the foreign subsidiaries can be discounted in 1920, since Allen & Hanburys' investments in this area were yielding few returns.)

The milk and malted food departments seemed immune to the effects of the downturn in the economy in 1919-20. This led to a severe drop in profits for Allen & Hanburys, from £100,000 to £32,560, but with its sales up by 20 percent, the infant foods section was "the outstanding and bright exception" in a bleak year. In 1922 the directors declared: "This wonderfully successful and profitable department has eclipsed all previous results." It was responsible for 80 percent of all the net profits of Allen & Hanburys. The board looked forward to the future with guarded optimism:

> We believe that the year under review [1921] will pass into the history of Commerce as one of the most – if not actually the most – difficult and serious ever experienced. Our experience is the experience of practically every commercial undertaking in the country, particularly of manufacturing concerns, and when we look round at the disastrous effect on large old-established businesses of world-wide reputation, we feel thankful that we have "weathered the storm", for we believe the worst is passed.

During the rebuilding of the Bethnal Green factory the opportunity had been taken to expand the analytical laboratory. Although much of Allen & Hanburys' trade was in the old galenicals, the technical aspects of pharmacy were becoming more complex in the inter-war period. Legislation was requiring that pharmacists should be in charge of the manufacturing and other departments of such a business: the Dangerous Drugs Act of 1922 which affected the manufacturing, wholesale and retail sides of pharmacy alike, necessitated the employment of trained and qualified men for carrying out many of its exacting provisions. The Pharmacy and Poisons Act of 1933 further tightened the regulations concerning the selling and dispensing of listed poisons and controlled drugs, which could now only be done by registered members of the Pharmaceutical Society.

A view of the analytical laboratory at Bethnal Green.

The laboratories occupied about half of the top floor of the new building at Bethnal Green and had an area of about 120 feet by 40 feet. There were separate analytical, research, bacteriological and experimental manufacturing divisions and also a well-stocked library. The director of the laboratory was Norman Evers, whose staff included seven chemists and a number of assistants. Allen & Hanburys claimed that "the newly equipped laboratories provide probably the best facilities enjoyed by any firm of manufacturing wholesale druggists in this country". According to another account, alongside the routine testing each year of over 8,000 samples of drugs: "In the research and experimental research laboratories work is carried out with an eye to the future: new preparations are made in small batches with the object of discovering how best they can be manufactured on a large scale; old methods of manufacture are examined in the light of recent knowledge: investigations are made upon vexed and troublesome problems in chemistry, pharmacy and pharmacology, and new manufacturing plant is tested."[3]

In short, an embryonic research division had been formed, which though small by American and Continental standards was immediately involved in exploiting one of the major drug breakthroughs of the twentieth century. In 1923 Allen & Hanburys became a pioneer in the production of insulin, a hormone treatment for diabetes, which had been discovered in Canada.

Insulin is secreted by the pancreas and is essential for the conversion of blood glucose to liver glycogen, the source of heat and energy for muscular activity. The pancreas of diabetics does not produce enough insulin to allow sufficient glucose to enter the cells. The result is that much of the blood glucose is unused and the blood glucose level rises: eventually the glucose passes out of the body, causing disorders of the metabolism that can lead to coma and death.

From the 1890s several investigators had managed to lower blood sugar levels by using pancreatic extracts. None of them, however, had succeeded in returning very ill patients to normal health and the pancreatic substance involved had not been isolated. In 1921 the search was taken up by two Canadians, Frederick Grant Banting and Charles Best, who began experimental work at the University of Toronto under a world authority on the subject of diabetes, Professor John Macleod. Using the pancreas of a dog and a previously tried alcoholic extraction method, by the end of the year Banting's and Best's efforts had resulted in a usable extract. It was given the name insulin, a hormone that was to save the lives of literally millions afflicted with what, until then, had been a fatal condition. The first to receive insulin, in January 1922, was twelve-year old Leonard Thompson, a dangerously ill diabetic who was being treated at the Toronto General Hospital and was not expected to live much longer. Unfortunately, the first injections had to be terminated due to local irritation and it became evident that further purification of insulin was needed. This was achieved by Professor J.B. Collip of the University of Edmonton, who precipitated insulin from aqueous alcoholic extract of the pancreas by pouring this into several volumes of pure alcohol. This time the effect of the injections was dramatic, for the boy was rapidly restored to health in only a few days. He was to remain in the best of health for several years, until his untimely death in a motor cycle accident.[4]

Banting and Best had agreed to apply for patents on the process on the understanding that the University of Toronto would accept and administer them. This it did by setting up an Insulin Committee, which at once put all the relevant information at the disposal of the Eli Lilly Co of Indianapolis. This altruistic gesture ensured the rapid production of insulin, and meant that the lives of as many diabetics as possible were saved. Similar arrangements were made with other responsible agencies throughout the world.

The British rights of the patent were offered as a free gift to the Medical Research Council of London, which was entrusted with the task of ensuring that commercial production was conducted in a safe and efficient manner. In early 1923 the MRC announced that it had entered into an agreement for the production of insulin with a number of British firms – namely Allen & Hanburys, The British Drug Houses Ltd, Burroughs Wellcome and Boots Pure Drug Co Ltd.

The quantities of insulin available at first were very small and Eli Lilly initially supplied the British demand. Owing to the comparatively small number of doses produced, only large hospitals and medical

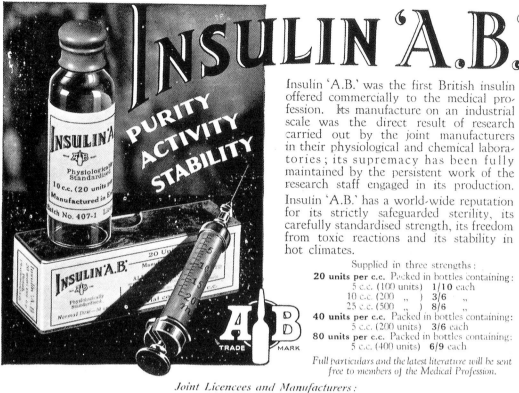

Insulin 'A.B.'

PURITY ACTIVITY STABILITY

Insulin 'A.B.' was the first British insulin offered commercially to the medical profession. Its manufacture on an industrial scale was the direct result of research carried out by the joint manufacturers in their physiological and chemical laboratories; its supremacy has been fully maintained by the persistent work of the research staff engaged in its production.

Insulin 'A.B.' has a world-wide reputation for its strictly safeguarded sterility, its carefully standardised strength, its freedom from toxic reactions and its stability in hot climates.

Supplied in three strengths:

20 units per c.c. Packed in bottles containing:
5 c.c. (100 units) 1/10 each
10 c.c. (200 „) 3/6 „
25 c.c. (500 „) 8/6 „
40 units per c.c. Packed in bottles containing:
5 c.c. (200 units) 3/6 each
80 units per c.c. Packed in bottles containing:
5 c.c. (400 units) 6/9 each

Full particulars and the latest literature will be sent free to members of the Medical Profession.

Joint Licencees and Manufacturers:

Allen & Hanburys Ltd.   The British Drug Houses Ltd.

Advertisement for insulin. Allen & Hanburys was amongst the first firms to market this new treatment for diabetes.

practitioners had access to the drug. The large quantities of alcohol used for extraction brought the manufacture under almost prohibitive restrictions, until the Customs and Excise allowed specially de-natured alcohol to be used duty free. The embargo on the importation of Canadian cattle had greatly reduced the supply of fresh pancreas material in the UK and a good deal of improvisation and initiative had been necessary to ensure adequate supplies.

Allen & Hanburys decided to join forces for the production of insulin with The British Drug Houses Ltd. This firm was better placed in its Graham Street premises for the erection of a large-scale production unit, which was accomplished under the direction of the research chemist, Francis Carr. Allen & Hanburys was able to add the expertise of its analytical laboratory. An agreement was drawn up between the two companies and the insulin produced by their joint efforts was marketed as "Insulin A.B.". By July 1923, the A.B. Partnership, which continued in operation until after the Second World War, was producing 50,000 doses of insulin a week – a supply which actually exceeded demand; and since then, no diabetic has been denied the drug because of manufacturing shortages. The insulin arrived at Bethnal Green as a solution, where it was taken to a special packing room to be bottled under sterile conditions. A high-pressure steam steriliser dealt with 3,000 insulin vials at a time.

Interior and exterior views of Plough Court, 1927.

By the end of 1923, the A.B. Partnership accounted for 95 percent of UK insulin production. It was a highly profitable activity for the company for the first two years, since the margin between the manufacturing cost and the selling price was considerable. But overproduction and the growth of competition meant that the selling price of 100 units of insulin fell dramatically from about 25/- in 1923 to less than 1/- in 1935. In 1925 the profit on insulin had disappeared, though it recovered thereafter and became a steady, if unspectacular, source of business.

The profits from insulin had contributed to the good financial results in 1924, which had seen the company largely recover the ground lost during the postwar difficulties. The company celebrated by paying a 10/- dividend on the deferred ordinary shares and capitalising £31,500 of its reserves to create 31,500 more deferred ordinary shares. It also paid a bonus to the work-force – a week's wages to all those of at least a year's service, which totalled some £5,000. A similar bonus was paid each year until 1929. Labour relations at Allen & Hanburys appear to have been very good during the inter-war period. A staff pension fund had been inaugurated from 1920, which paid half the salary (subject to a stated maxima) upon the retirement age of sixty-five.

"Allenburys" baby foods in miniature. These items were specially commissioned in the 1920s by Sir Edwin Lutyens when he was constructing a Dolls' House for Her Majesty Queen Mary. The feeding bottle is one inch long. (By gracious permission of Her Majesty The Queen)

An idea of what it was like to work at Allen & Hanburys in the mid-1920s can be obtained by a retrospective tour of its departments. These were still extraordinarily diverse: so much so, that when Allen & Hanburys' trade journal, *Plough Magazine*, published a "Round the Factory with a Notebook and Camera" series in 1925-9, it took ten parts, and even then many of the firm's activities were not covered.

The branches in the City and West End set the Allen & Hanbury style. Plough Court, despite its unprofitability, was still dispensing drugs in its impressive surroundings, a living testament to the firm's historical traditions and commitment to honest dealing. Prestige and the close ties with the medical world also radiated from Wigmore Street and Vere Street. At the former the ground floor was given up to the display and sale of instruments of hospital furniture. Large and comprehensive stocks of surgical instruments and appliances were in evidence as well as displays of aseptic hospital furniture, for which the company was increasingly noted. The First World War brought many surgical advances, and these were reflected in the appearance of a new Allen & Hanbury operating table, introduced in 1920. This table, designed with the help of Sir Holburt Waring of St. Bartholomew's Hospital (hence its familiar name of the "Bart's" table), was a recognisable ancestor of modern operating tables. It incorporated a hydraulic height adjustment, lever control of Trendelenburg and reverse-Trendelenburg positions, and a crank-operated back elevator. By 1930 this table had been further improved by hand-wheel controls and a wide range of accessories. On the first floor at Wigmore Street were rooms for the preparation and sterilisation of ligatures and the display of electro-medical apparatus. On the second floor were the fitting rooms, where patients were equipped with special appliances, such as artificial eyes and limbs. There were separate rooms for the hearing-aid section and the occasional demonstration of various surgical instruments to medical students by the manager. The third and fourth floors were principally devoted to stock, with the exception of a workshop for making belts and trusses and a room in which knives were specially set before despatch.

The main surgical instrument workshop was at Bethnal Green. Manufacture remained a highly skilled craft, with the company training many of its own apprentices. The work was extensively sub-divided: there were brass workers, who produced various non-ferrous articles; those who made electrical instruments for eyes, nose and throat; and steel workers, a class which included "blunt" workers, "bow" workers, and "edge" workers, who ground all the instruments (now made out of stainless steel) with a cutting edge. Ernest Cripps in his history of the company, which was published at about this time, noted a workman building a model "Bart's" operating table, an accurate and fully working scale model that could fit in a bowler hat and was produced as a salesman's sample. Also at Bethnal Green was the production of the full-sized tables, besides other items of hospital furniture and high-pressure steam sterilisers. There was a sheet-metal working shop and a complete nickel and silver-plating plant.

The Vere Street branch in the 1920s was described as the embodiment of the "concept of pharmaceutical perfection", where many of the staff were sons of leading manufacturing chemists. They regarded Vere Street as a kind of finishing school, whose different departments – retailing, wholesaling, compounding and dispensing – offered a complete grounding in all aspects of pharmaceutical work. This was no ordinary pharmacy and something of the awe it inspired is well caught in the following recollections of Vere Street in the 1920s, by a man who later became its manager:

> The windows were lead-lighted, coloured glass, devoid of display, and the handles at the swing doors of the entrance were of polished brass. The interior display involved little more than the old green ointment or extract jars, and recess-labelled dispensing rounds. The shop counter ran the length of the shop and had three desks equally spaced, one for each of the exalted personages who had, by seniority, qualified to wear a black alpaca jacket and serve the distinguished customers. On one occasion, during my first few months on the staff, I was detailed to relieve the assistant at the lowest desk for half a day. I was so overcome by the distinction that I wrote to my mother about it and entered it in my diary. The only other person permitted to be at the counter was a young lady who elegantly wrapped all dispensed medicines and arranged their dispatch. [The manager] W.H. McCallum's partially glassed office was in a prominent position, and there he held court with the dignity of a medical consultant. He had a fund of knowledge, medical and otherwise, such as few have attained, and his West Highland accent, tempered by many years in London, was a delight to hear.
>
> The dispensing, like the shop, had qualified staff who only numbered seven, including John Dickson, that unforgettable character – a lowland Scot and a schoolfellow of Sir James Barrie – who was known as the checker. When he was on duty nothing left the dispensary without the scrutiny of his eye, finger and nose. He often completed his inspection with a close inspection of the dispenser (I nearly said culprit). [At times of stress] John

Dickson's patience would evaporate and he would give vent to his feelings by throwing a heavy prescription book from one end of the dispensary to the other . . .

Vere Street consisted of a basement and four floors, with a staff in the 1920s of about fifty, a few of whom lived in. It was, of course, in the centre of the West End medical community and so, besides the ordinary customers, consultants often called in or sent orders from their practices. Orders came in at all times and were dispatched night and day, both locally and to the provinces. Vere Street's laboratory prepared every conceivable sterile medication, particularly the tuberculins; it also specialised in the culture of *B. bulgaricus* and *B. acidophilus* "witness tubes" for checking the temperature reached by dressings and sutures in autoclaves; vacuum tubes for the collection of blood; bee toxin (the stings for which were extracted on the spot); and solutions for skin testing and specific desensitisation. Some of the more lowly work at Vere Street was unpleasant:

> The last man to join the staff went straight on to the "pill bench". There he was the recipient of all prescriptions for pills, many of which were "stinkers" (containing asafoetida or the valerianates, for example), all of which had to be made and coated with either varnish, silver, salol, talc or powdered liquorice root. The first thing each morning it was his job to make the fresh infusions for the day and for some years it was his duty, every Thursday morning, to send one of the messenger boys to a local butcher's shop for marrow bones from which to extract the marrow. The hardest part of this job was to incorporate into the intractable mass a quantity of sodium chloride and sodium benzoate. This was done in the largest mortar by belabouring the material with the heaviest pestle available.
>
> The section next to "pills" was "ointments, suppositories and bougies", then came "capsules and cachets". Centrally situated was the checker and the assistant who answered the telephone and copied new prescriptions into the book. Finally, there was a very efficient lady, the dispensary's second in command, who dispensed the "waits". All poisons had to be checked by another pharmacist, and the details, together with the signatures of the two pharmacists, were recorded in the poison book.[5]

The main headquarters of Allen & Hanburys were now housed in the new factory at Bethnal Green. This stood as a large, central block, which consisted of five floors and a basement, with a square water tower, and was surrounded by a range of three-storied buildings. Here were the directors' rooms and main administrative offices of the company, which processed the huge number of wholesale orders. Here, too, as we have seen, were the analytical laboratories and the surgical instrument-making department. Pills and tablets and a large number of galenical preparations were also manufactured at Bethnal Green.

The entire length of the top floor of the main building was occupied by the general office, which was involved in dealing with the constant stream of postal orders that arrived at Bethnal Green early each morning. Photographs of the general office at this time show it looking very much like other offices in inter-war Britain. Many female clerks are in evidence – then, as now, women were regarded as being uniquely

Allen & Hanburys at the Manchester Surgical Exhibition, 1927.

qualified for such tasks – and the firm employed many of the latest office methods and machines, such as ledger posting machines, comptometers and "kardex" files. Processing such a large number of orders, with each order sometimes containing multiple requests from amongst Allen & Hanburys' thousands of products, was an administrative challenge. A special typewriter was used to copy each order and then prepare the other documentation – the invoice, the ledger docket, the pricing copy, the despatch copy, the receiving note and the multi-coloured requisitions for each department. These requisitions were then despatched to the appropriate parts of the building by enclosing them in a carrier propelled by compressed air.

On the floor below the general office was the packed drugs department. This was a comparatively recent development, since in the nineteenth century chemists and druggists had packed their own drugs, buying them in bulk from firms such as Allen & Hanburys. The expansion of the trade had made this an uneconomic activity for the druggist and so bottling, packing and labelling were now done by the wholesalers. Allen & Hanburys was proud of the world-wide trade and variety in this department:

(left) "Allenburys" showcard by Gladys Peto.

(right) "Allenburys" Rusks tin.

View of the Bethnal Green factory in 1927. The central block had a square water tower and flagstaff, the top of which was 150 feet from the ground.

Here is a girl labelling bottles of Castor Oil for a chemist in North London, next to her is another filling bottles of bath crystals, at the next bench tablets are being packed for the Company's branch house in Shanghai. Here is a consignment of Cod-Liver Oil and Malt being prepared for the Argentine, and there we have Skin Cream to be sold in an Egyptian druggist's shop. Capsules for Arabia, Diabetic Flour for Australia, Chemical Food for India, Easton's Syrup for Brazil, Syrup of Figs for Edinburgh, are a few of the orders one notices; the work is done by girls whose speed and deftness in packing and finishing are remarkable.[6]

The packed drugs department was divided into two parts: in one, packed drugs bearing the chemist's or druggist's name and address on a distinctive label were dealt with; in another, Allen & Hanburys' "Torch" brand products were prepared, which were sold to the trade at a lower price than the customised goods. There was also a washing plant and hot rooms for bottles.

Below packed drugs, on successive floors were the "dry" and "wet" departments. "Drys" were drugs which could be packed in parcels, as distinct from liquid or semi-liquid preparations: the department consisted of long rows of bales, boxes, canisters, bags and bins, containing roots, barks, leaves, gums, powders and chemicals. A poison "cage" contained the dangerous drugs – pills, powders, and other preparations of a certain strength of opium, morphia, cocaine and heroin. In the "wet" department the orders were drawn from rows of bottles and huge forty-gallon "stores" of Doulton-ware, containing such preparations as ammoniated tincture of quinine, oil of eucalyptus, syrup of figs and Parrish's Food. This section also had its own poison "cage", where dangerous drugs were dispensed under the most strictly controlled conditions.

Another department at Bethnal Green, separate from the main block, also dealt with a vast range of chemists' sundries. A section was devoted to dressings – stacks of wools, lints, bandages and gauzes. In another part were stored rubber goods, such as hot water bottles, sheeting, air cushions, enemas, india-rubber syringes and ice-bags. There was an extensive selection of hardware goods: pans and urinals, funnels, douches, footwarmers, ointment pots and a variety of scientific glassware. Weighing scales, from baby scales to full-size instruments for the pharmacy, were a speciality; and so, too, were thermometers of all types: room, bath, dairy, incubator, garden, chemical, and, of course, the clinical.

The whole of the ground floor of the Bethnal Green factory was devoted to the despatch of all these products. This was the busiest and noisiest part of the factory as the avalanche of items was sorted and checked, ready for posting and despatch world-wide. For UK deliveries, the firm had built up its own fleet of vans, beginning with the De-Dion Bouton and Commer vehicles. These distinctly coloured red and cream vans became a well-known sight in the area as they streamed out of the Bethnal Green factory according to a well-planned timetable.

An indication of the self-sufficient policy of Allen & Hanburys in its role as the "Universal Provider" is shown by the fact that in 1894 the firm had decided to set up its own printing department in the long east building at Bethnal Green. Here were the latest printing machines – for producing coloured labels, embossing box tops, and booklet covers – guillotines for cutting up sheets of cardboard and paper, and carton-glueing and box-making machines. The output included, besides the company's advertising material, calendars and chemists' showcards, numerous booklets for the medical profession, trade catalogues and price lists in many languages, and the trade journal, *Plough Magazine*. Ernest Cripps' history of Allen & Hanburys was also printed in this department in 1927. An important feature of the work was the printing of labels for packed drugs: these could be carefully overprinted with the chemists' name and address. There was even an artist's studio at Bethnal Green, where the advertising illustrations and designs were produced.

Most of Allen & Hanburys' manufacturing was conducted at Ware. However, the pill room at Bethnal Green produced one speciality of the firm, where intricate rolling, cutting and shaping machinery turned a stiff paste into round and oval pills ready for coating with sugar, "pearl" (sugar and talc) or gelatin. The pills were then brushed through a pierced tray on to another covered with minute raised cups, where they were held by suction. The entire tray was then turned upside down by hand, and the pills were dipped in liquid gelatin, off which the constantly forming scum had just been cleared. Near to the pill room was the oil refinery, which, now that it was no longer the manufacturing centre for the firm's cod-liver oil, dealt with large quantities of castor and olive oils as well as "Chrismol" (liquid paraffin). Finally, the Bethnal Green site also housed a tablet room, where noisy machines were engaged in turning out compressed tablets at the rate of several hundreds a minute.

At Ware the production of the famous "Allenburys" milk foods began on the nearby farms, from where the firm's supply of fresh milk was drawn. The manufacturing of dried milk was a relatively simple process, but great care was needed to prevent the formation of bacteria. This was achieved by the tuberculin testing of every animal, strict hygiene during the milking of the herd, high-pressure steaming of the churns and constant monitoring of the milk once it reached the Ware factory. All this contrasted with normal British milk production, which in the 1920s was still a national disgrace, with no systematic testing of cows and a consequent high incidence of bovine tuberculosis and infant deaths. The milk had to be modified considerably so that the proportions of its constituents approximated those of human milk. In the "Allenburys" system the 3 percent of casein present in cow's milk was reduced to about 1 percent (the level in human milk), the fat, albumen and milk sugar were adjusted to the correct proportions and sufficient quantity of dextro-maltose was added to ensure that the casein remained highly non-flocculent. The milk so humanised and adjusted was evaporated under reduced pressure and then dried and ground, care being taken to preserve the natural vitamins. The food was then automatically weighed and packed into decorated tins by machinery, using a continuous "runway".

Low temperature evaporation was also the main process in the production of Allen & Hanburys' malt preparations. Visitors could look through portholes in the malt extract vacuum pans to see the wort boiling vigorously inside. The vapour was carried by condenser into the river; the malt grains were fed to cattle; and the extract was drawn off, to be used as either a treacle-like substance (the main constituent in "Bynol" food and tonic products) or as a liquid (a vehicle for the medicinal specialities in the "Bynin" range).

On the other side of Priory Street in the Buryfield building were extensive flour stores and a bakery for the preparation of No. 3 Malted Food. Manufacture was a multi-level operation in the three-storied building. Mechanical blenders mixed the flour and malt extract, which was finely ground by disintegrators in the basement and then blown into a specially constructed chamber on the roof, whence it fell into mechanical tin-filling apparatus. The Milk Foods and Diet products were also mixed and packaged in this building, the dried milk being delivered in weighed bulk from the milk factory. Here, too, the "Allenburys" Rusks were made. The rusk bread, in long, flat loaves, was baked first in a 45-foot travelling oven, before being sliced up and toasted to give the rusks their familiar golden-brown colour.

In a building next to the foods section were the capsule, pastille and lozenge departments. In capsule manufacture, a solution of gelatin (the main constituent) was poured on to square metal sheets, forming a flexible mass that could be stretched over a mould. The medicant was

Allen & Hanburys' motor transport in the 1920s.

spread over the sheet and then sandwiched between another: it was then a simple matter to compress the capsules in a hydraulic press. Pastille manufacture was more complex. Essentially, these were of two types: confectionery pastilles – such as the popular glycerine and blackcurrant – and gum pastilles, which contained a whole range of medicaments, such as cocaine and eucalyptus. In one of the rooms at Ware was a row of boiling coppers, each capable of holding 1,000 lbs, in which the ingredients of the pastilles – gum, sugar, and fruit juice – were liquefied and mixed before being run into moulds. Originally, a primitive five-spouted filler had been used to fill these moulds, but this had been superseded by a giant filling machine, known as the "Mogul", which also automatically sifted and sorted the pastilles. There was still a large element of hand-labour as the account in the *Plough Magazine* made clear:

> The pastilles are now "pinned". Pins with their points out are set like the teeth of a comb in pieces of teak about 16 inches long; nimble fingered girls place a pastille upon the point of each pin. In this condition they are washed to remove all traces of starch, placed in suitable racks and dried. They are then dipped in liquid coating and emerge bright and shining. Once again they are dried and then are pulled off their pins by a most ingenious and simple contrivance; by the action of a lever the comb-back is pulled sharply back and the pastilles knocked off and piled in trays ready to be finally hardened off and then weighed and sent on to the packers.[7]

(above) Malt products at
Ware.

Advertisement for
pastilles, a perennial
money-spinner for the
firm in the inter-war
period.

Over a hundred different kinds of Allen & Hanbury pastilles were
produced, for which there was a heavy demand, especially in the winter
months. This was when the firm's lozenges also came into their own.
These were produced by a somewhat simpler process from a dough of
sugar, gum or fruit paste and the medicant. In parts the Ware factory
resembled a sweet factory rather than a pharmacy, since amongst the
output were acidulated fruit drops.

The Ware factory, like Bethnal Green, had a hankering for self-
sufficiency. It drew its own water from two wells, one in the old mills and
another on the Buryfield site. In the western strip of Buryfield, behind
the row of engine houses, the company had a witch's garden of
poisonous herbs, among which henbane (*hyoscyamus*) and deadly
nightshade (*belladonna*) grew in decorative rows like garden plants.
These could be ground in the Ware factory's extensive drug mills and
analysed in the adjoining pharmaceutical laboratories.

The Allen & Hanburys' food, drug, and surgical instrument trade, as it
was conducted in these separate locations, appears to have reached its
fullest extent in the mid-1920s. Some departments were more profitable

as I have just taken an —

Allenburys Pastille

Allenburys Glycerine and Black Currant Pastilles allay irritation and prevent infection. They are delicious and effective. Try them. Obtainable only from Chemists. In tins, 8d. & 1/3.

(right) Original five-spouted filler for pouring pastille juice into moulds.

"Pinning" pastilles at Ware in the 1920s.

than others, but generally they were operating smoothly. Turnover was £1,103,500 in 1925, earning a net profit of £118,140, which enabled a dividend of 7/- to be paid on the ordinary shares. "Allenburys" was now a household word.

But the company's niche in the food and drug market was by no means secure. Unknown to the directors the demand for dried milk had reached a peak, and thereafter the demand for this product and some of the other Allen & Hanbury staples, such as malt extract and cod-liver oil, was to slacken and then decline. This was partly the result of social and economic conditions, and partly due to increasing competition. Allen & Hanburys' dominance of the milk food business, for example, had not gone unchallenged.

The 1920s had seen the emergence of a major competitor in milk foods in the shape of Glaxo. The origins of this firm lay in the merchanting firm of Joseph Nathan, a Londoner who settled in Wellington, New Zealand, in 1857. At first Nathan dealt in a wide range of groceries and ironmongery imported from Britain, but later in the 1890s, with the development of refrigerated ships and the growth of New Zealand farmers' cooperatives, he switched his activities to the export of frozen meat and butter to Britain. As the century ended, the business was registered in London as a limited liability company. At this point, Joseph Nathan and his sons decided to try their hand at producing milk powder as a way of using the surplus skimmed milk of their New Zealand creameries and butter factory. Initially, they were not very successful: the patents purchased for the venture proved flawed and the syndicate of which the Nathans were a part became involved in litigation with the patentee. By 1908, however, the Nathans' dried milk business had been successfully launched under the brand-name "Glaxo", run by a newly formed Glaxo department within the Nathan firm. Joseph's youngest son, Alec Nathan (1872-1954), was brought over to head the department, which he did with considerable skill for almost three decades.[8]

Glaxo lacked Allen & Hanburys' status and its close association with the medical world; on the other hand, Alec Nathan showed no hesitation in using the brashest publicity techniques. Unlike Allen & Hanburys, which usually advertised its products in the staid pages of the *Chemist and Druggist* and felt most at home in the dignified atmosphere of the medical and nursing exhibitions, Glaxo went directly to the public. In the *Daily Mail* on 27 May 1908 a full-page advertisement announced Glaxo as the "Food that Builds Bonnie Babies". This catchy slogan was backed by a skilful press and postage campaign to the public, doctors, nurses, and to the retail pharmacists. A *Glaxo Baby Book* was produced, which gave practical guidance to mothers on every aspect of infant growth and feeding. Once established, Glaxo shared in the expansion of the milk food business from which Allen & Hanburys was also benefiting. Before 1914 turnover was less than £80,000, but by 1921 sales had reached their peak of over £1.5 million, far outstripping Allen & Hanburys' business from all its branches.

In 1923 an event occurred that was to alter the scale and scope of the Glaxo operations, as well as ultimately to affect profoundly the

development of Allen & Hanburys. The quality of milk supplied from New Zealand for marketing in Britain fluctuated considerably, and in 1919 Alec Nathan recruited a young chemist, (Sir) Harry Jephcott (1891-1978), to monitor the quality and set standards. His first laboratory was in a tiny room about 20 feet square in a warehouse off the Harrow Road in West London, where his establishment was regarded by one of the Nathans as "Alec's b..... folly".[9] Jephcott's formidable business talents (which were eventually to propel him to the chairmanship of Glaxo) were not yet apparent, but his superb sense of the technical possibilities of the pharmaceutical industry was demonstrated immediately when he persuaded the Nathans to send him to the International Dairy Congress in Washington, D.C., in 1923.[10] While in the USA, Jephcott took the opportunity to visit Professor Elmer V. McCollum and Dr. Theodore Zucker to discuss their recent work on "accessory food factors", subsequently termed "vitamins".

At that time no vitamins had been isolated, though their existence was recognised.[11] In particular, the animal experiments of Professor Frederick Gowland Hopkins of Cambridge University, published in 1912, demonstrated scientifically that minute amounts of unknown substances present in normal foods were essential for healthy nutrition.

Glaxo

Built us a Bonnie Baby

Thousands of letters from happy mothers give testimony to the wonderful results of Glaxo feeding. Health, contentment, a robust constitution — all come normally to the Glaxo fed baby

Glaxo is a humanised milk easily digested and free from any risk of tuberculosis

Glaxo

THE SUNSHINE BABY FOOD

GLAXO HOUSE, 6, OSNABURGH STREET, LONDON, N.W.1

147

In a less scientific fashion, firms such as Allen & Hanburys carefully prepared their milk foods to preserve these substances and also mixed them with other ingredients, such as malt and cod-liver oil, that were known to have beneficial effects. Elmer McCollum's breakthrough at Wisconsin University was to detect fat- and water-soluble accessory food factors in milk, which he designated as "fat-soluble A" and "water-soluble B" (vitamins A and B). Continuing his work at Johns Hopkins University, McCollum identified the antirachitic factor in cod-liver oil, known after 1925 as vitamin D, since it was the fourth to be discovered (vitamin A had been isolated in the previous year). Shortly after McCollum's announcement of the new vitamin, Theodore Zucker of Columbia University introduced a process which achieved a thousand-fold concentration of it by treating cod-liver oil.

Jephcott immediately grasped the importance of these developments for Glaxo milk powders. At his instigation, the Nathan company secured the licence for Zucker's process, so laying the foundation for its development as a pharmaceuticals manufacturer. The immediate result was "Sunshine Glaxo – the baby food reinforced with sunshine vitamin D to build strong bones and teeth". In 1924 the Nathan's Glaxo department began production of "Ostelin", the company's first pharmaceutical product, and the first vitamin-concentrate to be made on a commercial scale in Britain. Then in 1928 Dr. Harry Steenbock of Wisconsin University patented a method of irradiating certain foods by ultra-violet light to improve their antirachitic properties. When Steenbock's process superseded Zucker's, the Nathans again became the first to obtain a British licence. By the 1930s the Glaxo department was being transformed (and was transforming the Nathan firm) into a modern pharmaceutical company, which from 1935 was based at Greenford and known as Glaxo Laboratories Ltd.

At a stroke Allen & Hanburys had lost its lead in dried milk production to a relative newcomer. Of course, it was not long before the company was successfully adding vitamins to its "Allenburys" foods. In 1928 synthetic vitamin D was added to the Foods, Diet and Rusks, using the Steenbock method of irradiating ergosterol. But by the early 1930s the milk food business was in decline. Allen & Hanburys' difficulties were exacerbated by a production method that was becoming increasingly uneconomic and out-dated. In contrast to Glaxo, which imported milk that had been produced by the relatively simple method of drying unmodified milk on hot rollers, Allen & Hanburys continued the two-stage process of evaporating *modified* milk to a thick paste, which was then tray-dried in an oven. The Allen & Hanburys' system had its merits, but economy was not one of them and by the Second World War the business was commercially doomed. In retrospect, it is a moot point whether the firm should have switched to the roller method in the inter-war period. Actually, it was never considered. A retired director has stated: "We could have sold a roller powder, but I don't think we wanted to. We'd had at least two generations of throwing out our chests and talking about modifying the cow to suit the human baby, [so] it would have been like betraying our birthright to go into roller powder."[12]

Advertisement announcing the introduction of vitamin D into Allen & Hanburys' products.

148

Vitamin D in the 'Allenburys' Products

The following well-known 'Allenburys' Products have for some time been enriched by the addition of synthetic Vitamin D prepared by the new process of Ultra-Violet Light Irradiation.

The 'Allenburys'
Foods for Infants

The 'Allenburys'
Malted Rusks

The 'Allenburys' Diet

'Bynotone'

Amongst other notable advantages these products are therefore fully protective against rickets and allied disorders. *No change has been made in the packing or the directions for use.*

Allen & Hanburys Ltd.

Bethnal Green, London, E. 2.

TOILET SPECIALISTS · THE Boots CHEMISTS · DISPENSING CHEMISTS.

PRESCRIPTIONS

PERFUMERY.

Muswell Hill
Feb 14. 1920

In 1932 the directors undertook a survey of the drop in infant foods. The main contributory factors were the decline in the birth rate and the increasing popularity, especially in times of depression, of whole milk, which was now safer and more reliable, even if it was not entirely free of bacteria. But the directors also highlighted the influence of the newly emerging Infant Welfare Centres, which had been founded to improve the well-being of mothers and babies by providing free medical care, qualified nursing guidance and subsidised nutrition. These clinics supplied infant milk foods at, and even below, cost price. Allen & Hanburys shunned this trade, preferring to remain tied exclusively to its old allies, the chemists. The firm did put up Infant Welfare packs of the Nos. 1, 2 and 3 Foods, which were stocked by selected chemists, but these were only supplied on the official order of the Infant Welfare Centres. The company, because of a desire to protect the chemists, stipulated that if "Allenburys" was supplied to Infant Welfare Centres it should only be sold at full price. But, as the directors admitted: "This policy, adapted in the interests of our general business, has probably been inimical to the business in infants' foods." Other firms, particularly Glaxo, which introduced its "Ostermilk" exclusively to the clinics, showed no hesitation in providing cut-price milk foods. Increasing volume as sales of Ostermilk mounted compensated for the lower profit and, by bypassing the chemists (who Alec Nathan accused of being too greedy), Glaxo hit Allen & Hanburys where it hurt most.

Allen & Hanburys had no choice but to follow this lead and in 1934 the "Allenburys" foods were being introduced to the clinics at special prices. The company also engaged a lady doctor to organise a mothers' bureau, to give lectures to nurses, and to apply her knowledge of infant feeding problems to this side of the business. An "Allenburys" Half-Cream Food was introduced and, following Dr. Helen Mackay's research on nutritional anaemia resulting from the deficiency of iron in cow's milk, small additional amounts of iron were added to the "Allenburys" Foods. A new publicity campaign was begun to bring these products to the attention of the public. A colour magazine, *Wise Mothercraft*, was issued and about 10,000 copies were circulated to a select number of proud mothers (Allen & Hanburys had long since developed a policy of watching the "births" column in the press for such details). A specially qualified medical man was also hired to bring the merits of the infant foods to paediatricians and other specialists.

Since obtaining adequate supplies of milk became difficult at this time, in 1931 a creamery in the village of West Pennard, near Glastonbury, was acquired and two tank wagons were purchased. Under a Milk Marketing Scheme it proved possible to manufacture in bulk full cream and machine-skimmed condensed milk for confectioners. By 1935 this creamery was producing 9,702 cwts of full cream and 1,412 cwts of machine-skimmed milk and a butter and cheese department was set up. Allen & Hanburys was now actively involved in the dairy industry.

The decline of the dried milk trade came at a bad time for the company, since by then the effects of the world depression were making themselves felt. In the period 1928-34 Allen & Hanburys' net profits

The emergence of national retailing outlets in the pharmaceutical trade, such as Boots, signalled the demise of Allen & Hanburys' major customer – the retail chemists.

The Nicest Way

of taking

HALIBUT LIVER OIL

Halibut Liver Oil, exceptionally rich in Vitamins A & D because it is extracted by our own process from the finest halibut caught by British seamen . . . juice expressed from sun-ripened oranges and full of the precious fresh fruit Vitamin C . . . made into Haliborange to help you and your children keep summertime health all through the rain, fog and cold of the winter.

CHILDREN AND THEIR PARENTS

love the fresh juicy orange flavour of Haliborange—no fishy taste whatever. Just half a teaspoonful for baby, rising to a dessertspoonful for adults. (Exact directions are given on every bottle.) Start Haliborange now.

British line-fishing vessels returning from their long stay in Northern waters with their catch of halibut.

Haliborange
VITAMINS A · D · C

LOOK FOR THE NEW CREAM and GREEN CARTON

Haliborange is now in a new carton to protect it from all damage. The price remains the same at **2/6 & 4/6**

ALLEN & HANBURYS Ltd., 37 Lombard St., London, E.C.3

H3.

plummeted from £118,370 to £26,100 and in 1934 the final dividend on the ordinary shares was passed. The firm was feeling the effects of increased competition in virtually all spheres of its activity. Even the drug and chemical side of the business, once so buoyant, had been hit. This was partly due to Allen & Hanburys' policy of selling only to the established trade – in other words, the retail chemists. The firm's loyalty to the thousands of chemists' shops in the country was only natural, but it was also increasingly out of step with the times. Despite the depression, the growth of other retail outlets was phenomenal. The early 1930s was the period, for example, when "Woolworth" became a household word as its stores opened at the astonishing rate of one every eighteen days. By 1931 Woolworth's had almost 500 branches in operation. Allen & Hanburys was slow to realise the implications of this. At about this time a young accountant, Leslie Lazell (who was later to become an influential managing director of Beechams), left Allen & Hanburys to take up a post at Macleans Ltd. Lazell recalled, Allen & Hanburys "thought I was mad", and the sales manager "asked me if I knew that Macleans were supplying toothpaste to Woolworths. He prophesied that the chemists would break them."[13] Unfortunately for Allen & Hanburys, the opposite happened and a few years later the company had to admit that: "As year by year the multiple shop companies – some of whom manufacture for themselves – take over established chemists' shops throughout the country (often those of the best character) the scope for business in drugs and chemicals with the retail chemist becomes more limited".

The company also had to deal at this time with the falling demand for cod-liver oil. In the early 1920s this had never been a very profitable activity, due to failures in the Norwegian fishing grounds and increasing competition, and in 1924 in an attempt to stem the losses a new factory for processing the oil was opened in Aberdeen. Allen & Hanburys recognised that the business remained "highly speculative". By the mid-1930s a Hull cooperative of trawler owners was able to produce 8,000 tons of cod-liver oil each year, enough to satisfy the whole of the UK demand, which meant that it was no longer profitable for Allen & Hanburys to produce its own oil at Aberdeen. The research on vitamins had, of course, hit the trade and after 1932 it was possible to produce synthetic vitamin D. Moreover, cod-liver oil was being replaced by halibut-liver oil, since it had been discovered that the livers of this fish were richer in vitamin A. Here Allen & Hanburys was able to overcome the unpalatability of the oil and score a notable success with the marketing of liquid "Haliborange" and "Halibol" in 1934. Noted the company: "Haliborange has come into steady recognition as the nicest way of taking halibut-liver oil, presenting at the same time the three vitamins A, C and D." Together with the new Allen & Hanbury laxative "Lixen", this was to be one of the best selling lines in the 1930s.

In the 1930s the company also expanded its facilities for surgical instrument production. The factory was re-equipped with new machinery; the nickel-plating plant was modernised; a chromium-plating plant was established; and electric welding machines were installed. A

"Haliborange", first marketed in 1934, was a great success for the company. It combined vitamins A, C and D.

(left) Arthur J. Firkins (left) and F. W. Gamble in Australia, during the latter's world tour, 1925.

Allen & Hanburys' South African branch at Smith Street, Durban. Exterior and manufacturing laboratory.

range of stainless steel goods was introduced and the "Bart's" operating table was remodelled, culminating in the world-famous model E design of 1940, which featured adjustable lateral lift and the provision of side bars for accessories. At Wigmore Street a new department for the deaf was set up and arrangements were made to produce surgical dressings. Unfortunately, although the turnover of the surgical instrument side was well over £100,000 per annum by 1934, profit margins continued to be slim: most of the business was done with Government departments and public bodies at unremunerative prices and a considerable proportion was sent to the overseas subsidiaries at factory cost.

Allen & Hanburys had tried hard to make its foreign ventures pay in the inter-war period. The years in the aftermath of the confiscation of the Russian plant had been a low point. Until 1922 the South African company was the only subsidiary to return a dividend; all the others made losses. Frederic Gamble, who had previously visited the Canadian branch, set off in 1924-5 on an eight-month inspection of the firm's foreign holdings, touring Canada, South Africa and the Far East. At this time Allen & Hanburys had £156,150 invested in these subsidiaries, of which only India was making good progress. Gamble returned very much impressed by the Canadian and US prospects and in 1927, although the Canadian company was making a loss, Allen & Hanburys purchased the whole of its shares, transferring W.T. Thorne from the Shanghai branch to run it. The malt extract plant was enlarged and an extensive business in all types of malt products was begun. But Gamble's hopes for the Canadian market were not fulfilled and the firm made steady losses, which had reached $20,000 a year by 1934, necessitating another visit by Gamble. In 1937 Gilbert Gamble (the son of Frederic) was elected to the Canadian board in an effort to return it to profitability.

As in the period before 1918, poor trading in some overseas areas was offset by success in others. The South African company generally did well, benefiting from trade with the many new hospitals. In 1922 a surgical branch was opened in Plein Street, Johannesburg. The main offices, processing and packing division remained in a large block of buildings in Smith Street, Durban. Here, the *Plough Magazine* informed its reader, the practice of pharmacy was very different from that at home, especially amongst the native population:

> The usual 6 or 8 oz. bottle is of no earthly use to "Wenna", as the native is generally called. He will take a minim of Croton Oil [a drastic purgative] and think nothing of it; in all probability more Croton Oil is sold in South Africa per head of the population than in any other country. An order to our Durban House for a *gallon* is by no means rare, smaller quantities are going out daily. "Elegant pharmacy" does not attract the native, what he requires is something evil smelling and evil tasting, the more so the greater the price he will pay for it.[14]

The South African company made profits even during the depression and these had reached the record level of £11,000 by 1935. The firm had outgrown its Smith Street site and in 1939 Thomas Walton acquired land at Congella, a few miles outside Durban, on which to erect a new factory (plans which were inevitably delayed until after the Second World War).

India was also buying many of Allen & Hanburys' products at this time. In 1921 the first Allen & Hanbury office was opened in Calcutta, under A.H.P. Jennings, who had previously been associated with the Shanghai branch. His territory included India, Burma, Ceylon, Malaya and Siam. No stocks were held by the company, but were shipped direct from Britain to the principal centres. Under the "indefatigable" Jennings this trade prospered, and India rapidly became one of the world's best markets for "Allenburys" products. But elsewhere, the political troubles in China had disrupted the trade and in 1931 the Chinese office was closed; whilst in Australia tariffs prompted the directors to close the drug side of the business altogether and transfer it to a Sydney agency. Thus, as it had in the period before 1918, the company found that operating foreign companies was not the road to easy riches.

In retrospect, it can be appreciated that it would have been better for Allen & Hanburys to divest itself of its unprofitable overseas and domestic ventures in the 1930s and, instead of becoming involved in distracting activities such as milk production, to concentrate its efforts, as Glaxo was doing, in establishing itself as a modern scientific pharmaceutical company marketing high value-added products.

Some progress was made in this direction. In the early 1930s it had been hoped that the growth-controlling hormone of the parathyroid gland might prove of value in limiting the spread of cancer. "G.R.H." (Growth Retarding Hormone) was prepared in the Allen & Hanburys' laboratories and the firm subsidised tests at the Royal College of Surgeons and at King's College and by a few medical practitioners. But the early promise of the work was not fulfilled. Simultaneously, a more successful investigation led to the production of a preparation containing the active principles of the adrenal cortex. This was "Eucortone", which was used in the treatment of Addison's disease (a chronic condition caused by under-activity of the thryoid gland). Subsequent research by other workers showed that the Allen & Hanbury substance contained aldosterone, which was identified as a major causative factor in certain types of oedema.

But Allen & Hanburys lacked an outstanding character on the research side, such as Harry Jephcott. The company was still very much a family-run concern, with a Hanbury as chairman (in 1937 F. Capel Hanbury occupied this position in succession to his father, who had retired from the chairmanship in his eighty-sixth year), and it maintained its organisation and style as set out in the nineteenth century by Cornelius.

In fact, Allen & Hanburys epitomised the British pharmaceutical industry at this time, one in which centuries-old remedies sat alongside the new, advanced medicines. F.W. Gamble and Norman Evers, writing in 1935, summarised it thus: "When we survey the progress that has occurred in this period, we see that it is due chiefly to the introduction of new types of pharmaceutical products which have required improvements in methods and in plants. These have grown up alongside the old

Intestinal Toxæmia with Hypertension Gastric Fermentation and Distension

CHARKAOLIN adsorbs toxins and gases in the stomach and intestines. An index of its adsorptive activity is its complete deodorisation of the intestinal contents.

CHARKAOLIN has given remarkable results in some cases of hypertension with intestinal auto-intoxication.

CHARKAOLIN is the original preparation of activated charcoal with Osmo Kaolin.

CHARKAOLIN GRANULES
In bottles at 2/6

CHARKAOLIN TABLETS
In bottles at 1/6 and 2/6

Prices in Great Britain and Northern Ireland.

Descriptive literature and clinical sample on request.

CHARKAOLIN

Allen & Hanburys Ltd., London, E.2
Telephone: Bishopsgate 3201 (12 Lines)   Telegrams: Greenburys, Beth, London

158

products, which have continued to be manufactured by the old methods, though often improved in detail."[15] The "new" products were drugs such as insulin, which were based on hormones and were described at that time as "organo-therapeutic" remedies. Nearly all of these – such as adrenaline, ergotoxine, thyroxin, oestrone and, of course, insulin – were developments of the early twentieth century. By the 1930s the chemotherapeutic revolution was underway with major advances in the field of antibiotics that would make themselves felt after the Second World War (see the following chapter). These drugs demanded more advanced and efficient manufacturing methods: greater control of the pH; the introduction of the new stainless steels for chemical plant; more sophisticated techniques for sterilisation; and the use of centrifuges for filtration. The "old" products were the traditional vegetable drugs, foods, and patent medicines, which still enjoyed a wide sale at this time with all the household names well to the fore – Beecham, Veno, Scott, Eno, Fulford and Steedman. Allen & Hanburys had a foot in both camps, selling both technologically sophisticated drugs and popular remedies. Thus insulin and eurcortone jostled in Allen & Hanbury advertisements with "charkaolin", a mixture of activated charcoal and kaolin, which was said to prevent "intestinal auto-intoxication" and so catered for the British public's obsession with its bowel movements.

In this context, the firm's record in the inter-war period was still a creditable one. Despite a falling turnover, profits had been maintained and showed signs of rising to their old levels at the end of the 1930s; whilst a conservative policy had amassed reserves of over £372,000 by 1938 (equivalent to well over half the paid up capital). Perhaps, too, a major reorientation of its products was too much to expect from the firm at this time and its policy was perfectly understandable: the impact of science on the pharmaceutical industry was still relatively small and the major selling lines remained the old-fashioned medicaments in which Allen & Hanburys specialised. This was to change dramatically after the Second World War, when both Allen & Hanburys and the pharmaceutical industry became science-based.

6

AN END AND A BEGINNING, 1940-58

Allen & Hanburys Ltd . . . announce that, on June 30, 1958, they are discontinuing the manufacture and supply of traditional drugs and galenicals.

Chemist and Druggist 169 (1958), p. 64

Prior to the Second World War, the pharmacists' armoury for attacking disease was relatively limited. A reader leafing through the pages of journals such as the *Chemist and Druggist*, even as late as 1945, would find good ground for believing that the pharmaceutical trade had changed relatively little since the nineteenth century. The advertisements and articles are dominated by many of the old Victorian favourites: cough syrups, pastilles, herbal tablets, embrocations, veterinary products, tonics and laxatives. Modern synthetic drugs appear but rarely. This was a reflection of the fact that before 1935 there were very few medicines capable of either attacking the causes of major diseases or of offering any really effective treatment: these included vitamin therapy, quinine, digitalis, insulin, aspirin, thyroxine, ipecacuanha, mercury and "salvarsan". But only a very few of these, such as Ehrlich's "salvarsan", were truly modern preparations.

Despite Ehrlich's work, not until 1935 was the chemotherapeutic revolution underway. In that year, Hildegarde Domagk was dying from severe septicaemia caused by pricking her finger with a needle. Her father was Gerhard Domagk, a research director in the laboratories of the German chemical giant I.G. Farbenindustrie, who was searching for a drug effective against generalised bacterial infection. Domagk's research had focused on a red azo dye called "Prontosil Rubrum", derived from coal tar, which he had tested on mice. He found that small, non-toxic doses of the brick-red dye prevented every single mouse which had received it by stomach tube from succumbing to an otherwise lethal inoculation of streptococci. But would it be a safe and effective treatment in humans? Domagk decided to try it on his daughter. "Prontosil" saved her life.

"Prontosil" became the first of the sulpha drugs, so named because their therapeutic properties derived from the sulphonamide group in their structure. Since sulphanilamide had been investigated some twenty-five years previously, it could not be patented and so any manufacturer was free to incorporate it in his own formulation. A massive

Advertisements from the Chemist and Druggist 1945, *showing the traditional nature of the pharmaceutical industry at that time. (Courtesy Royal Pharmaceutical Society of Great Britain)*

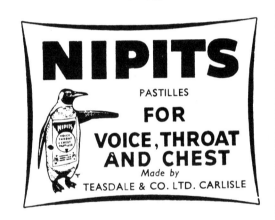

A Non-Griping and Palatable Preparation of Senna

"LIXEN"

1. "Lixen" is a safe aperient, without toxic effects.
2. It is a thorough aperient, efficiently emptying the colon.
3. "Lixen" is made from senna pods which are considered to be more effective than senna leaves.
4. In "Lixen" the griping action of senna is allayed, but the activity of the senna is not destroyed.
5. The "Lixen" preparations are agreeably flavoured, and are readily taken by children and adults.

"LIXEN"
Brand
Elixir of Senna Pods

1 teaspoonful is equivalent to 10 large senna pods.
In bottles : For Prescribing, 4 oz. and 8 oz.
For Dispensing, 40 oz. and 80 oz.

"LIXEN"
Brand
Laxative Lozenges

Each lozenge is equivalent to 6 large senna pods.
In boxes of 12 and 24 lozenges.

Descriptive literature and a clinical sample will be sent on request.

ALLEN & HANBURYS LTD., LONDON, E 2

Telephone : Bishopsgate 4201 (12 lines)   Telegrams : "Greenburys, Eth London"

162

research effort was soon underway as the leading chemical manufacturers began searching for even more effective sulpha drugs. Despite innumerable attempts, few of the resulting preparations offered much of an advance. But the British firm, May & Baker, was successful in achieving a breakthrough when in 1937 its research chemists synthesised sulphapyridine ("M & B 693"). This compound was more potent than sulphanilamide and also had a wider spectrum of antibacterial activity, being effective against pneumococci, meningococci, and other organisms. "M & B 693" caught the popular imagination when it saved the life of Winston Churchill during his visit to North Africa in 1943. According to Churchill, during an attack of pneumonia, "admirable M & B from which I did not suffer any inconvenience, was used at the earliest moment and, after a week's fever, the intruders were repulsed".[1]

Sulpha drugs were a powerful therapeutic tool, but they had one drawback – although they killed off bacteria, they had a limited spectrum and occasional toxicity. What was needed was an equally powerful antibiotic that was also safe. Unknown to researchers in the 1930s, such a drug had already been identified, but the scientific paper describing it lay forgotten. The coming of war at the end of the 1930s provided the stimulus that brought it to attention.

Alexander Fleming's discovery of penicillin at St. Mary's Hospital, Paddington, in 1928 is probably the most famous story of drug discovery in the twentieth century. Fleming was a leading authority on antiseptics, but it was a remarkable series of events in the summer of 1928 that led him to discover the antibacterial activity of penicillin. The probable sequence of events has been reconstructed in an account written by his former assistant, Professor Ronald Hare.[2] Fortuitously, a colleague on the floor beneath Fleming was working with moulds, the spores of one of which probably wafted into Fleming's laboratory to settle on a petri dish coated with staphylococci. Not only that, but the mould was a rare strain of *Penicillium notatum*, which produced relatively large amounts of penicillin. Finally, a series of climatic and local temperature variations in the laboratory favoured the growth of the mould, so allowing Fleming to observe a zone of inhibition of staphylococcal growth when he examined the plate in September 1928. Fleming did not overlook the therapeutic potential of penicillin and in further investigations he was able to demonstrate its antiseptic properties. But early trials with the mould proved disappointing, especially since the medications from this early penicillin proved unstable and difficult to produce in any quantity. Unfortunately, he never injected penicillin into infected mice, and it was left to others to discover its outstanding therapeutic powers.

The driving force behind subsequent investigations of penicillin was (Lord) Howard Florey, an Australian who had moved from Sheffield University to take up the chair of pathology at Oxford University. In 1938 Florey and (Sir) Ernst Chain, a young Jewish refugee from Hitler's Germany, began work with a culture of Fleming's original mould and accepted the challenge of producing a culture medium from which to extract the active material. Eventually, they succeeded in producing penicillin as a brown, dry powder of sufficient potency to be tested on

One of Allen & Hanburys' best-sellers in the 1940s, the laxative "Lixen".

163

patients. In February 1941, Albert Alexander, a forty-three-year-old policeman, who was dying from a mixed staphylococcal and streptococcal infection that had spread throughout his body and had already necessitated the removal of his eye, was injected with penicillin. His condition began to improve immediately, though, heartbreakingly, not enough penicillin could be produced by the Oxford team to cure him completely and he died from a residual lung infection. Nevertheless, the powerful antibacterial activity of penicillin had been successfully demonstrated and within a few years it was routinely curing fatally ill patients. Large-scale culture of the antibiotic was still in the future, however, and was only accomplished under the urgency of wartime conditions and with the greater resources of the Americans.

Not surprisingly, the success with penicillin triggered a search through many other kinds of moulds, spores and growths to find other antibiotic agents. Penicillin attacked a wide variety of germs, but was ineffective against others, especially the tuberculosis bacillus – the "white plague", which was still responsible for millions of deaths each year. In 1943, Selman Waksman a microbiologist at Rutgers University in America, isolated streptomycin, an antibiotic that was not only effective against tuberculosis, but also against a variety of other diseases that had been unaffected by penicillin, including plague, brucellosis, and various forms of bacterial dysentery.

Following the discovery of streptomycin, the pharmaceutical industry began a massive screening programme of soil samples in the search for more antibiotics. Many were discovered, though only a handful proved to be major breakthroughs. One of them was chloramphenicol ("Chloromycetin"), which was discovered in 1947 by the American firm Parke Davis and swiftly confirmed as the first broad-spectrum antibiotic. Another was tetracycline, developed in 1953 by two US firms, Pfizer and Cyanamid, which was the first semi-synthetic antibiotic to be prepared. By the 1950s the chemotherapeutic revolution was well underway with the appearance of corticosteroids, anti-depressants and diuretics.

The rate of discovery and wartime demand caused a rapid expansion of the drug industry. Pharmaceutical manufacture was now big business, in which massive financial and technical resources were needed to develop and market new drugs. The development of penicillin by Florey and Chain was only possible because of a remarkably generous donation from the Rockefeller Foundation. The initial research on streptomycin had cost nearly a million dollars to finance, and the US industry was to spend twenty times as much again on production plant. Pfizer spent some four million dollars in developing oxytetracycline, but in two years the company had spent almost double this amount on advertising the drug.

The industry after 1945 was increasingly dominated by the large German and American firms. But the British pharmaceutical industry was also expanding. In the period 1937-46 sales of drugs nearly trebled to £58 million and by 1946 the industry employed over 44,000 people, almost double the 1937 figure. Britain emerged from the war as second only to America as a drug exporter. In 1938 Britain exported only about

Aerial view of Ware in 1947.

£3 million worth of pharmaceutical products, but by 1946 this figure had risen to over £12 million.[3]

After the Second World War the fortunes of the major British drug companies were transformed. The Beecham Group and ICI provide an illustration (the development of Glaxo is considered in the following chapter). Beecham's original success had been based on the old proprietary medicine trade, with its pills and powders becoming household words through skilful advertising. It had little concern with the manufacture of "ethical" medicines and at the end of the 1940s it presented an old-fashioned image: a third of the company profits came from the glucose drink, "Lucozade"; the group comprised no less than 105 companies, with little overall corporate strategy; and it had at one point diversified into wholesale groceries, in which it had little expertise. But under the guidance of a new managing director, Leslie Lazell, a research division was set up at Brockham Park, near Dorking, and the firm began to move forward in the direction of an international science-based and market-oriented firm. Beecham Laboratories achieved brilliant success in 1957 when it isolated the basic core of penicillin, which enabled scientists to produce a whole range of penicillins with

broadened-spectrum and antibacterial resistance. In 1959 Beecham's launched its own semi-synthetic penicillin ("Broxil"), which was soon followed by others, notably ampicillin ("Penbritin"), carbenicillin ("Pyopen"), carfecillin ("Uticillin") and amoxycillin ("Amoxil"). The impact of these discoveries on the company was dramatic: Beecham's turnover in 1951-2 had been £25.4 million, with profits of £2.6 million (a ratio of 10 percent); by 1968-9 turnover had reached £134 million and profits £25 million (a ratio of nearly 19 percent).[4] The lesson was simple: investment in R & D bred new products, which generated profits and growth.

Prior to the Second World War, ICI had only manufactured small amounts of synthetic drugs. But the war had focused its activities on pharmaceutical research, particularly in the field of anti-malarial drugs. ICI's principal success was based on the discovery that the newly developed antibacterial sulphonamides also contained an anti-malarial property. This led to the development of "Paludrine", which was used extensively in the armed forces and later in malaria eradication programmes. In 1957 the Pharmaceutical Division at ICI became a separate entity and went on to discover a wide range of drugs, including the widely used fluorocarbon anaesthetic, "Fluothane", and the anti-convulsant primidone ("Mysoline").

One other event, political and administrative, rather than scientific, shaped the British (and international) pharmaceutical industry after the Second World War. This was the foundation of the National Health Service in 1948, which further stimulated pharmaceutical development. As the NHS's drug bill rose – from £6.8 million in 1947 to £55.6 million in 1955-6 – it heralded the demise of the old proprietary drug trade (at least as the leading sector of the industry) and further intensified the search for new synthetic drugs.[5] It also attracted more than a score of the leading foreign drug companies, particularly American firms, such as Pfizer, Smith Kline & French, Merck, Parke Davis, and Wyeth, who in the early 1960s soon pushed aside most of the British competition. The American invasion had important repercussions for firms such as Allen & Hanburys and Glaxo: henceforth they would need their own research-based products to compete and it was no longer enough to purchase licences from across the Atlantic.

By then the nature of the industry was apparent: it was a high risk business, increasingly dominated by large-scale firms (invariably multi-nationals), which could afford to pour the necessary resources into research and product development. But it was clearly no place for a small, family-owned concern, heavily dependent for its income on a range of old-fashioned medicaments. Allen & Hanburys had emerged from the War amongst the top ten British pharmaceutical companies: staying there on its own was obviously going to prove difficult. It was evident that few of the old-established houses were succeeding in the new environment: the future lay with the newer firms, which were switching to research-based high technology.

An historian looking for a symbol of these profound changes in the story of Allen & Hanburys might be tempted to choose the closing

Bomb damage at Bethnal Green (above) and Plough Court in 1940.

168

months of 1940. The company had emerged relatively unscathed from the First World War; in the Second it was not to be so lucky. Allen & Hanburys had a taste of things to come, when one night in August 1940 three incendiary bombs hit the roof of the sundries department of the Bethnal Green factory, causing slight fire damage. On Friday 20 September 1940, however, a brilliant moon brought with it a fresh attack. A German bomber appeared to the north-east, picked out by searchlights. Firemen on duty at the Bethnal Green site were "commenting on the absence of any gunfire when the sprinkler alarm bell rang. A brilliant, blinding blue flash of light followed immediately to the accompaniment of what those who heard it described as a 'ripping, tearing, explosion', caused, as was afterwards found, by a 'D' type of bomb holding about a ton of high explosive striking the roof of the laboratory."[6] A parachute had brought the bomb through the wall of the printing department – so setting off the alarm – before it exploded with such devastating effect above the stockroom.

No lives were lost during this attack, but the bomb and subsequent fire completely destroyed major sections of the Bethnal Green factory. The manufacturing laboratory, which included the pill and tablet plant, and the dispatch and records department, with its many thousands of customers' records, were lost. The printing and advertising departments in the east block were gutted and demolished. In the central building, fire, blast and water damage wrecked the packed drugs and insulin departments, while on the top floor of this building, an incendiary bomb destroyed the analytical and research departments and the large library.

On 12 November 1940, Plough Court itself fell victim to a bomb which landed on the building next door. Allen & Hanburys' pharmacy avoided total destruction, but the effect of the blast – which blew out windows and ceilings – was enough to cause the firm to transfer its dispensing and wholesaling activities to Vere Street and the repaired parts of Bethnal Green. While the rebuilding of the Bethnal Green premises was proceeding some of the head office staff continued to work in considerable discomfort at Plough Court. But in January 1943 Bethnal Green was ready to receive the last of them and the premises in Plough Court, where the firm had had its home since 1715, were left empty and derelict.

In the wake of the bombing, Allen & Hanburys' immediate concern was to repair its productive capacity. The most serious loss was the destruction of the sterile filling rooms and apparatus for insulin, which by then was an essential drug for many people. This was given the first priority. Fortunately, the firm had its factory at Ware, where a pre-war development proved fortuitous.

In 1939 Allen & Hanburys had begun commercial production of intravenous fluids supplied in "Sterivac" containers which, suitably prepared, could also be used for blood transfusions. "Sterivac" was not entirely an Allen & Hanbury innovation, though the company was soon to become widely known for this speciality. Sterile intravenous fluids were already being marketed at that time in America by Baxter Inc., which exported litre and half-litre bottles to Britain through an agent,

"Sterivac" was another surgical speciality for which the firm became well known. Here "Sterivac" products are being capped.

"Sterivac" packing.

John Bell & Croyden of Wigmore Street. One of Bell & Croyden's representatives, however, George Emrys Jones, patented a much improved bottle seal, which broke the Baxter patents and gave British firms access to the technology. F.W. Gamble recognised the potential of Emrys Jones's patent and Allen & Hanburys acquired it for use at Ware. A newly appointed pharmacist, E.K. Samways, took charge of setting up a laboratory for the "Sterivac" line, which he soon accomplished with the help of another pharmacist, Joan Iliffe. By 1940 an output of about a thousand bottles a day had been reached in a facility which included bottle-washing and autoclaving equipment. This equipment could be – and was – readily adapted for the filling of insulin solutions and suspensions under aseptic conditions. Thus within ten days insulin was being filled at Ware. The filling team was partly made up of "Sterivac" personnel, but was supervised by Margaret Simpson, the pharmacist who had been in charge of the filling room at Bethnal Green and who brought with her (by lorry!) some of her skilled girls: a comment perhaps on the speed with which industry recovered from the Blitz.

Gradually, other aspects of the business took on some semblance of order. Since practically everything inflammable had been destroyed at Bethnal Green, many orders had been lost and needed transcribing from memory. The firm's original printing blocks and labels had been lost, so that the wreckage had to be searched for days to rescue one copy of every piece of printed matter, so that it could be photographed and reproduced! In many instances, packages of the firm's products had to be procured from wholesalers or retailers to obtain a record. Nissen huts were built at Ware to house the transferred production facilities for packed drugs. As the new buildings were occupied and stocks replenished, new work began to pour in, such as bottling Ministry of Food orange juice at the rate of more than 150,000 bottles per month; packing household milk powder and rose hip syrup; and producing a number of special medicines and products for the Ministry of Supply and the British Red Cross.

For the Allen & Hanburys' management it was a difficult time, as it was for other pharmaceutical firms. Aside from the loss of manpower, which drew 250 Allen & Hanbury workers into the armed forces, the importation of many foreign drugs and raw materials was disrupted or completely dislocated by the war. Soon after war was declared, certain statutory rules and orders were issued by the Government, which ordained that rigid economy was to be exercised in the use of certain scarce drugs, and that more plentiful drugs were to be used instead. The Vegetable Drugs' Committee was also formed to collect voluntarily many drugs and vegetable substances which, although native to Britain – such as belladonna, digitalis and colchicum – had previously been imported. Other materials were strictly controlled. Alcohol, a key ingredient in so many pharmaceutical processes, was rationed. So, too, was sugar. This hit the Allen & Hanburys' pastille business particularly, and, in a situation in which the firm had to scramble for every ton of sugar it used, new formulations had to be devised using syrup, malt, and glucose as a substitute for cane sugar. Government control of prices also

"Sterivac" bottles.

had a negative effect on profits: although sales increased by 85 percent during the war years, average yearly net profits showed virtually no increase at all and remained at about £100,000.

In some areas, though, the war brought new opportunities. Following approaches from Alexander Fleming, late in 1942 the Ministry of Supply established a Penicillin Chemical Committee, to coordinate industrial manufacture along the lines already being pursued in America. Boots, Burroughs Wellcome, Glaxo, ICI, Kemball Bishop, and May & Baker eventually began making arrangements for the production of penicillin, using the tried and trusted surface-culture method. Allen & Hanburys came into the picture later, having been slow to recognise the potential of penicillin in the early days, and paid the penalty for its late start. Again, it was Glaxo under the able direction of Harry Jephcott, who seized the main chance and took the leading position in the production of the drug.

In America important developments had taken place during the war years in the production of penicillin by deep fermentation. At the US Department of Agriculture's Northern Regional Research Laboratory at Peoria, Illinois, intensive efforts were made to find a strain of penicillin-producing mould that would grow in deep tanks and have a high yield. Thousands of samples of soil and soil-organisms were examined.

Notwithstanding, one of the best improvements in penicillin yield was obtained with a strain of *P. chrysogenum* growing on a cantaloup melon in the fruit market at Peoria! After intensive treatment, this strain led the way to the production of mutants yielding nearly a thousand units per millilitre (in contrast to the Oxford process, which had yielded only 1-2 units per millilitre). By the end of the war, American companies, such as Charles Pfizer & Co, were able to satisfy all military requirements.

As a chemist, Jephcott well understood the magnitude of the technical difficulties involved. He also appreciated the commercial possibilities, especially when they were backed by the Government. Jephcott led Glaxo to construct a purpose-built antibiotics factory at Barnard Castle, County Durham, in 1944, and another at Ulverston in 1946; he also visited the US in 1945 to negotiate licensing agreements with Merck and Squibb, which enabled Glaxo to use deep-culture techniques for the production of penicillin. By the end of the war, Glaxo was supplying about 90 percent of British output. At Barnard Castle, a specially devised brew of corn-steep liquor modified by other chemicals was fed into tanks surrounded by batteries of 5,000-gallon vertical fermenters. Commented the *Chemist and Druggist*: "To see, at Barnard Castle, penicillin produced from natural material at such relatively low cost is to place in its true perspective the rumoured production of penicillin by synthetic means. It is also to have the imagination fired. . . A new industry has been born, and one which offers an opportunity for British pre-eminence."[7]

Allen & Hanburys, though, was not entirely out of the picture. Its directors, aware that the company had fallen behind in an expanding field, towards the end of the war entered into an agreement with the Government for the production of penicillin by surface culture. The agreement gave access to the penicillin expertise of other UK producers, for a limited period, but bound the company to only the initial stage of a rapidly developing technology. Manufacture began using sterile milk bottles – a method that was relatively unproductive and extremely wasteful of space, especially when compared to the flat glass flasks (nicknamed "bed-pans") that were used by Glaxo. Allen & Hanburys was aware of the research into deep fermentation: indeed John C. Hanbury and Dr. Glyn Owen Richards, who managed the firm's penicillin pilot plant, had visited US firms in 1945. But, as Capel Hanbury had complained: "Even at that late stage, we were not allowed to carry on research into alternative processes. The reasons for the Government ban were by no means obvious, although it was plain that the surface-culture process was already out-dated, and the American manufacturers were abandoning it."[8] Actually, the Government's attitude was plain enough: it needed a guaranteed supply of penicillin and did not want too many firms dabbling in experimental technologies. Allen & Hanburys had no choice but to comply. A pilot bottle plant was set up (named "P1") and began selling its first penicillin at £24 per mega-unit (in the 1980s the price was about 4 pence per mega-unit!). But within a week of the plant successfully running its first trials, the

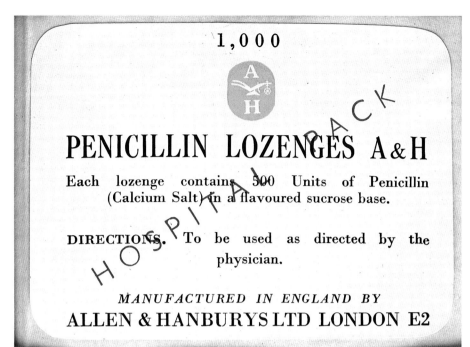

The age of antibiotics. Allen & Hanburys begin the marketing of penicillin lozenges.

Government announced early in 1946 that bottle culture was dead.

Allen & Hanburys had its own 500-gallon penicillin fermenter at Ware, as part of a private venture, which had shown that large-scale production was well within the company's capabilities. On the other hand, there was a leeway of several years to be made up and the total commitment required was beyond the firm's resources. Thus, the translation of the pilot production plant to a newly erected three-storeyed "P" building was never completed, and the premises were gradually taken over for other purposes.

The situation, however, was not entirely beyond redemption. To begin with, the company secretary, W.J. Rennie, had shrewdly secured a promise from the Ministry of Supply that, if Allen & Hanburys was compelled to manufacture penicillin by bottle-culture, then the Government would indemnify the firm for its losses if the process was proved redundant. Secondly, the fact that it was not involved in the actual manufacture of the product did not mean that Allen & Hanburys was prevented from exploiting the breakthrough in antibiotics in other ways. Thus, it was one of the first firms to market penicillin preparations. The company began to market lozenges, which sold by the million and the firm installed its first roll-wrapping machine for them. It also led the way in supplying penicillin in vials for injection. Here the expertise of Allen & Hanburys' head of pharmaceutical research, Cyril J. Eastland, proved invaluable in devising formulations that delivered the injectable dose in anhydrous oil, which (although extremely painful) ensured that it could be stored for up to three months (whereas normal aqueous penicillin solution had to be mixed on the spot for immediate use only). Although the penicillin had to be purchased, the technology of all these preparations was "in-house", and became a profitable line. Vere Street provided a useful initial outlet for these new preparations, which were dispensed round the clock – a unique service at that time.

The Second World War was important for Allen & Hanburys in another respect, for it saw the timely emergence of an effective managing director in the shape of Cyril Wheatley Maplethorpe (1898-1983). It had always been the good fortune of the family members of the firm to ally themselves with capable and industrious managers: William Allen drew on the talents of John T. Barry; Cornelius and Frederick Hanbury had the support of W. Ralph Dodd and then F.W. Gamble; and Capel Hanbury had Gamble and then Maplethorpe, with the latter also providing help for Capel's son, (Sir) John C. Hanbury.

Maplethorpe had qualified as a pharmaceutical chemist at the Pharmaceutical Society's College (or "the Square" as it had come to be known) in 1920. After a spell in the Society's research laboratories and museum, he joined Allen & Hanburys in 1924 as a research chemist, becoming head of the pharmaceutical production department in the following year. By 1932 Maplethorpe had become manager at the Ware factory on the death of Harry Radford (the son of William Radford, who had been responsible for the building of the original factory), and was able to bring with him some much-needed scientific expertise. He was, in fact, only the second technically qualified pharmacist to work at Ware in this period (the other was Capel Hanbury, who had made his headquarters there, since he disliked working at Bethnal Green). Maplethorpe involved himself with research and product development in the 1930s and was responsible for "Isogel", a bulk laxative made from the husk of the Indian *Isphagula* seed – a traditional, but profitable, product. But Maplethorpe was more than simply a good chemist. Described as "probably the most influential pharmacist of his generation . . . who had elements of greatness in him",[9] he worked untiringly through the Pharmaceutical Society (of which he became President in 1963-5) to achieve better educational standards.[10] This commitment stemmed from an awareness that the days of the old galenicals and food products were numbered and he began to push the company, as far as he was able, towards a more scientific future.

In 1944 Maplethorpe's talents were recognised by his appointment to the Allen & Hanburys' board as managing director, on the retirement of F.W. Gamble. Henceforth, he could exert more influence in leading the company away from its traditional practices and product lines. For, if the implications of the advances in chemotherapy for Allen & Hanburys were appreciated by Maplethorpe, this was far from the case with the older members of what was still quintessentially a family firm.

Capel Hanbury was the chairman of the company in the immediate postwar period, with his son, John, as vice-chairman. (John C. Hanbury was to succeed his father in 1954.) These men presided over a company that, to all appearances, at the close of the war still retained an air of the nineteenth century: had Cornelius Hanbury returned he would have found things very much unchanged. Plough Court, it is true, had closed, and the cod-liver oil factories were soon to be relinquished. But the firm still had its main West End outlets – Vere Street and Wigmore Street –

and the same spread of products at Bethnal Green and Ware: Allenburys' specialities, surgical instruments, and bulk drugs and galenicals. The 1946 product list gives a good indication of the main lines: these included liver extracts, the "Bynin" malt products, "Haliborange", various ampoules for injections, insulin, "Lixen", pastilles, and "Sterivac" apparatus – and the company also took on commercial analyses. The Hanburys' attitude to this plethora of products also remained unchanged, believing that this "spread gives a stability to the business and enables full advantage to be taken of changes in the character of the markets".

In surgical instrument manufacture, Allen & Hanburys was still a name to be reckoned with. Its introduction of the model E operating table in 1940, which, amongst other things, featured adjustable lateral lift, was a major success and secured for the firm an international reputation. As a response to more specialised surgical techniques, the firm designed an operation chair for neurosurgery, which enabled intra-cranial procedures to be conducted with the patient in a sitting position. These developments led Allen & Hanburys' designers and engineers to consider the possibility of producing a table that could be used for *all* specialised types of surgery. This ambition was to be realised with the

175

176

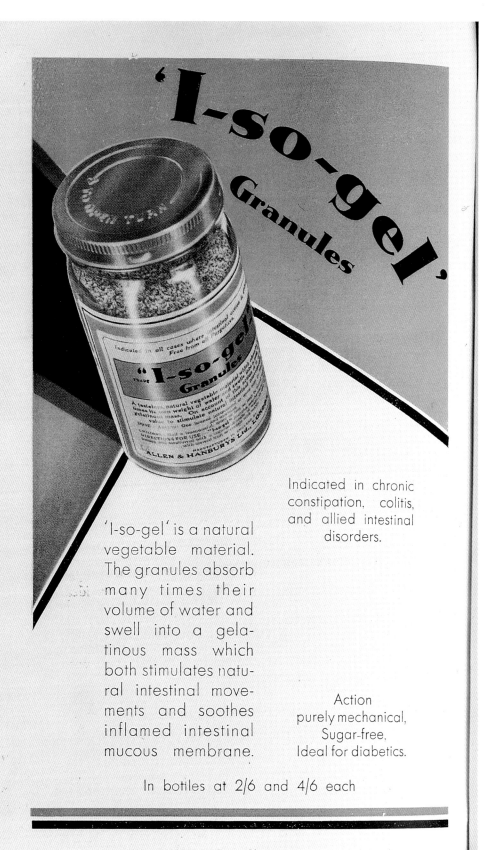

'I-so-gel' Granules

Indicated in chronic constipation, colitis, and allied intestinal disorders.

'I-so-gel' is a natural vegetable material. The granules absorb many times their volume of water and swell into a gelatinous mass which both stimulates natural intestinal movements and soothes inflamed intestinal mucous membrane.

Action purely mechanical, Sugar-free. Ideal for diabetics.

In botiles at 2/6 and 4/6 each

Page Twelve

(left) Cyril Wheatley Maplethorpe (1898-1983), who was the architect of the firm's fortunes in the 1950s and early 1960s and masterminded its move out of the traditional galenical sector of the industry. Oil portrait by Anna Zinkeisen. (Courtesy Royal Pharmaceutical Society of Great Britain)

(right) "Isogel", a bulk laxative, was formulated by Maplethorpe in his early days with the firm.

(right) Operating table assembly. Allen & Hanburys maintained a high reputation in surgical products manufacture in this period.

(below) Operating theatre equipped by Allen & Hanburys at the Queen Victoria Hospital, East Grinstead, in the 1940s. The hospital was associated with the eminent plastic surgeon, Sir Archibald McIndoe.

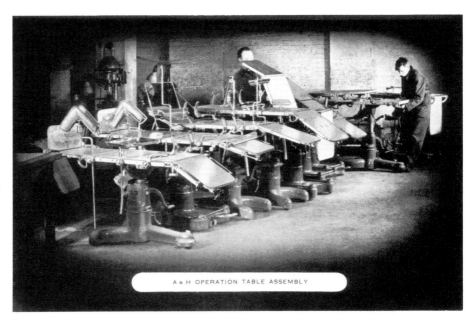

A & H OPERATION TABLE ASSEMBLY

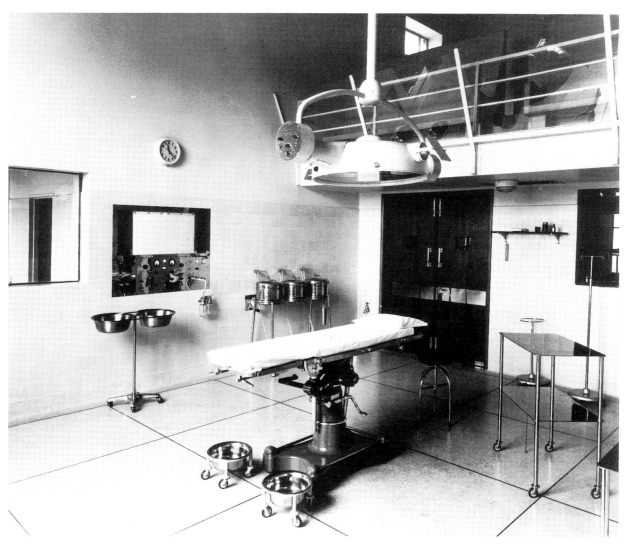

model MC table, which allowed surgeons and anaesthetists a complete range of adjustments that made the table serviceable for neuro- and orthopaedic surgery, and radiography.

In the 1950s some of the older lines enjoyed a new lease of life. The company found that there was still "an unlimited market for all types of malt products". In 1954 the chairman stated that "Allenburys Pastilles . . . have a bigger sale today than ever before in the Company's history." This was particularly true in the US, where the Americans accorded pastilles a respect that they reserved for such traditionally sought-after English goods as country tweeds. Once sugar rationing had been removed, pastille-making became more mechanised: a new Baker Perkins "Master" machine, with an automatic stacking and drying facility, replaced the old inter-war "Mogul". Gone, too, was the laborious method of hand-pinning the pastilles for the final finishing, which was replaced by an invention made by two carpenters in Allen & Hanburys. Even as late as the 1960s, however, the work was still relatively labour-intensive and individual workers continued to plunge rows of pastilles into troughs of coating compound.

The manufacture of one old-established favourite did cease, however. In 1953 Allen & Hanburys announced that its infant foods had been discontinued: dried milk was no longer economic to produce by the firm's vacuum evaporation process and the company now rid itself of "a thoroughly unprofitable anachronism", though the "Allenburys' Diet for Invalids" was retained because of its popularity with the public. But, ironically, this was far from the end of the firm's involvement in the milk business. Allen & Hanburys' acquisition of its own dairy before 1940 to secure supplies of milk has already been mentioned. In the Second World War these facilities for handling and processing milk became of national strategic importance, since Allen & Hanburys' location to the north of London was in an area not relatively well endowed with dairies. The Ministry of Food asked Allen & Hanburys to fill this gap by processing liquid milk, which it did by setting up a batch pasteurising system. In return, the firm was allowed to use a fixed allocation of milk in its own products. Towards the end of the war, more investment in pasteurising plant followed and the company also began bottling. At the end of the war, Allen & Hanburys found itself with a profitable milk business, which was growing steadily, and it seemed perfectly reasonable to enter the milk business by forming its own company – Lea Valley Dairies. Apparently, Maplethorpe found nothing incongruous in this; it was a sound business opportunity and, always the entrepreneur, he took it. The subsidiary grew quite rapidly in the period 1945-55 and it acquired other milk businesses over a considerable area, embracing not only Hertfordshire, but Luton and other parts of Bedfordshire, Essex and Suffolk. In 1957 Gates Bros offered to buy Lea Valley Dairies, but its profitability meant that Allen & Hanburys was in no mood to sell. But two years later, when there was a trend for merger and rationalisation in the milk industry, and when United Dairies and Cow & Gate merged, Allen & Hanburys faced severe competition if it chose to continue independently. In 1959, therefore, the company resigned itself to the inevitable and sold its entire milk wholesaling and retailing interests – numbering some 150 milk rounds and 150,000 customers – to Unigate Ltd for £1.1 million.

In the early 1950s, Maplethorpe began grappling with the problem of Allen & Hanburys' diverse overseas trading activities. Not only was the performance of its overseas companies mixed, but Allen & Hanburys had never had a coordinated strategy for them: run in a largely *ad hoc* fashion, rarely visited by the firm's directors, and often regarded as simply a useful outlet for excess capacity, the overseas trading companies were contributing little to the overall performance of the parent. In 1946, as ever, the chairman's outlook was optimistic: some profits were being made by all the subsidiaries, the Canadian trade was expanding, and South America wanted more Allen & Hanbury products. On the other hand, both Africa and Canada needed more working capital, and so too did Australia, where the company had decided to open a new factory. By the early 1950s the company was finding the export trade "strenuous and costly" and profits were hard to generate. As Capel Hanbury stated in 1953: "The great competition in the pharmaceutical and surgical fields, the protection by many countries of their home markets and the greater facilities available to many overseas countries for expansion in outside markets have made, and are making, the increase of a profitable export market extremely difficult."

To maximise Allen & Hanburys' potential in this area, in 1948 Maplethorpe decided to strengthen the firm's control of its overseas partners by giving fellow board member William M. Clayson specific responsibility for liaison with the overseas subsidiaries. The boards of the subsidiaries in Canada, Africa, Australasia and South America were then reconstituted, with Maplethorpe and Clayson at the head of each. Thereafter, the company had a directed overseas policy, with more frequent consultation and visits overseas, facilitated by the development of air travel. In particular, Maplethorpe wished the overseas companies to become more actively involved in manufacturing. Up to that point, most of the Allen & Hanburys' overseas businesses did little in the way of large-scale manufacture: most of the work entailed packaging materials and medicines supplied from England.

In South Africa – easily the most successful of the firm's overseas ventures – Maplethorpe sent out Harold Goodson, from the bulk drug manufacture department at Ware, to manage a new factory at Congella, near Durban. This venture had been planned before the war by Thomas Walton and had been opened with due ceremony by Capel Hanbury in October 1950. But three years later the premises were completely destroyed by fire. This misfortune allowed Maplethorpe, who was on the spot within days of the disaster, to become more actively involved. E.K. Samways, by now manager of the Ware factory, was promptly sent out to replace the old Congella premises with a new factory twice the size, with expanded facilities for tablet manufacture. By then Allen & Hanburys was also active in West Africa, having in 1954 formed a new subsidiary, Allen & Hanburys (Nigeria) Ltd, with its headquarters in Lagos.

In Australia in 1945 D.O. Evans, the Australian-born manager of the

Above, L. to R.
Mr. S. P. Sen, President, Indian Pharmaceutical Association.
General Manager, Bengal Chemical and Pharmaceutical Works Ltd.
Dr. B. Bannerjee; Mr. S. H. Merchant; Mr. C. W. Maplethorpe,
Mr. M. Tiche, Calcutta Manager, May & Baker (India) Ltd.

Left, L. to R.
Mr. S. H. Merchant, Assistant Drugs Controller, Government of India.
Dr. B. Bannerjee, Deputy Director, Central Drugs Laboratory.
Dr. P. K. Sanyal, Drugs Analyst, Public Health Laboratory.
Mr. C. W. Maplethorpe.

Cyril Maplethorpe takes tea in the School of Tropical Medicine with the pharmacists of Calcutta, 1952. A page from an album of the visit.

Vere Street branch, toured the continent and secured the lease on a suitable factory building at St. Mary's, on the outskirts of Sydney. By 1947 the manufacture of some Allen & Hanbury staples, such as tablets, sterile products and "Lixen", had begun and a little later a new showroom was opened in Melbourne. At the same time, a pharmacist was sent from England to New Zealand and the tempo of the company's activities in that area began to quicken in association with its agents, Sharland & Co, who had a network of factories and depots in that country.

In Canada in 1950 a new factory was opened on an industrial site in the north-western outskirts of Toronto, where Donald McClaren, a pharmacist and member of the Allen & Hanburys' sales staff, ran its activities for a time. An attempt was also made to revitalise the Indian branch, which until then had always been a depot for the parent company's sales of such specialities as the "Bynin" preparations. In the mid-1950s attempts were made to begin some manufacturing at Karachi and Chittagong in Pakistan. In 1957 negotiations also began for a prestigious joint venture with the Iranian Government, which was to result in a £1.5 million factory near Teheran in the early 1960s (a project which is discussed in the next chapter).

Besides rationalising the firm's overseas subsidiaries, Maplethorpe did

181

Interior of Allen & Hanburys' surgical instrument showroom, Cape Town, 1949.

what he could to extend its research activities. He hired more technically qualified personnel, beginning in 1938 with a new technical assistant for himself, E.K. Samways – only the third qualified pharmacist (again from "the Square") to work at Ware. After the war, Maplethorpe took the opportunity to bring in more such recruits, notably Dr. Harry Collier, who became head of the pharmacology department at Ware in 1945 and whose particular field of research was in neuromuscular blocking agents. The first research chemist, Norman R. Campbell, was also hired to investigate sex hormones. In 1950 after the chief chemist and director of research, Dr. Norman Evers, had retired, Allen & Hanburys recruited a new research director, Dr. F. Arnold Robinson (1908-88), to coordinate the development of new drugs. Robinson had previously been at Glaxo Laboratories at Greenford, where he had worked alongside Dr. Lester Smith and had gained experience with a wide range of synthetic medicinal chemicals, such as stilboestrol, aneurin and other B vitamins, besides wartime work on essential drugs, formerly obtained from Germany. He was also involved in establishing the corn products process for the production of penicillin. A brief spell at the Distillers Co followed, before he began work at Ware on a variety of modern chemotherapeutic endeavours. None of the resulting products was a major advance and some were based on licences: nevertheless, on their own terms they included some notable successes and showed Allen & Hanburys embarking slowly on a proper research programme – still a new idea amongst British pharmaceutical companies. By the mid-1950s, this policy began to bear fruit and Allen & Hanburys' product line began to acquire a more modern look.

By 1953 Allen & Hanburys had introduced a range of chloramphenicol products, which were close in composition to those of Parke Davis. The company had also brought out "Guanimycin", a preparation for oral use in the treatment of the common bacterial dysenteries, combining sulphaguanadine with the streptomycin. In September 1953 Allen & Hanburys introduced a cough linctus under the name "Ethnine", which was based on a non-addictive French derivative of morphine, pholcodine, which was considered at the time to have many advantages over the traditional cough depressants. "Ethnine" became one of the premier cough mixtures of the day.

During and after the Second World War, the company had been closely involved with the production of drugs used by surgeons to produce muscular relaxation during operations. The most important long-acting drug of that kind was tubocararine, an alkaloid derived from tropical plants used by the inhabitants of tropical forests to tip their hunting arrows and weapons. In view of the uncertainty of supplies of such material, Allen & Hanburys undertook a research project designed to synthesise chemicals having properties comparable to those of tubocararine. The successful result of the project was "Laudolissin", an effective substitute for tubocararine. With the return of peace, supplies of curare once more became available and the synthesised drug was abandoned (unfortunately, the paralysis induced by it was prolonged, a disadvantage in surgery). From the company's viewpoint, it had proved a pointless development, though a spin-off from it was the isolation of a new compound, dequalinium ("dequadin"), which exhibited potent antibacterial properties when used topically. The most valuable use of this drug was in treating mouth and throat infections and it was first marketed in the form of lozenges in 1956, which gained immediate acceptance and became one of the firm's most widely used products. Although hopes that "dequadin" could be used as an antibacterial paint were to be disappointed (on open wounds, it later proved to be toxic and had to be withdrawn), it did become the subject of many licensing agreements under which other companies in the US and Europe utilised "dequadin" salts as active ingredients in their own products. The royalties and profits were a valuable return on the original research project, and no doubt helped to rub in the lesson that resources spent in such activities was money well spent.

Also in 1956, the rights on other drugs were purchased and developed into new Allen & Hanbury products. Arrangements were made for the manufacture under licence from Warner-Lambert Laboratories of choline theophyllinate, a bronchodilator with demonstrable superiority over earlier oral spasmolytics in the treatment of asthma and chronic bronchitis. The production of choline theophyllinate itself and the tablets made from it under the name "Choledyl" entailed a considerable research effort as the product was potentially unstable. The problem was solved by avoiding the use of wet syrups and employing the relatively new compression coating techniques to produce a "tablet within a tablet". From the Schering Corporation in America, a new range of products based on piriton chlorpheniramine was introduced. This chemical was a potent antihistamine and was used to treat a wide range of allergic disorders, either with injections, tablets or linctus. Marketed by Allen & Hanburys as "Piriton", it was widely regarded as one of the best antihistamines available, being relatively non-sedative, and succeeded in exploiting the popularity of such drugs at that time and enjoyed a large sale.

The summer of 1957 also saw the culmination of an unusually interesting project involving the company's chemists and physicians at the Birmingham Childrens' Hospital. Here a prolonged investigation had been taking place into the rare disease of phenylketonuria, a disorder of the metabolism in new-born babies. The treatment of this condition involved feeding such children on a diet from which the amino acid phenylalanine had been removed. A process involving the hydrolysis of casein was evolved by Evers and Eastland. Using this material, dietetic regimes were introduced in Birmingham and in other childrens' hospitals which enabled the phenylketonuric children to be reared successfully and to the great advantage of their mental health. "Cymogran" resulted from this work and provided a blend of all the essential amino acids round which a comprehensive diet could then be built. The availability of this product and others devised on similar lines transformed the lives of phenylketonuric children, whose previous outlook had been either premature death or mental retardation. Although an important medicine, "Cymogran" was not very profitable and never could be because there are relatively few patients. Scientists at Allen & Hanburys and elsewhere had not yet identified the need to seek better treatment for common illnesses if clinical and financial success are to go hand in hand.

Allen & Hanburys also catered for the growing market for anti-depressants and sleeping tablets. "Anxine", a tablet for the treatment of anxiety was introduced in 1954, to be followed a year later by "Bidormal", an "alarm-clock pill", containing a sleep-inducing barbiturate and a delayed-action amphetamine, which was designed to overcome the hangover associated with tranquillisers. In 1957 Allen & Hanburys introduced "Fentazin", a phenothiazine derivative, which controlled anxiety and tension and was useful in treating "morning sickness".

Finally, the company maintained its status as a "household" word with the introduction of an improved form of "Haliborange", which had first been introduced in 1933. Using a process pioneered by Collett & Co of Oslo, in 1956 Allen & Hanburys introduced a compressed

184

An improved tablet form of "Haliborange" was marketed by Allen & Hanburys in 1956.

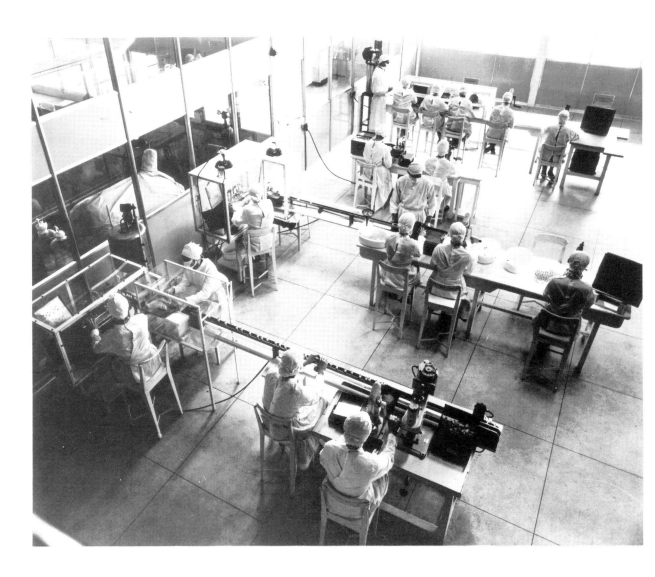

(above) Sterile products department, Ware.

(right) Scrubbing up and robing area in the sterile products department, Ware, 1957.

"Haliborange" tablet in which the fat-soluble vitamins A and D were presented in a non-fatty but stable form, together with vitamin C. The tablets were thus free from a fishy taste and remained "the nicest way" to swallow a vitamin supplement.

The main focus of Allen & Hanburys' production and research activities had shifted to Ware. After the war, the Bethnal Green factory was rebuilt, but now served as the administrative headquarters of the company and manufacture there had almost ceased. (Surgical instrument making continued for a time in the 1950s, but that, too, was eventually transferred elsewhere.) The branches in the West End were also relatively less important. In March 1958 the Wigmore Street premises were evacuated on the expiry of the lease and the business incorporated into the Vere Street branch. At Ware the "P" building, situated in the middle of the Buryfield site and adjacent to the older part of the works, now dominated the site. Originally intended for penicillin manufacture, it had soon been utilised for other purposes, such as "Sterivac" production and tablet manufacture. There was also an "X" building, which had absorbed the old crude drug and galenical manufacturing plant from Bethnal Green. But the days of this business were numbered: Maplethorpe was increasingly committed to closing a department in which, despite some modern equipment, "many old implements [were] still in evidence, percolators and copper stills abound[ed] and the wooden paddle [had] not quite disappeared".[11] The sterile filling and packing of solutions was now of much more importance and in 1957 a new block for this activity was opened at Ware.[12] Finally, in a symbolic gesture, Maplethorpe announced in the following year that Allen & Hanburys' production of traditional drugs and galenicals would end.

Maplethorpe's reforms, however, took place within a family firm that was still very conservative. In retrospect, what Allen & Hanburys needed in the face of the dramatic new advances in the pharmaceutical industry, was a daring and imaginative management, with a financial commitment to research and development. These had never been conspicuous Hanbury virtues, and their absence was to lead to the family losing control of the business in the 1950s when economic circumstances finally overtook the firm.

The problem was essentially a simple one: though Allen & Hanburys remained a profitable business, turnover was no longer sufficient for it to remain in the race with the bigger pharmaceutical firms. As Capel Hanbury admitted in 1946: "The position is then, that the need and opportunity for expansion in every direction are present, but the means are extremely limited." Annual working capital was usually well below £100,000 for most of the period from 1941 to 1958. Hit by postwar inflation in materials and labour, with high taxation, the directors found it "almost impossible to 'plough back' sufficient to maintain a business". The time was ripe for the issue of new capital, but this the firm was reluctant to contemplate. For generations the ordinary shareholders had enjoyed comfortable dividends (even during the difficult years of the Second World War and after, the dividend on the ordinary shares was never less than 15 percent) and retained complete control of the business, preferring to plough back resources into reserve rather than the research side. If the firm went public it would signal the end of this situation. At the annual meeting in December 1946, Capel Hanbury commented:

> It would be possible to raise fresh capital from the public as so many other companies are doing, but the amount of money which would be required would be so large as to overwhelm the existing ordinary share capital and probably the present controlling interests. [Therefore] the issue of fresh capital should be postponed until the directors consider the interests of those who have built up its resources in the past and of those who are bearing the burden today can be properly safeguarded.

Instead Allen & Hanburys utilised its friendly connection with Barclays Bank and reached an agreement which allowed the firm to borrow up to the limit of its paid-up capital. By 1950 the bank loan stood at £740,000. The loan bought time, but it was conditional: when it saw fit Barclays could twist the firm's arm to issue capital. Inevitably, in 1951 £1 million 4 percent debenture stock was issued, to be followed in the next year by the raising of the authorised capital of the firm to £1 million (of which £800,600 was issued). This involved an issue to the existing ordinary shareholders of 203,500 ordinary shares of £1 each. This resulted in the ordinary shares of the company being available to the public for the first time and marked the beginning of the end of the Hanburys' control of the business.

The chairman, John Hanbury, still attended daily to the business and was an eloquent spokesman for the interests of the industry. As president of the Association of the British Pharmaceutical Industry (ABPI) in 1950-2, for example, he opposed the price-cutting recommendations of the Joint Committee on Proprietary Preparations (the Cohen Committee). But the changing climate of the industry meant that the direction of Allen & Hanburys could no longer be under the Hanburys' sole control, so allowing Cyril Maplethorpe an increasingly free hand.

Maplethorpe's presence gave the firm a strong central direction, but its financial problems remained. How was Allen & Hanburys to maintain its position and reputation in the face of increasing competition at home and overseas? The question was answered on Tuesday 8 April 1958 when the boards of Glaxo Laboratories and Allen & Hanburys issued a surprise joint press statement:

> The Directors of Glaxo Laboratories Ltd and Allen & Hanburys Ltd announce that discussions have been taking place with a view to a merger between the two Companies. It is intended that each Company would retain its own name, individuality and pattern of business, and would continue to trade as at present. The Directors are satisfied that financial and technical co-operation will increase the effectiveness of both Companies at home and abroad. The two businesses are complementary rather than competitive and the merger should establish a concern of great strength and comprehensiveness in the pharmaceutical field.

The news of the Allen & Hanburys and Glaxo merger came as a surprise to both the City and those within the pharmaceutical industry.

The negotiations leading to it had been conducted for many months amongst the respective board members, particularly Sir Harry Jephcott and Cyril Maplethorpe, but they had been kept secret. John Hanbury later recalled how the negotiations began:

> My first serious contact with Harry Jephcott had been when I was President of the ABPI in 1951, when I exchanged correspondence with him on the need for closer collaboration and rationalisation between British pharmaceutical manufacturers. Even at that early stage we were seriously concerned about the activities of the Americans and the need for British firms to come closer together. At about the same time I visited him at Greenford and I suspect that these exchanges may have sown the first seeds from which the merger eventually came.[13]

Thereafter, Maplethorpe led the negotiations with Glaxo. In private he admitted his preference for preserving Allen & Hanburys' independence, especially since the company had promising developments underway, such as a new veterinary vaccine. In short, he wanted to manage his own research-based company. But given Allen & Hanburys' severe cash-flow problems, Maplethorpe had little choice but to settle for the best deal he could. His position was not entirely without strength: Allen & Hanburys had some useful assets to bargain with and there was also its prestigious name to consider. But Glaxo's position was stronger.

Jephcott had built up the company enormously since its dried milk days. The contrast with Allen & Hanburys is a fascinating one. Both had been family firms, which owed much of their early success to milk food manufacture. As we have seen, the companies began to diverge in the inter-war period, when Glaxo (as part of Joseph Nathan & Co) stole a march on its rival by its more scientific approach. Undoubtedly, Glaxo had been helped by the fact that it was not committed, as Allen & Hanburys was, to providing such a wide range of medical and surgical specialities. More important by far, it had a man of vision at the helm. Jephcott had continued his rise within the company: in 1935 he became managing director of Glaxo Laboratories Ltd, which was set up as a subsidiary of the Nathan Co, and succeeded Alec Nathan as managing director of the parent company in 1939. At a newly built site at Greenford, Jephcott continued to exploit the work on vitamins (though the firm still manufactured more traditional products, such as dried milk and iron tablets) and also began manufacturing purified anti-anaemic liver extracts.

The Second World War was a turning point in Jephcott's career and that of Glaxo Laboratories. Prior to the War, Jephcott "had contemplated resigning to become a New Zealand fruit farmer when he was particularly discouraged at Glaxo's continuing commitment to unexciting and only moderately profitable food subsidiaries";[14] but by 1943 he had persuaded his colleagues that fine chemical production should be given priority. Under Jephcott's guidance, the company undertook the licensed production of penicillin, with Jephcott himself visiting the USA on behalf of the Ministry of Supply in 1945 to report on production of the drug. This firmly launched Glaxo into the era of antibiotics by allowing it to seize the leading position amongst British manufacturers in the latest deep-fermentation techniques.

Building on this success, in 1948 Glaxo achieved its own major break-through when a research team at Greenford under Dr. Lester Smith isolated vitamin B_{12} (the anti-pernicious anaemia factor) in the liver. But mostly, Glaxo provided the chemical development for other people's research. In 1950 development work began on cortisone, which had been found to have beneficial effects on rheumatoid arthritis. Basing its research on hecogenin, a steroid that could be obtained in quantity from the juice expressed in the manufacture of sisal, Glaxo was able to begin the commercial production of steroids. By 1955 it was able to market a successful range of corticosteroids, such as "Cortelan" and "Efcortelan".

Jephcott was now chairman of Glaxo Laboratories, having succeeded Alec Nathan in 1945, and had been knighted a year later for his wartime work. In 1947 Sir Harry Jephcott arranged for Glaxo Laboratories to go public and divest itself of many of the non-pharmaceutical interests of its parent, Joseph Nathan & Co, which ceased to exist. The share capital consisted of £700,000 in preference shares and £80,000 in ordinary shares, a highly geared arrangement that was to result in particularly high earnings for the ordinary shareholders as Glaxo's new products paved the way for spectacular growth. Within ten years the capital was increased from the original £80,000 to £3.2 million, solely by the capitalisation of retained profits.

By 1958 Glaxo's financial position was impressive, particularly when it is compared with Allen & Hanburys' (see Table below), and it was well placed to put in a generous bid for its competitor. In 1958 Glaxo's equity earnings were reported to be fourteen times those of Allen & Hanburys'; ordinary share capital was £4.7 million and £488,400, respectively; and the capital and revenue reserves were £7.6 million compared to £1.7 million.

Capital and profits of Allen & Hanburys Ltd and Glaxo Laboratories Ltd (initially J. Nathan & Co), 1915-55.

	(£) Issued Capital		(£) Net Profit	
Year	A & H	Glaxo	A & H	Glaxo
1915	273,210	166,140	?	9,570
1925	569,500	1,013,540	118,140	50,694
1935	575,000	731,854	50,000	74,432
1945	575,600	779,635	50,752	87,988
1955	800,600	3,885,400	105,429	1,556,501

Source: Allen & Hanburys' Minute Books; Glaxo figures from R.P.T. Davenport-Hines, "Glaxo as a Multinational Before 1963", in G. Jones (ed.), *British Multinationals* (Aldershot, 1986), p. 140.

The *Daily Mail* described Glaxo's offer as "a takeover bid of the best kind"; and, indeed, there was something for everyone in the eventual agreement. For an outlay of £633,000, Glaxo took control of assets valued at £1.5 million, whose real value was to prove several times as

Merger of Allen & Hanburys and Glaxo, 1958.

much. For Jephcott, as the chairman of what was, after all, a relative parvenu in the world of pharmaceutical manufacture, there was the satisfaction of having acquired one of the most prestigious names in the industry. Allen & Hanburys had lost its independence: on the other hand, it was difficult for its shareholders to resist a chance virtually to double their money, and Glaxo's greater resources offered the chance to realise at last some of Maplethorpe's long-term research plans at Ware. Generally, the move was welcomed by both companies. Therefore, on 6 May 1958 Allen & Hanburys Ltd wrote to its ordinary shareholders recommending that an offer received from Glaxo Laboratories Ltd – to exchange three ordinary stock 10/- units for each £1 Allen & Hanburys' share – be accepted.

7

ALLEN & HANBURYS AND THE CHEMOTHERAPEUTIC REVOLUTION

With the advent of greater understanding of physiological mechanisms it has become possible to take a more mechanistic approach to research and start from a rationally argued hypothesis to design drugs. The target diseases selected for study are generally those prevalent in western society and progress depends largely on the current state of understanding of physiology in relation to diseases. This is the modern "rational approach" to drug design which is becoming increasingly important with the development of information in cell biochemistry, especially where this is understood at the molecular level.

C. Robin Ganellin, "Discovering New Medicines", Messel Medal Address, 1988, *Chemistry and Industry*, 2 January 1989, p. 12.

The thirty-year period from 1958-88 has been one of dramatic expansion for the British pharmaceutical industry. It has also seen a remarkable transformation in the fortunes of Allen & Hanburys and its parent. At the beginning of the 1960s, Glaxo ranked roughly fourth in pharmaceutical sales in the UK (behind Pfizer, Lederle (Cyanamid), and Smith, Kline & French), with Allen & Hanburys in about sixteenth place.[1] The British pharmaceutical industry was still relatively small, accounting for only about one percent of the country's Gross National Product. By 1988, however, Glaxo and Allen & Hanburys had emerged as the UK's leading drug companies and the parent, Glaxo Holdings p.l.c., was ranked only second in the *world* to the American firm Merck. In the UK, Allen & Hanburys had also become the market leader in what was an entirely new speciality for the firm – respiratory medicines. The way in which this remarkable turnabout was achieved forms the subject of this chapter.

In retrospect, it might be imagined that Jephcott's policy of bringing together British pharmaceutical companies under the Glaxo umbrella had shown considerable foresight and had been triumphantly vindicated. The truth is perhaps more prosaic. After the Second World War, Glaxo acquired other companies from the traditional sector of the British pharmaceutical industry: Evans Medical Ltd (1961), Edinburgh Pharmaceutical Industries Ltd (1962), The British Drug Houses Group Ltd (1967). Mainly because of the possible use of griseofulvin as an antifungal agent, in 1954 it also bought Murphy Chemical Co Ltd, a company engaged in

*Sir John C. Hanbury,
Allen & Hanburys'
chairman, addressing the
British Pharmaceutical
Conference, 1962.*

agricultural chemicals. Farley Infants Foods Ltd was another acquisition in 1968. Jephcott's policy undoubtedly contributed to the rationalisation of the UK industry, but it is difficult to discern any industrial strategy behind these acquisitions, for which the company issued a third of its share capital. Acquiring sound products from other companies or institutions was, it seems, more attractive to Jephcott than outright speculative research.

The result was that Glaxo became bigger and its product range was considerably extended: but ironically, the company now found itself with exactly the same problem that had dogged Allen & Hanburys in the early twentieth century. Glaxo had itself become something of a "Universal Provider", involved in a wide range of products. These included: pharmaceutical specialities; vaccines; veterinary medicines and animal feedstuffs; laboratory chemicals; surgical equipment; hospital and specialised medical furniture; farm and garden products, such as insecticides, weedkillers and fertilisers; milk products, baby and invalid foods; and finally, pharmaceutical wholesaling (Vestric), supplying prescription and other products to retail chemists. As the present chairman of Glaxo, Sir Paul Girolami, has remarked: "It is difficult to make an assessment of the balance of advantage to Glaxo, or of the process of rationalisation, brought about by these acquisitions . . . [since] . . . with the exception of Allen & Hanburys, there is little evidence of any long-term benefit, either financial or industrial, to the [Glaxo] Group."[2]

Not surprisingly, in the absence of a coherent strategy, it took some years before Glaxo and Allen & Hanburys were merged in more than name only. At the board level, the two companies were integrated by Maplethorpe taking a seat as director of Glaxo Laboratories, and by Herbert Palmer (the managing director of Glaxo) becoming a director of Allen & Hanburys. E.K. Samways was also elected to the Allen & Hanburys' board at this time. John C. Hanbury remained chairman of the firm and was Maplethorpe's alternate on the Glaxo board, in the unlikely event of the latter's absence. The takeover involved no great loss of prestige for Maplethorpe. Jephcott and Maplethorpe had a healthy respect for each other and their views coincided: both men grasped the essential fact that the future of the industry lay in synthetic drugs and not the old galenicals. They also had dominant personalities and considerable presence – characteristics perhaps helped by the fact that both men were well over six feet tall!

Herbert Palmer proved a wise choice as the Glaxo representative on the Allen & Hanburys' board, helping to re-direct the firm's energies in the early 1960s. As E.K. Samways recalls, Palmer helped to dampen Allen & Hanburys' over-exuberance with its new-found position and act as buffer between the company and Sir Harry Jephcott. Samways remembers Jephcott sending for the whole of the Allen & Hanbury board in about November 1958, when "he outlined some of his ideas for the development of the company. He indicated that his shares never paid investors more than 2 percent – and he wanted it that way – he wanted to have blue chip status, he wanted growth, and he believed in ploughing back."

Having paid a good price for Allen & Hanburys, however, Jephcott needed to maximise its potential and in the event proved unwilling to tamper with its working too much. During the 1960s, therefore, Allen & Hanburys continued very much as an independent company. Some of Glaxo's acquisitions were dismembered and these Allen & Hanburys were asked to assimilate. Glaxo (now known as Glaxo Group Ltd), after it had acquired Edinburgh Pharmaceutical Industries Ltd (EPI), set up a committee to study ways of rationalising production. The speciality sales companies of Duncan, Flockhart & Co and Allied Laboratories (which were part of EPI Ltd) also became part of the pharmaceutical business of Allen & Hanburys.[4] When The British Drug Houses Group joined Glaxo in 1967, it was split in two: its laboratory and pure chemical side was separated from its pharmaceutical business. Ian Smith of Allen & Hanburys became managing director of the latter and set about drastically pruning the BDH, Duncan Flockhart and EPI lists of their more old-fashioned preparations and of the weaker of any duplicated products.

These additional companies created inefficiencies and problems of

(above) Cyril W. Maplethorpe.

(above right) Sir Harry Jephcott (1891-1978), chairman of Glaxo until 1963, who grasped early the importance of scientific research in the pharmaceutical industry.

(right) E.K. Samways, production director of Allen & Hanburys, and one of the longest-serving members of the company.

overlapping, which were not seriously tackled until the late 1960s. At that time, in 1968, the deputy chairman (Sir) Austin Bide appointed E.K. Samways, production director at Allen & Hanburys, to head an investigatory team into pharmaceutical manufacturing in the Glaxo Group.[5] The team's report provided the basis for rationalising the production of ampoules, tablets and pharmaceutical liquids at Greenford, Ware, Barnard Castle and Speke. Besides economising on labour, space and capital equipment, the report also provided important provision for dealing with the accidental loss of production facilities at any one site.

Thus Allen & Hanburys' business grew in size and scope in this period. It remained a profitable business, helped by the astute financial direction of Arthur Axe, who introduced an integrated system of modern cost accounting in the company, and Berkley E. Baker, who introduced modern marketing methods for its products. Allen & Hanburys' headquarters and surgical instrument division remained at Bethnal Green, where a new block was completed in 1959 to house new directors' offices and a new boardroom. The Bethnal Green offices controlled the showroom at Vere Street and the main research and manufacturing activities at Ware.

At the Ware site the product range continued to be diverse. Reference has already been made to the introduction of "Sterivac". During the late 1950s a long programme of research and development led to the introduction in 1959 of intravenous infusion solutions presented in flexible plastic containers in place of the "Sterivac"-type glass bottles. The research workers who were tackling this programme first had to find a plastic which met the necessary physical requirements and which was biologically and chemically totally inert and safe. Ultimately, with the help of a licensing agreement with the Geneva company VIFOR, a plastic of suitable composition was found and a lengthy programme of development began to perfect production methods involving the manufacture, filling and sterilisation of the plastic bags. The technical difficulties were incomparably greater than those involving the same solutions in glass containers, but they were all mastered and the new containers, for which the word "Steriflex" was coined, soon superseded glass bottles: the plastic bags were disposable, were much less bulky and fragile, and were lighter and more easily transported. The "Steriflex" products proved particularly useful for military use, and were also soon introduced into civilian hospitals.

Alongside these more novel products and the production of important pharmaceutical preparations, such as insulin, there was still much that was traditional at Ware. Despite the so-called chemotherapeutic revolution, it should be remembered that it is only within the last twenty years that the modern high-technology profile of the pharmaceutical industry has appeared. A visitor to Ware in the mid-1960s would have been able to see pastille manufacturing, which in its basic techniques had changed little since the nineteenth century. Commented the *Allenburys Bulletin* in June 1966: "Various processes in the making of pastilles have been mechanised but even today they still receive a considerable amount of personal care and attention. Their production can still justifiably be described as a craft." One of the duties of the head of the pastille department was to carry out the "3 o'clock test, when he tastes the glycerine and blackcurrant mixture – a function which, in fact, he takes extremely seriously for, as with wine-tasting, this is the only way by which it is possible to guarantee the flavour of every batch."[6]

Craft skills were still very much in evidence in surgical instrument manufacturing. Remarkably, despite its consistently poor performance, this section of Allen & Hanburys continued to lead a charmed life and had survived intact through all the mergers, upheavals and changes of location. In 1966, for a time, the business had been transferred from Bethnal Green to Leyton in east London, where the production philosophy remained the same: the highest quality instruments, produced by hand, often by request for particular surgical operations. The company reported proudly: "The skill of the craftsman has remained unchanged – he takes a bar of stainless steel, places it in the furnace and when red hot beats it into shape. The production of surgical instruments calls for innumerable stages of work. There are very few which can be made by die-stamping or mass-production methods so that for the most part each instrument has to be passed to a number of different people."[7] While certain members of the Allen & Hanburys' board despaired of the way in which this activity drained resources from the more profitable sides of the business, Maplethorpe, who entertained notions of mass-producing surgical instruments by machinery and also may have had a soft spot for craft workers in a declining industry, continued to support it.

In the 1960s, however, the surgical instrument business was being seriously eroded both by domestic competition and by the import of instruments produced by low-cost foreign labour. Increasingly, the company was pushed towards the equipment side: operation tables, sterilisers, hospital furniture, and disposable plastic products, such as catheters. In 1963, as Bethnal Green became increasingly cramped, a new factory was purchased at Portsmouth under the name of Swanbrig Engineers Ltd, and some of the skilled workers from Bethnal Green were transferred there. Besides operation tables and steriliser bodies, Swanbrig Engineers also began producing the tubular steel frames used for hospital furniture manufacture in the Buckingham factory of another Allen & Hanburys' surgical subsidiary company, W.H. Deane (High Wycombe) Ltd. Meanwhile, plastic products, including catheters, and a range of surgical instruments were being manufactured in the factories of another subsidiary, Eschmann Bros & Walsh Ltd, in Sussex and London. Wardco Ltd at Sheffield were also making surgical instruments and scissors for the group. In 1963, to bring all these subsidiaries together, Allen & Hanburys (Surgical Engineering) Ltd was incorporated with its registered office at Bethnal Green. Gradually, the manufacturing of surgical instrument specialities at Bethnal Green ceased and its function became purely administrative.

In 1965 Allen & Hanburys celebrated its 250th anniversary. Turnover had reached £8 million and the number of staff had grown to about 2000. John C. Hanbury was chairman and was to remain so until his retirement

in 1973 (when he was knighted for his work as chairman of the Central Health Services Council), with Cyril Maplethorpe as managing director. In 1963, as his career was drawing to a close, Maplethorpe was elected President of the Pharmaceutical Society (the first director or partner of Allen & Hanburys to hold the post since William Allen in 1841) and was to remain in the position until 1965. By then Maplethorpe had retired, handing over the managing directorship to David Smart, who had become a director of the company in 1961.

David Smart was a Cambridge graduate, who had read medicine, but had not qualified as a doctor because of illness. Instead, he brought his medical knowledge to bear on the marketing side of Allen & Hanburys. He also modernised the management function with clearly defined, written-down areas of responsibility. Under Smart, who was to succeed John C. Hanbury as chairman, a number of key changes, both internal and external, conspired to fuse together Allen & Hanburys and its parent. In the early 1960s two important decisions were taken by the Glaxo board: to introduce an international strategy and organisation for marketing its products; and to concentrate more of its resources in basic research. These two decisions were inter-connected: without an expanding international market, particularly in the developed countries which had been neglected by both Allen & Hanburys and Glaxo, the increasing costs in research could not be contemplated or supported; secondly, the old policy of developing and improving compounds discovered by others could not, in the increasingly competitive post-war

(above) The Shah of
Iran greets Sir Harry
Jephcott at the
opening of the
Teheran factory in
May 1963.

(right) The Shah and
his Queen inspect a
tableting machine at
the Darou Pakhsh
factory, with the help
of an Iranian
pharmacist trained at
Ware.

200

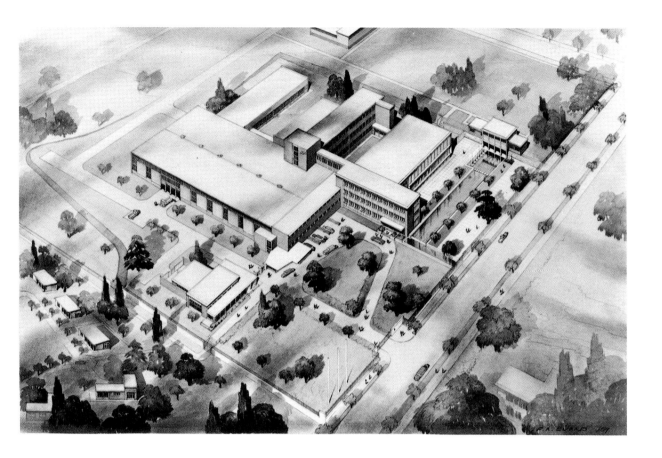

Architect's drawing of the Darou Pakhsh factory in Teheran.

world, be expected to work as well as in the past. Giving direction to these new strategies, at the end of 1961, Glaxo Research Ltd was set up by Jephcott to centralise the research function of the company.[8] More importantly, after 1962, Allen & Hanburys' research division at Ware became an independent entity with the specific task of discovering new medicines. The success with which it did so and its remarkable impact on the Glaxo Group is related later in this chapter. As part of the new strategy, in 1966 Glaxo International Ltd was formed to co-ordinate the expansion of Glaxo's new overseas markets.

In some areas Allen & Hanburys, in the immediate aftermath of the Glaxo merger, continued to operate its foreign projects very much independently. Some of these were the result of plans hatched before 1958. Perhaps the most prestigious and successful was the building of a pharmaceutical factory in Teheran, on behalf of the Imperial Royal Welfare (Darou Pakhsh) Organisation. This was the result of contacts by Keith Maidment, Allen & Hanburys' sales representative in the Middle East, who heard that a consortium under the patronage of the Shah wished to build a pharmaceutical factory in Iran. Maplethorpe, with Raymond Greenwood's advice, decided to bid for the contract, which was duly won in 1958. Darou Pakhsh agreed to provide the total capital involved, some £1.5 million, with Allen & Hanburys to receive substantial royalties for its pharmaceutical formulations, its technical expertise and design know-how in building the factory, and in training Iranian students at Ware. An Iranian Projects Committee was set up under Greenwood's chairmanship, with E.K. Samways as technical adviser, to co-ordinate operations. The factory was officially opened in 1963, when Jephcott, Maplethorpe and Hanbury attended a ceremony hosted by the Shah. With a small permanent staff of Allen & Hanbury workers, headed by Peter Hanbury (John C. Hanbury's younger brother), the factory proved a profitable undertaking until the Shah was ousted in 1978. A comprehensive selection of Allen & Hanburys' products was manufactured and later it was agreed that the Darou Pakhsh factory could also produce a selected range of products of Glaxo and ICI.

It was in the international sphere that Allen & Hanburys and Glaxo first began to work closely together. There was considerable overlap in their trading overseas, since both companies had in the early twentieth century been attracted by colonial markets and undeveloped countries. A study of Glaxo's overseas operations has highlighted that by 1957 Glaxo Laboratories was represented in nearly seventy countries, and had nine overseas subsidiary headquarters with manufacturing facilities at Verona, Wadeville (South Africa), Karachi, Bombay, Melbourne, Palmerston North (New Zealand), Niteroi (Brazil), Montevideo and Buenos Aires. In addition there were other major overseas headquarters, or territorial offices, such as Cairo, Singapore, Toronto, Havana and Santiago, and separate factories in Argentina, Australia and New Zealand. As with Allen & Hanburys, the performance of these operations was mixed.[9]

Some rationalisation of these overlapping overseas ventures was inevitable. This was largely effected by Glaxo-Allenburys (Export) Ltd, which had its headquarters in London, and was formed in 1960 to direct the export activities of the two companies. The directors were Sir Harry Jephcott, Herbert Palmer, Cyril Maplethorpe, John Hurran, Arthur Langridge and Raymond Greenwood, who began re-organising the overseas subsidiaries. The result was that a string of Glaxo-Allenburys companies appeared in Canada (1958), New Zealand (1958), Australia (1960), South Africa (1960), Nigeria (1960) and Ghana (1962). In the 1970s the success of Glaxo's strategy allowed it to give even more attention to overseas marketing. The board set themselves the task of correcting a weakness in the Glaxo-Allenburys empire – the company's absence in certain major markets, most notably the US, and its poor performance in certain other markets, such as Japan, Germany and France. The fact was that even if Allen & Hanburys and Glaxo had produced world-beating products in the 1960s, they would have been incapable of reaping the benefits overseas because an efficient marketing organisation was lacking. Even in Europe there were serious marketing deficiencies. In 1978, however, Glaxo renounced its policy of using marketing and licensing agreements with US firms as a way to penetrate that market, and instead entered America directly. In 1978, Meyer Laboratories Inc, a small but vigorous marketing concern with 150 staff, based in Fort Lauderdale, Florida, was bought as the starting-point for a new American initiative. In 1972 Glaxo also decided to compete more strongly for the Japanese market by buying into Shin Nihon, a Japanese company with which it had been trading since 1954.

Thus by the 1970s, when Maurice Smith had assumed the mantle of managing director of Allen & Hanburys in succession to David Smart, the marketing function of the company was being more effectively merged into its increasingly successful parent. Glaxo's confidence and new ambitions stemmed partly from the increasing strength of its research programme, to which Allen & Hanburys had made a striking contribution. Allen & Hanburys' research activities at Ware had also maintained their independence in the aftermath of the merger with Glaxo. No plans were made to merge the Glaxo and Allen & Hanburys' efforts in this sphere – indeed, it would have proved difficult. At Greenford the Glaxo laboratories were increasingly involved with work on ways to treat and control infections and on steroids; while at Ware, pharmaceutical research had yet to become properly focused. In the early 1960s, Allen & Hanburys still remained something of a "Universal Provider", with its laboratories engaged in a wide range of products. The Allen & Hanbury medicine-chest at that time included the vitamin and iron supplements "Haliborange" and "Ferrodic"; decongestants and common cold relievers, such as "Hazol" and "Capriton"; tranquillisers, notably "Fentazin"; and antibacterials, such as "Dequadin" (see below). The key feature of many of these products was that they were developed by companies abroad, particularly American ones. Allen & Hanburys merely purchased the licences. The firm also modified popular formulations, up-dated its traditional products, and attempted to discover new money-spinners: in short, any strategy was tried that would generate enough cash to keep the company in the race with its competitors.

Guanimycin	1953	antibiotic/sulphonamide mixture
Ethnine	1953	cough linctus
Anxine	1954	tranquilliser
Bidormal	1955	tranquilliser
Haliborange	1956	vitamin supplement
Choledyl	1956	bronchodilator
Piriton	1956	antihistamine therapy
Cymogran	1957	food supplement for phenylketonurics
Dequadin	1957	antibacterial
Fentazin	1957	tranquilliser
Dictol	1959	lungworm vaccine for cattle
Ferrodic	1962	mineral supplement
Euvitol	1962	central nervous stimulant
Capriton	1962	common cold reliever
Hazol	1962	nasal decongestant

An important line for Allen & Hanburys at this time was veterinary drugs. The firm had always sold a number of such products and in the 1950s the marketing policy was revised and a new veterinary division was established. By far the most important of the drugs marketed by this division was "Dictol", launched in February 1959 as an orally administered vaccine for the immunisation of cattle against lungworm. This is a

Product literature for "Dictol", the oral vaccine for lungworm. It had a shelf life of only twelve days, requiring correspondingly fast distribution, and could only be produced from January to July.

(left) The Bethnal Green factory in 1967.

"Dequadin" mailing item and showcard.

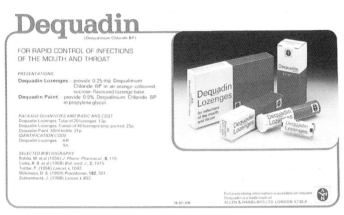

disease – commonly known by farmers as husk or hoose – caused by the parasitic nematode *Dictyocaulus viviparus*, whose larvae invade the lungs and bronchi of young cattle, producing a distressing cough and pneumonia. In the UK alone this resulted in the deaths of many thousands of young cattle each year, while a much greater number received a serious check to their development. For many years a successful vaccine had eluded scientists, but in a brilliant piece of research, the veterinary school of the University of Glasgow discovered that an oral vaccine might be prepared from the infective larvae, provided these were treated with controlled doses of X-rays to render them sterile, but still sufficiently active to penetrate to the lungs and induce an immune response.

The work came to the attention of Allen & Hanburys' "circus", the travelling team (E.K. Samways, David Smart and Francis Conduit) which scouted for new ideas and opportunities for the firm. Large-scale production was beyond the capabilities of the University, so Allen & Hanburys in a joint project with the Glasgow team developed methods whereby an adequately stable, standard and effective vaccine could be prepared in large quantities. E.K. Samways persuaded the Glasgow researchers of the necessity of scaling up the production process (one which involved the culture of large quantities of cattle faeces, in order to recover the larvae), which Allen & Hanburys achieved in giant trays. Other work involved the isolation of parasites from infected calves, determination of the correct dosage of X-rays to be used in their inactivation without risk to the staff, and the bacteriological control procedures that were necessary to ensure the vaccine's safety.

The final development stages of "Dictol" occupied a period of two years and involved, amongst other things, trials on thousands of farm animals throughout the country. On its introduction, its power to confer immunity was amply proved and by the 1960s over a quarter of a million calves were being immunised in the UK alone. "Dictol" benefited from a new marketing policy, the work of Berkley E. Baker: advertising and sales promotion were directed towards the veterinary surgeon rather than the farmer, and selling was supported by specially trained representatives, with the help of graduate veterinarian staff. Unfortunately, there was no great need for the vaccine in overseas markets.

During 1961, however, Allen & Hanburys' research director, Arnold Robinson, left the firm and accepted a post as head of the Twyford Laboratories of Arthur Guinness & Sons. This marked a turning point in the fortunes of Allen & Hanburys' research activities (and, ultimately, it was also to herald a remarkable change in those of Glaxo, too), for it brought to Ware a new research director, Dr. David Jack.

David Jack's career before he joined Allen & Hanburys had been unusually varied.[10] After a pharmaceutical apprenticeship in his native Fife, he studied at Glasgow in the University and the Royal Technical College and in 1948 graduated as a BSc with a first in pharmacy and pharmacology. Thereafter, he taught pharmacology in the University and physiology in the Technical College for brief periods, interrupted by a two-year spell of National Service. In 1951 he decided that he did not wish to pursue a career in experimental pharmacology and joined Glaxo Laboratories as a research chemist, thinking that industrial experience would be of value in any subsequent academic career. In the event, however, he found that he preferred the practical problems of industry; but not in pharmacy, which, though important, was not very exciting, and not in Glaxo, where he thought he had no real future.

He therefore joined Menley & James Ltd in 1953 as their senior development chemist responsible for pharmacy and chemistry. Fortunately for him, that small British pharmaceutical company was the UK agent for Smith Kline & French and for Eaton Laboratories, a subdivision of the Norwich Pharmacal Co of New York, so that a substantial number of varied products had to be developed. Smith Kline & French soon acquired Menley & James and Jack became head of laboratory services, which ultimately involved about a hundred workers in pharmacy, chemistry and pharmacology. During this period his interest in chemistry grew and in 1960 he obtained his PhD in medicinal chemistry at London University.

Fortuitously, therefore, he had acquired formal qualifications in chemistry, pharmacology and pharmacy and had practised all three to varying extents. He was, however, beginning to tire of a diet containing

Dr. David Jack,
appointed research
director of Allen &
Hanburys in 1961.

so much pharmaceutical development and wanted new opportunities. The first possibility that came his way was an invitation to apply for the Headship of the School of Pharmacy in Glasgow, but he was not appointed. Cyril Maplethorpe was, however, a member of the interviewing panel and, as a result, Jack went to Allen & Hanburys instead, having been mailed an unsolicited copy of their advertisement for a new research director. Thus, nearly thirty-nine years old, he arrived in Ware at the end of 1961 with a useful background in pharmaceutical development, but with little experience of drug research.

David Jack appreciated the level of commitment required as research director of Allen & Hanburys and took up the post on a firm undertaking from Sir Harry Jephcott and Maplethorpe that he would be given the resources and, above all, the time to develop a new research programme. As a starter he asked Maplethorpe to increase the R & D

207

staff from 120 to 200 and for at least five years to show what he could do. This was agreed, but very soon a complication arose when Jephcott decided to set up Glaxo Research Ltd in order to coordinate the Group's R & D activities. Jack was asked via Maplethorpe to be a director of the new company, but he declined the offer because he had already found Jephcott's attitude to research to be in conflict with what he proposed to do at Ware. Comments Jack: "Jephcott may well have been the greatest man who worked for Glaxo, but he was suspicious of speculative research and was a champion of development activities, of products licensed from other companies, especially the American ones, or government sponsored projects." This was perhaps not so surprising, since this was the way Jephcott had built up Glaxo. But Jack's view was that major products were no longer available and that Glaxo would have to find and develop its own if it was to continue to grow. But true to their word, Jephcott and Maplethorpe agreed that the research activities at Ware should proceed independently of those at Greenford and appointed Jack to the board of Allen & Hanburys in June 1962. Thus, as much by accident as by design, Glaxo found itself with two independent research organisations, both pursuing different lines of investigation.

The prospects at Ware for Jack initially did not look promising. There was hostility from a few of the senior staff at Ware, but this was more than compensated by the quiet but friendly welcome from nearly all the rest. The problem was that about three-quarters of the research effort was directed to the control of bacterial and parasitic infections which, in view of the great Glaxo expertise and effort at Greenford and elsewhere, was irrelevant to the overall needs of Glaxo and worse than that, thought Jack, had little hope of success. He decided, therefore, to transfer the parasitology to Glaxo Research, discontinue the rest and start again with projects clearly different from the many at Greenford on antibiotics, corticosteroids and vaccines.

He started by "taking a hammer to the crystalline organisation" he had inherited. This was not entirely popular, but the unease of the staff steadily changed to willing cooperation as he assembled his own "task-force" and they set to work. The new leaders came both from within Allen & Hanburys and from outside. Dr. Roy Brittain, who had joined Allen & Hanburys from the School of Pharmacy, London University, in 1955 (coincidentally, on the same day as Larry Lunts, who was later to synthesise many of the firm's most important drugs), became head of pharmacology. He had attracted Jack because of his "irrepressible enthusiasm and optimism, and his receptivity to new ideas". Desmond Poynter – "a naturally sensitive biologist" – agreed to forsake parasitology and set up a new department of pathology; Alec Ritchie joined from Glaxo and Norman Harper from Chelsea College to strengthen the chemistry; Les Martin from Bengers Laboratories became head of biochemistry; Deryck Rhodes from Pfizer took pharmacy; and Ivor Mitchell from Glaxo Ulverston became senior administrator and head of product registration. Denis Cahal, later chief executive of the Committee on Safety of Drugs, was briefly medical director and was succeeded by Wilfrid Simpson in 1964 and by David Harris in 1969. According to

David Jack: "Whatever was achieved in our Ware laboratories and its consequences resulted, above all, from the efforts of these men."

Jack's task was made easier by the appointment of Sir Alan Wilson as Jephcott's successor, in 1963. As a Fellow of the Royal Society, Wilson was more committed to speculative research and he and, in time, his successors (Sir) Austin Bide and (Sir) Paul Girolami, saw that adequate funding was directed towards this activity, even during some difficult financial times. But the task of finding a suitable line of attack for the discovery of new drugs at Ware was by no means easy, even with a more closely defined research programme.

At this point, it is worth examining some of the recent trends in drug research from about 1960 to the present day. This period has seen no slowing of the process of the discovery and marketing of new drugs: indeed it has seen it accelerate. A select list of the major drugs that have been discovered (or entered regular use) over the last three decades would include, *inter alia*: oral contraceptives, semi-synthetic penicillins, tranquillisers, beta-blockers, anti-tumour agents, immunosuppressants, anaesthetics, analgesics, anti-coagulants, anti-ulcerants, broad-spectrum antibiotics, bronchodilators, cardiac stimulants, hypnotics and hypogly-caemics. The history of the pharmaceutical industry has shown that there is no single method by which drug discovery can proceed: indeed, serendipity has always played an important role, even in the major breakthroughs. Nevertheless, the sophistication of many of these modern drugs – especially those for controlling high blood-pressure, ulcer disease and asthma – show that a more "rational", mechanistic approach to drug design has been emerging in recent years.

Increasingly, the approach that modern drug researchers find the most rewarding is one that takes as its starting point a thorough understanding of the underlying biological processes. The key to modern drug design is the recognition that the body is controlled by chemical messengers. In this communication system two types of messengers are particularly important – enzymes and physiological mediators (including nerve trans-mitters and hormones) – both of which have specific actions and only operate at certain sites. Enzymes have active sites which specifically recognise the appropriate substrates which they can process. Similarly, physiological mediators act as chemical messengers and combine with their own receptors; they are remarkably specific, since the mediators are not recognised by other receptors. This "selectivity" is the key to modern drug design: enzyme inhibitors can be designed using the chemistry of the substrate as the starting point; while mediators can be blocked by using antagonists at their receptors.

These developments had a number of important implications for the major drug companies. Above all, firms now needed to invest heavily in the more rational approach, which alone could bring long-term success and a sufficient return on the heavy capital investment. This demanded close collaboration between chemists and biologists, who now needed to be organised in project teams rather than in separate disciplines. The scope of the research activities of companies, such as Allen & Hanburys, would also in many cases need to be enlarged. As David Jack has written: "Manipulation of intracellular mediators is a powerful method for achieving selective drug effects because of the great variety and selectivity of the physiological mechanisms in the cell membrane. To be successful, however, the process has to be understood and backed by first-class medicinal chemistry and painstaking *in vitro* pharmacology and then by studies in whole animals to confirm the reality and possible clinical relevance of any selective activity found."[11] The thalidomide tragedy in about 1960 also vastly expanded the scale of the pharmaceutical industry's research activities, particularly in the area of testing and clinical trials.

It was the modification of the actions of non-peptide physiological mediators that David Jack and his colleagues accepted as their personal challenge in drug research and was to dominate the direction of the programme at Ware. But the strategy emerged slowly. The development of the Ware research programme after 1962 was a learning process for all concerned. Work on the central nervous system was aimed at better medicines for controlling pain and anxiety, depression and schizophrenia, and the major psychoses, and the cardiovascular effort at better control of blood pressure. The projects were simple and based for the most part on making and testing analogues of known drugs with a view to eliminating use-limiting side effects, and on pharmacological screening of numerous other compounds to try to establish new leads. The test systems consisted of well-established pharmacological preparations. The respiratory project, started in 1963, was similar in kind and its first objective was an improved bronchodilator which would selectively mimic the relaxant effect of adrenaline on bronchial muscle. Its outcome was, however, quite different, because in 1966 the discovery of salbutamol ("Ventolin"), which was unique in being hundreds of times more active on respiratory muscle than on the heart, changed everything – the commercial standing of Allen & Hanburys, the future of drug research at Ware, and, not least, Jack's understanding of how to look for drugs.

Bronchial asthma is a common disease, its wheezy symptoms being familiar to most by personal experience, since about one in twenty adults and rather more children are affected. Indeed, because of this familiarity, the serious nature of asthma is often forgotten; asthma can kill if it is badly treated.

Asthma, though, has long been recognised (indeed the word is Greek in origin). An English physician in the second half of the seventeenth century described the "tyranny" of the disease: "The asthma is a laborious respiration with lifting up the shoulders and wheezing . . . , 'tis observed that the asthmatic cannot cough, sneeze nor speak easily, because a sufficient quantity of air cannot be drawn into the lungs to support those actions."[12] Attempts to treat the affliction date back many centuries, too. Five hundred years ago stramonium – a preparation of the dried leaves of the thorn apple – was smoked in India to relieve attacks: it contained atropine, which blocks the muscarinic receptors for acetylcholine. By 1900 many mild bronchodilators of herbal origin were recognised and used. A popular asthma cure in England in the early 1900s, for example, was tea and stramonium sprinkled with a solution of potassium nitrate and then dried and allowed to smoulder, so that the fumes could be inhaled. The inhalation was a mixture of bronchodilators, which helped reverse the contraction of the bronchial smooth muscle and lessened the secretion of mucus in the airways. Such mixtures were inhaled through a variety of devices that could be bought at the chemist's shop. Naturally, in the early twentieth century Allen & Hanburys was amongst the leading suppliers.

We now know that the wheezing and difficulty in breathing is caused by narrowing of the airways, firstly because of the contraction of the muscles which surround the bronchi (bronchospasm), and secondly, because of damage to the lining of the bronchi which results in accumulation of cell debris and mucus in the lumen and progressive blockage of the airways. These changes are caused by an inflammatory process in the lungs which in most, but not all, cases is due to allergy to foreign proteins, most commonly those from house mites and pollens. The purpose of drug treatment today is to prevent or correct both the bronchospasm and the physical occlusion, in the former by bronchodilator treatment and in the latter with anti-inflammatory steroids. Much of this modern treatment is based on work done at Ware between 1963 and 1972.

The bronchodilators in common use when the asthma project was started were adrenaline, a physiological bronchodilator, which was given by injection to relieve severe asthma, and ephedrine, which acts similarly but is active by mouth. Both, however, affect many kinds of cells in the body apart from bronchial smooth muscle and cause powerful and unwanted stimulation of the heart and other undesirable effects, even at therapeutic dosage. Theophylline, given by injection or by mouth, was usually better tolerated and, unlike the others, is still in fairly common use. Its disadvantage is that it, too, causes cardiovascular side effects and can induce dangerous convulsions after even modest over-dosage.

The story of modern bronchodilators began in 1948 when an American pharmacologist Raymond Ahlquist showed that there are two quite different cellular receptors through which adrenaline exerts its many actions. They are alpha-receptors, which control contraction of involuntary muscles; and beta-receptors, which control relaxation of involuntary muscles, including those in the bronchi, *and* stimulation of the heart. In particular, he found isoprenaline to be more active than adrenaline at beta-receptors and virtually inactive at alpha-receptors. Its action on the bronchi is, therefore, more selective than that of adrenaline, but it too is a powerful cardiac stimulant. Nevertheless, it came into common use to treat asthma when formulated in a pressurised inhaler (Riker & Co's "Medihaler") in the late 1950s because it gave almost instantaneous relief which persisted for an hour or so. Unfortunately, many patients with worsening asthma overdosed themselves with these inhalers and as many as 3000 asthmatic teenagers died in the early 1960s because, it is thought, of excessive cardiac stimulation when they were already oxygen-deficient and for want of steroid treatment to prevent mucus plugging their bronchi. There was clearly need for better adrenaline analogues to relax the bronchi without stimulating the heart.

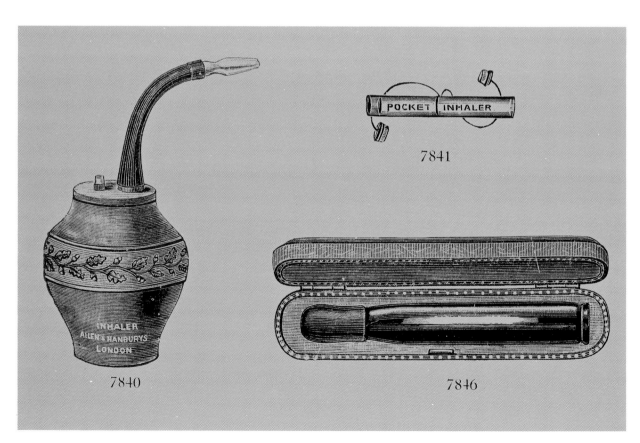

7841

7840

7846

But how was this to be achieved?

In Ware the chemists started by making analogues of isoprenaline which, like adrenaline, contains a catechol grouping. Catechols of this kind are short-acting because this group is unstable in the body. Larry Lunts suggested, therefore, that non-catechol analogues of adrenaline be made since they might be more stable and longer-acting. A model compound was orciprenaline ("Alupent"), newly discovered by Boehringer in Germany, which is relatively stable in the body and is active by mouth as well as by inhalation; it is, however, about equiactive on the bronchi and the heart.

Roy Brittain recalls how the Ware project reached a successful climax. Initially, the chemists had difficulty in providing the compounds that the biologists had requested. Brittain dealt with the disappointment of the latter by calling a meeting, which prompted Larry Lunts' proposals. Some of them did not look particularly exciting, but that was "one of our first important lessons", says Brittain. "You don't have to make big changes in a molecule to change its properties profoundly." Almost the first compound on the list was AH 3021, the saligenin analogue of isoprenaline. In June 1966 it was duly sent for testing and Brittain awaited the results. He remembers how Valerie Cullum, then a junior pharmacologist:

> came into my office on this afternoon and said that there was something funny about this beta-stimulant: it relaxed the bronchial smooth muscle, but it wouldn't stimulate the heart. The result was in front of us! and all I did was to send her back to the laboratory to do the experiment again. She came the next day and said exactly the same thing. I still didn't exactly believe it, so I sent her back again. On the third day she came back yet again and I went and did an experiment for myself. Then we realised there was something uniquely different in that molecule. But when everything suddenly lands almost in your lap, you don't actually believe it.[13]

Soon after, a related compound, salbutamol (AH 3365), was made and tested and found to be even more selectively active on the bronchi and also more potent. Immediately, it was subjected to intensive investigations in animals and man. Its properties were first described in 1968 in *Nature*[14] and it was marketed by Allen & Hanburys as "Ventolin" Inhaler in 1969 and as "Ventolin" Tablets in the following year.

The much greater activity of salbutamol on bronchial smooth muscle than on the heart muscle was not compatible with Ahlquist's simple alpha- and beta-receptor hypothesis, since the adrenaline receptors in both types of cells are of the beta-type. Clearly, further subdivision of beta-receptors was required. In 1966, however, A.M. Lands and his colleagues at the Sterling-Winthrop Research Institute in the US announced that they had found similar, but much less selective action, results in modified catecholamines and proposed that beta-receptors be further divided into $beta_1$- and $beta_2$-sub-types. Their proposal is now well accepted and $beta_1$-receptors are known to mediate cardiac stimulation and $beta_2$-receptors to mediate relaxation of involuntary muscle in the bronchi, uterus, and vasculature of skeletal muscle, and

In the 1900s there were few effective treatments for asthma, though Allen & Hanbury inhalers offered some relief for sufferers.

Dr. Roy Brittain, head of pharmacology in the 1960s.

accelerated recovery of skeletal muscle from contraction. The Ware workers were naturally disappointed that their discovery of sub-types of beta-receptors had been anticipated, but were comforted by the fact that salbutamol was clearly a much better drug than any of the catechols. It was the first of a new kind of drug – a highly selective beta$_2$-stimulant bronchodilator!

Salbutamol is at its best by inhalation because its intrinsic beta$_2$-selectivity is enhanced by local application within the airways. By this route, as little as 100 or 200 microgrammes rapidly induces intense bronchodilation without significant side effects and its action persists for about four hours. The use of the drug by mouth is complicated by tremor of skeletal muscles and increased heart rate in sensitive individuals because of activation of beta$_2$-receptors in skeletal muscle and its blood vessels. Its bronchodilating action occurs gradually after the usual 4 mg. dose, is maximal after one hour, and persists for three to four hours. Although the side effects with oral doses are troublesome to a few patients, it is at least as effective and much safer to use than theophylline. Fortunately, chronic asthmatics do not become tolerant to the beneficial effect of salbutamol and the drug is increasingly used for maintenance treatment. The use of salbutamol has increased steadily during the last twenty years and new dose forms of the drug have been developed to supplement the original "Inhaler". The "Rotahaler" is a powder inhalation device which releases the drug in response to the act of breathing, as does the more recent "Diskhaler", which is loaded with a disc of the drug sufficient for two days' treatment. "Ventolin CR" tablets are a much improved sustained release form of the drug (based on the technology of the ALZA Corporation), which extend its duration of action to twelve hours. The salbutamol is released in aqueous solution through a minute hole pierced by laser in a special plastic coating through which water slowly penetrates, so dissolving the drug and discharging through the hole.

With the bronchodilator programme under way, the Ware group turned its attention to two other approaches to asthma. The first, based on disodium cromoglycate, which had recently been discovered by Fisons, proved abortive; the second, an attempt to achieve a selective anti-inflammatory steroid effect in the airways, led to another very significant advance in the treatment of the disease.

Cromoglycate ("Intal") is undoubtedly a useful anti-asthmatic drug, especially in children, but its mechanism of action remains a mystery. It is easy to show in acute tests that inhaled cromoglycate, and drugs like it, can inhibit constriction of the bronchi caused by exercise or by inhalation of specific allergens in asthma volunteers. Their beneficial effects are, however, much more difficult to detect in well-controlled clinical trials and for this reason Jack and his team abandoned work on cromoglycate-like drugs after testing several in man, including AH 7725, the first orally active drug of this kind. ICI, Wellcome and other companies also gave up soon afterwards and so after twenty years Fisons, with the original cromoglycate and the recent nedocromil ("Tilade"), have a near monopoly of this kind of drug, which must be a unique situation.

The steroid hormones of the adrenal cortex have many functions and are essential to life. For example, they are involved in the metabolism of carbohydrates, proteins and fats, in the body's ability to deal with stress (glucocorticoid actions) and in the control of salt and water balance (mineralocorticoid actions). Cortisol, the principal physiological hormone, exerts all three effects, but synthetic analogues such as prednisone or betamethasone have selective glucocorticoid effects and are therefore less likely to cause accumulation of salt and water. These drugs, which first became available in the 1950s, are, of course, used to treat patients with impaired adrenal function of different causes. They are, however, more often used to treat bronchial asthma and other immune disorders, because of their ability to suppress inflammatory responses. They are uniquely effective for this purpose, but unfortunately the effective treatment requires greater than short-term physiological exposure to the drugs and long-term treatment is associated with dangerous side-effects, not least of which is inhibition of the body's own capacity to make cortisol. Glucocorticoid steroids are, therefore, used only for severe asthma in the minimum effective dosage and, for this purpose, they are indispensable. Indeed, it is probable that inadequate use of steroids was a major contributory factor in the epidemic of unexplained deaths of young asthmatics that occurred around 1960.

Having achieved selective beta$_2$-stimulant activity in the lungs by modifying adrenaline, the Ware researchers considered the possibility of a selective anti-inflammatory steroid action in the lungs. A possible answer was prepared by Wilfrid Simpson, namely the use by inhalation of a potent topical anti-inflammatory steroid of a kind that had been developed for treating skin diseases, such as eczema or psoriasis, and which was remarkably effective for that purpose. (Eric Snell, medical director of Glaxo Laboratories, made a similar proposal independently in that company.) The idea was interesting, but three questions immediately arose. Would the airways respond like the skin to local application of such a drug? And if so, would the collagen-forming cells be inhibited in the lungs as they were in the skin? (Potent topical steroids cause skin thinning in man.) Finally, would the symptoms of lung infections be suppressed and the infections, therefore, spread? Beclomethasone dipropionate (BDP), a topical steroid licensed from Glaxo for use in "Propaderm" skin preparations, was known to have high topical anti-inflammatory activity in man and low glucocorticoid activity in the rat. It was formulated in a pressurised inhaler similar to "Ventolin" and the Ware workers were encouraged when the preparation was found to be well tolerated by inhalation in animals. For example, although typical glucocorticoid side effects occurred at high dosage in the dog, which proved to be more sensitive than man to BDP, the collagen fibres in their lungs were normal and the animals were not obviously prone to infections. Inhaled BDP was also well tolerated by man and had a clearly significant anti-inflammatory action in the lungs of asthmatic patients, not as intense as that achieved by glucocorticoid steroids by mouth or injection, but nevertheless clinically valuable. Inhaled BDP was marketed as "Becotide" Inhaler in 1972. Together with inhaled salbutamol and systemic glucocorticoids such as prednisone, it quickly established itself in the modern treatment of asthma. Topically applied BDP is also effective for hay fever and "Beconase", a spray especially designed for intranasal use, was marketed in 1974.

The Ware group was also involved in one of the continuing achievements of medical science that has occurred since the 1950s – the control of high blood-pressure. Its importance is obvious in view of the prevalence of heart and kidney disease, and strokes, in western society. The early effective drugs, because of their side effects, were a mixed blessing for many patients. Today a range of much more selectively acting drugs is available and amongst them are the beta-blockers originally developed by (Sir) James Black and his colleagues in ICI Pharmaceuticals. They are called beta-blockers because they antagonise the actions of adrenaline and sympathetic nerve stimulation at Ahlquist's beta-receptors which, amongst other things, control the rate and force of cardiac contraction. Black's starting hypothesis was that a specific beta-blocker would diminish the physiological effects of the sympathetic system on the heart, making it beat more slowly and less forcibly and become a more efficient pump. In particular, it would consume less oxygen and this would benefit patients with angina pectoris, whose pain is caused by a deficient blood and, therefore, oxygen supply to the heart due to narrowing of the coronary blood vessels. This brilliant insight proved to be correct and propranolol, launched by ICI in 1964 as "Inderal", became the first of the beta-blockers, which greatly improved the life of anginal patients. In 1969 the drug was found by Dr Brian Pritchard, a physician at University College Hospital, to reduce the blood-pressure in hypertensive patients and this became the commonest therapeutic indication for beta-blockers, because they were better tolerated than previously available drugs.

Following propranolol, the Ware researchers set out to find a better beta-blocker. As a minimum, a much longer-acting drug was required or, preferably, one which acted selectively on the heart and not on bronchial beta-receptors, since propranolol and similar drugs are contra-indicated in asthmatic patients, because they induce bronchospasm by blocking these receptors. The Ware team's long-acting drug proved to be toxic in animals and their cardio-selective drugs were not good enough, but their efforts were nevertheless rewarded by the serendipitous discovery of labetolol which, *mirabile dictu*, was derived from one of the structures prepared by Larry Lunts in the asthma project. Labetolol was clearly different, because it was found to reduce the blood-pressure in man from the very first dose, whereas the effect of propranolol developed slowly over a period of seven to ten days. The reason for the difference is that propranolol blocks only beta-receptors and its effect on blood pressure results from adaptation of the circulation to the chronic reduction in cardiac output caused by the drug. By contrast labetolol blocks not only beta-receptors, but also the alpha-receptors in the arteries of the skin and abdominal viscera, which in consequence become dilated. The end result is that the resting cardiac output is normal in patients treated with labetolol and their peripheral blood vessels are dilated, a situation which is more nearly normal than in patients on propranolol, whose cardiac output is low and peripheral blood vessels relatively contracted.

David Richards played a key role in the clinical development of labetolol, which was marketed as "Trandate" in 1977. As a specific anti-hypertensive drug, with a special place for treating emergencies, it has been modestly successful, but its performance remains a disappointment to its originators. The reason for its limited usage may be that, for optimum results, it is desirable to titrate the dose for individual patients, whereas simple standard dosages are the rule with ordinary beta-blockers.

The Ware team was more successful, spectacularly so in commercial terms, with their work on inhibition of gastric acid secretion as a means of healing and preventing duodenal and stomach ulcers. This began in 1969 as more research staff were authorised. Success in this sphere would obviously bring great dividends (though perhaps no one at that time realised how great they would be): ulcers are a relatively common complaint, only poorly controlled by existing treatments at that time. Until the 1970s there was little relief from the troubling symptoms of ulcers, apart from the administration of antacids, which did nothing to tackle the underlying causes of the disease, and surgery, which was painful, dangerous and not always successful.

217

Aerial view of Ware, 1966.

The Ware researchers were well aware of the efforts of Black and his colleagues at Smith Kline & French at Welwyn Garden City, and of others in Pfizer and Lilly in America, to inhibit the stimulant action of histamine on gastric acid secretion in the hope that it played a controlling physiological role in acid secretion. The acid is secreted by specialised cells, called parietal cells, in the lining of the stomach and the secretion was known *not* to be inhibited by anti-allergic antihistamine drugs pioneered by Daniel Bovet, a Swiss physiologist, in 1940. The histamine receptors had been shown to be different from those blocked by Bovet's antihistamines. Nevertheless, although histamine was a powerful stimulant of acid secretion in animals and man, there was enough doubt about the reality of its physiological role for Jack and his colleagues to wait until the position had been clarified and to try other approaches to the problem, including inhibition of the acid-stimulating effect of gastrin, a peptide hormone known to have a physiological role. The latter was obviously a much more difficult problem, which incidentally has not yet been solved, but was chosen because a gastrin antagonist would almost certainly inhibit acid secretion stimulated by taking food, whereas a histamine antagonist would do so only if histamine had a controlling effect on the physiology. By developing the experimental methodology the Ware team was well placed to switch to the easier project when and if histamine was shown to have such a role. The position became absolutely clear in 1972 when Black and his team showed that burimamide, a specific inhibitor of acid secretion induced by injecting histamine, also inhibited secretion stimulated by ingesting food. This was a historic discovery, since it proved simultaneously the physiological role of histamine and provided a new, highly selective means of inhibiting acid secretion and healing peptic ulcers. For this and his work on beta-blockers, Black shared the Nobel Prize for Medicine in 1988, a well-earned recognition of his unique ability to interpret the clinical relevance of basic scientific data and to find the new drugs implied in his hypotheses. Following this research, the histamine receptors specifically blocked by the anti-allergic antihistamines were called H_1-receptors and those blocked by burimamide, H_2-receptors.

Researchers at Ware set out to find a specific histamine H_2-antagonist immediately Black's results were known, but the job proved more difficult than expected since the structural requirements for this new kind of antagonist were not easy to satisfy. Burimamide itself was not of practical value because of low potency and inactivity by mouth. However, Smith Kline & French ultimately solved these problems and cimetidine ("Tagamet") was marketed in 1976, twelve years after the Welwyn project had started. The drug has been described as "the current state of the art of the medicinal chemist at his best, especially as it was necessary for a lead compound to be generated by rational approaches".[15] Cimetidine transformed the treatment of peptic ulcers and greatly reduced the need for surgery and its attendant risk of deaths. It also transformed the fortunes of Smith Kline & French, since by 1981 "Tagamet" was the best selling prescription drug of all time, with sales in that year of $620 million.

The only significant disadvantage of cimetidine was that its action on acid secretion was not totally selective, because at therapeutic doses, it inhibited enzymes in the liver which are normally involved in certain oxidative processes, including oxidative deactivation of drugs such as the bronchodilator theophylline. As a result, standard doses of these drugs have a more intense prolonged action and serious side-effects can occur. Cimetidine, in higher dosage, also antagonises the actions of male sex hormones in man, but this is of importance to relatively few patients. At Ware in 1976, a chemistry team led by Barry Price and exploring a structural modification suggested by John Clitheroe came up with ranitidine, a new histamine H_2-antagonist. David Richards, by now medical director at Ware, again led the development team, which showed that ranitidine had the required increased selectivity of action. This proved sufficient for it ultimately to become the dominant drug of this kind after its marketing by Glaxo as "Zantac" tablets in 1981.

By then, in 1979, the research activities centred at Ware and Greenford had been unified under one company, Glaxo Group Research Ltd, with Dr. David Jack as its chairman and chief executive. Jack also took a seat on the main Glaxo board. His policy of enlarging Allen & Hanburys' research activities, so that it was an important entity in its own right, had brought rich dividends. The Ware site, where new facilities had been constructed east of Harris's Lane to house the 500 members of Glaxo Group Research, was now generating products under the direction of Roy Brittain for the whole Group. Meanwhile, Allen & Hanburys had acquired its own drugs with which to carve its niche in the increasingly competitive pharmaceutical market of the 1980s.

8

ALLEN & HANBURYS LTD
IN THE 1980s

[Glaxo is] now, by deliberate policy, wholly devoted to the discovery, development, manufacture and sale of prescription medicines . . .

Glaxo Holdings p.l.c., *Annual Report and Accounts 1988*

In William Allen's day the pharmaceutical industry was still in its infancy: though its products were important to sufferers, it hardly featured as a national industry alongside textiles, coal, and iron and steel. The picture has changed dramatically since then. Whilst the "old" industries upon which Britain launched its Industrial Revolution have declined in recent years, the "new" high-technology industries such as pharmaceuticals have expanded. So much so, that in the decade 1977-87 pharmaceuticals was the country's fastest growing manufacturing sector, surpassing even electrical engineering. In constant price terms the industry's production has grown by some 40 percent since the start of the 1980s, more than twice the expansion achieved by the economy as a whole. Aside from the therapeutic gains, the industry provides jobs for about 87,000 and indirect employment for almost three times that number. Britain was the world's third largest medicine exporter throughout the 1980s, with exports of about £1700 million in 1988. This resulted in a net positive UK trade balance in pharmaceuticals of about £850 million per annum, making this sector the most significant contributor to the UK balance of trade after oil and "other transport".

In the technical sphere the UK has a high reputation for developing and marketing innovative products, reflecting the growing impact of R & D. In 1988 R & D spending in the UK pharmaceutical industry was about £700 million. Around ten percent of all British manufacturing industry R & D spending is contributed by the pharmaceutical sector, which benefits from only two percent of manufacturing industry's gross earnings. Other countries, it is true, have been spending even more heavily than this on pharmaceutical research: nevertheless, British R & D appears to be offering excellent value for money. In 1986 eight of the year's "top" 50 medicines (by value) world-wide were discovered and developed in Britain, as were 11 of the "top" 20 medicines available in the UK in 1987.[1] Clearly, the industry has come a long way since the First World War, when it was heavily dependent on German imports.

Some idea of these momentous changes may be gained by a visit to Ware. A visitor retracing the path of Ralph Dodd, who, we may recall, came to Ware in the 1890s searching for a new site for Allen & Hanburys, might be forgiven for thinking that little had changed in a hundred years. Turning into Priory Street the view along the River Lea, with a pharmaceutical factory straddling the mill stream, can have changed little in that time. Quiet and picturesque, it is easy to see why Ware became a favoured location for milk and malted food production. Closer inspection even reveals the Allen & Hanbury name on the front of the Priory Street factory on the Buryfield site. Here, however, all similarity with the past ends, for at close quarters the scene is one of intense activity. At various locations on the site building work is in progress; old parts of the factory are being demolished and new extensions planned. Turning the corner into Harris's Lane, the changes from the nineteenth century are even more dramatic. Where once open fields stretched away into the distance, the landscape is dominated by the large buildings housing the research laboratories that are now part of Glaxo Group Research Ltd and from which new products have emerged that have contributed much to Glaxo's growth.

In the 1980s that growth, in which Allen & Hanburys has shared, has been spectacular. During the 1970s Glaxo's results were relatively flat while it was developing new products and preparing to penetrate the American market; but the 1980s have seen the fastest growth in the company's history (see p. 225), the result of successfully executed research and marketing initiatives, especially in the US, and a more open, delegated and international organisation. The architect of these strategies is Sir Paul Girolami, who joined Glaxo in 1966, and was appointed chief executive in succession to Sir Austin Bide at the end of 1980. Under Girolami, the successful blending of basic research and shrewd marketing has made Glaxo the world's second largest pharmaceutical company in terms of sales, which totalled £2059 million in the financial year ending in June 1988. As shown below, only the American firm Merck surpasses that figure.

Leading Pharmaceutical Corporations 1988

 1. Merck & Co
 2. GLAXO
 3. Ciba-Geigy
 4. Hoechst
 5. American Home/A.H. Robins
 6. SmithKline
 7. Pfizer
 8. Sandoz
 9. Bayer
10. Lilly

Of Glaxo's sales, 87 percent are generated outside the company's UK base, with the US being the firm's largest single national market with sales of almost $1300 million. An important, though not the only, factor in this growth has been the sales of "Zantac", the anti-ulcerant treatment discovered by the research team headed by Dr. Roy Brittain. Girolami

Allen & Hanburys at Ware. The company's name still appears on the front of the restored nineteenth-century building in Priory Street, on the Buryfield site.

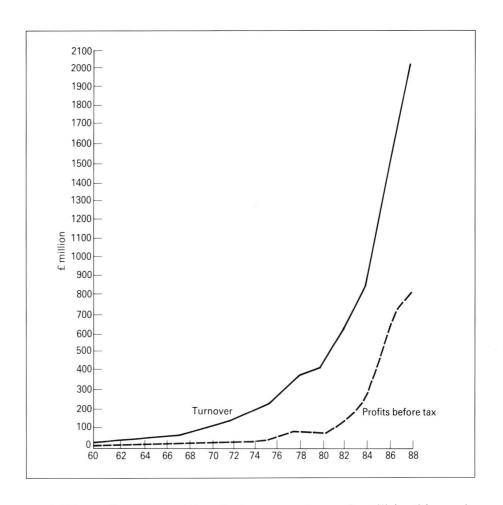

used "Zantac" to power Glaxo's phenomenal growth, utilising his newly created world-wide marketing organisation as a launching pad. Remarkably, "Zantac" was the first Glaxo compound to be developed concurrently in countries throughout the world and this happened because Jack had been appointed to the main Glaxo board and was able to unify product development programmes. In 1988 "Zantac" became the first pharmaceutical product in history to pass the £1 billion per annum sales mark.

What has been Allen & Hanburys' contribution to this record? Now that Glaxo and its old rival have become properly merged, this becomes increasingly difficult to assess. Undoubtedly, the work of Allen & Hanburys' research division in the 1960s and beyond had a major impact on the development of Glaxo, the repercussions of which are still being felt today (though Allen & Hanburys was only able to be successful because of the encouragement, backing and support of Glaxo). In the last six months of 1988 anti-ulcerants and respiratory drugs accounted for almost 75 percent of Glaxo's turnover of £1120 million. The Ware site itself proved a great asset to the Glaxo Group, allowing it space to expand outside London, and providing some first-class production facilities.

Turning to the performance of Allen & Hanburys' specialities, here the contribution is more easily calculated. In the 1980s Allen &

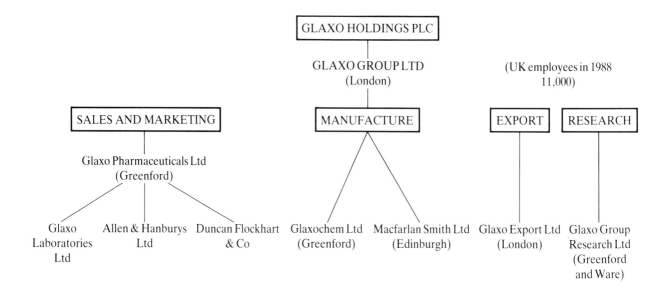

```
                        ┌──────────────────────┐
                        │  GLAXO HOLDINGS PLC   │
                        └──────────────────────┘
                                   │
                            GLAXO GROUP LTD              (UK employees in 1988
                              (London)                         11,000)

┌──────────────────────┐    ┌────────────────┐    ┌──────────┐ ┌──────────┐
│  SALES AND MARKETING  │    │  MANUFACTURE   │    │  EXPORT  │ │ RESEARCH │
└──────────────────────┘    └────────────────┘    └──────────┘ └──────────┘

   Glaxo Pharmaceuticals Ltd
        (Greenford)

  Glaxo    Allen & Hanburys  Duncan Flockhart   Glaxochem Ltd  Macfarlan Smith Ltd   Glaxo Export Ltd   Glaxo Group
Laboratories      Ltd            & Co           (Greenford)      (Edinburgh)            (London)        Research Ltd
   Ltd                                                                                                 (Greenford
                                                                                                        and Ware)
```

Hanburys, along with Glaxo Laboratories Ltd and Duncan Flockhart & Co, has formed a triumvirate in the sales and marketing division of Glaxo Pharmaceuticals Ltd (see above). Allen & Hanburys now concentrates entirely on respiratory and allergy medicines and herein perhaps lies the greatest change in the firm's historical evolution. In the 1980s Glaxo shed any pretence to being a "Universal Provider". It is a reminder of how swiftly the pharmaceutical industry has changed within recent times to realise that in 1980 Glaxo still produced milk and invalid foods, children's rusks, vitamin tablets, laxatives, veterinary products and hospital furniture. All that has now gone. By 1986 Glaxo had disposed of its wholesaling, generics and food and surgical products side of its activities as part of its policy of concentrating entirely on pharmaceuticals. The result of this policy has seen the divestment of what many of the old partners would have regarded as the Allen & Hanburys' heritage – its surgical engineering activities, for example. Even some of Allen & Hanburys' famous pharmaceutical specialities, such as insulin, are no longer produced. Gone, too, is Cornelius Hanbury's cherished West End "shop-window" at Vere Street: it was closed in 1973. In 1982, Horsenden House, a new administrative block for Glaxo Operations was opened at Greenford. Joining Glaxo and Duncan Flockhart employees, Allen & Hanburys made its headquarters there and Bethnal Green was closed. Apart from Ware, there is nothing left of the house that Cornelius and his partners built.

Company policy in the late 1980s has been to increase the firm's UK dominance of the respiratory and allergy drug markets. A primary aim was to bring sales and marketing closer together, so that Allen & Hanburys became a less sales driven company. Another strategic objective was to give more attention to the selling of the inhaled anti-inflammatory steroids. The result of these policies has been impressive. Bronchodilators have now become the foundation stone of modern asthma therapy: within the very broad range of intermediate degrees of airway obstruction from mild to moderately severe, bronchodilators are extremely effective at relieving symptoms. Salbutamol ("Ventolin") is now the most widely prescribed anti-asthma product; indeed, in 1988 it ranked twelfth in the world as a prescription drug with a 19 percent increase in sales. Meanwhile, the steroid aerosols – "Becotide" and "Becloforte" – that Allen & Hanburys pioneered have transformed the management of asthma in recent years and are the major preventative treatment in current use in the UK. Sales of these products have grown by 41 percent in 1987-8. In hay-fever treatments, "Beconase" is the world's leading nasal decongestant, with a 27 percent increase in sales in 1987-8. Total sales of these respiratory medicines in that period were £457 million, from total Glaxo sales of a little over £2000 million.

Despite these impressive figures, Allen & Hanburys, in common with other chemical and pharmaceutical companies, operates in a difficult environment. As one study of the pharmaceutical industry has remarked: "The story of the drug makers is a story of an industry with higher-than-average achievements yet dogged by more-than-average criticisms."[2] The criticisms most often voiced are: that the industry makes excessive profits (a reproof that would have sounded very familiar to the Bevans and William Allen[3]); that it makes too much money from the National Health Service (pharmaceuticals now account for about ten percent of the NHS's annual bill of about £2 billion); that the pharmaceutical industry has a multi-million pound vested interest in illness and ignores preventive measures; and that the cash and lobbying power of the giant companies is too great.[4] Environmental pollution, the use of animals in experiments, and marketing techniques in developed countries have also become areas of controversy.

The modern pharmaceutical industry is also a high-risk business. The market is an extremely competitive one: the top ten companies account for only 26 percent of the world market. Even the world leader, Merck, has only a 4 percent share of the international market. To achieve even that share demands extremely costly R & D. Glaxo earmarked £300 million a year for R & D by 1989; it has plans to open a new facility for Glaxo Group Research at Stevenage in the south of England; a new research development building is nearing completion at Glaxo S.p.A.'s site in Verona, Italy; and a substantial complex is under construction at the Glaxo Inc headquarters within Research Triangle Park in North Carolina.

Drug design also remains, to a certain extent, a speculative activity. The body's control system is more complex than the brief account of receptor theory presented in this book suggests: for any function there are usually several messengers and several receptors, besides amplification and modulating systems, feedback inhibitory mechanisms and various ion fluxes. Since enzymes and receptors are so ubiquitous, blocking them at one site may have undesirable effects at another location. The safety of medicines therefore remains hard to predict and mistakes still happen. The period after 1960 may have seen the major advances in drug therapy marked by the discovery of beta-blockers,

Overleaf:

(above left) A research biologist at Glaxo Group Research, Ware, measuring the effects of drugs on the diameter of small arteries and veins. Blood vessels are viewed under a microscope, linked via a camera to a microscaler and TV screen.

(below left) A research chemist at Glaxo Group Research at Ware purifying a drug by column chromatography.

(below right) Structural elucidation using 2-D spectroscopy at Glaxo Group Research, Ware.

(above right) Researchers at Glaxo Group Research, Ware, designing new chemical entities.

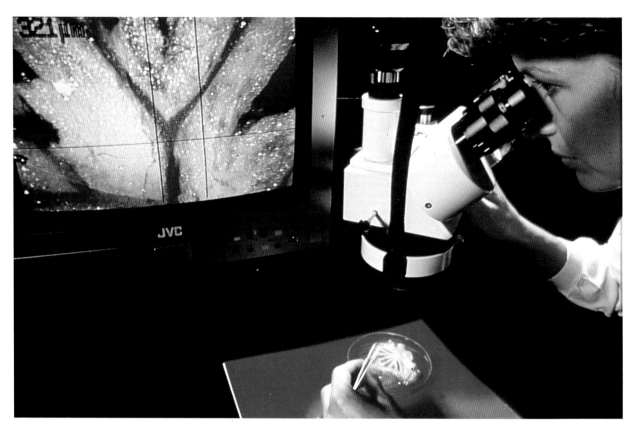

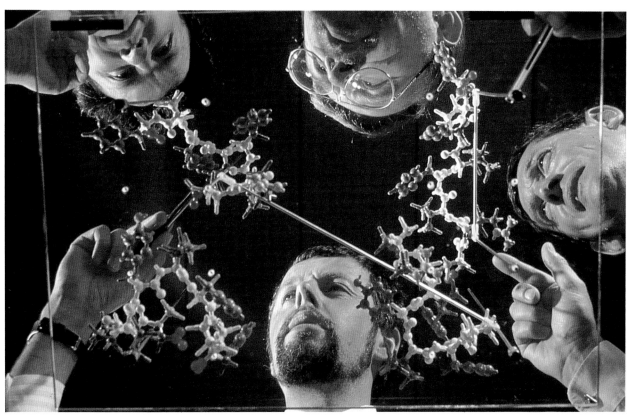

anti-ulcerants and bronchodilators, but it also witnessed the tragedies of thalidomide and the anti-arthritic drug "Opren".

Finally, for any leading pharmaceutical company, particularly one which derives its success from a single money-spinner, there is no room for complacency. The history of Allen & Hanburys shows that no matter how profitable and prestigious a firm becomes, it can never afford to stand still. One never knows when an unforeseen event may occur. At Ware, therefore, the search for new medicines goes on. Aside from the economic logic, this is hardly surprising. The pharmaceutical industry has made excellent progress in tackling disease and, although it can easily be overstated – since medical and social historians have reminded us of the importance of better nutrition and other aetiological factors – this has increased life expectancy (according to some estimates by some 5-10 years for each individual) and improved the quality of life. The control of bacteria and high blood-pressure, the new treatments for bronchial asthma and peptic ulcer disease, and progress in surgery made possible by new drugs have been the most notable advances. Nevertheless, drug discovery has yet to make a real impact on autoimmune diseases, cancer and virus infections; and some of the major killers in western society, such as coronary artery disease, remain intractable (even though their causes are broadly known).

To the research team at Ware, the success of drugs such as salbutamol and ranitidine was by no means the end of the road. The market for these products is highly competitive: effective patent lives are short in comparison with research and development and competitors soon introduce their own versions of successful medicines. Moreover, the receptor theory which had been used to devise drugs such as salbutamol had by no means exhausted its potential and David Jack and his colleagues soon began to look for improvements and further advances. Two projects at Ware had assumed particular importance by the 1980s: the search for an even better bronchodilator than salbutamol, and the investigation of new kinds of drug activity in analogues of 5-hydroxytryptamine (5-HT, or serotonin). These projects were aimed at different diseases, but both stemmed from Jack's interest in explaining the widely differing selectivity of adrenaline and salbutamol.

Adrenaline activates all known alpha- and beta-receptors with almost equal intensities; its fairly close analogue salbutamol is inactive at alpha-receptors and about a thousand times more active at $beta_2$- than at $beta_1$-receptors. How was this great difference to be explained? David Jack reached four broad conclusions, which have guided his subsequent efforts.

Firstly, the receptor proteins for adrenaline in the cell membranes are chemically different in each kind of cell, the difference between alpha- and beta-receptors being more profound than those between $beta_1$- and $beta_2$-receptors. Variations in the chemistry of receptor proteins is the essential prerequisite for selective alpha- and beta- and selective $beta_1$- and $beta_2$-adrenergic activity in analogues of adrenaline. Secondly, the activity of adrenaline or an analagous compound on a particular cell depends on the qualitative nature of the complex it forms with the receptor protein, because this determines how well it can initiate the cascade of events that constitute the cellular response, and on how long, on average, the complexes persist. The pharmacological term for the former influence is efficacy; the average life of the receptor complex is determined by the chemical affinity of the drug for the protein which is a measure of how firmly it sticks to the small part of the protein with which it interacts. High efficacy and high stickiness enhance activity, the stimulus applied to the cell being proportional to the product of the two. Thirdly, salbutamol is inactive at alpha-receptors because it has little affinity for them and is more active at $beta_2$-receptors than at $beta_1$-receptors, mainly because the efficacy of its $beta_2$-receptor protein complex is much greater than that of the corresponding $beta_1$-complex; it is, in fact, only a little more sticky at the $beta_2$-protein. ·Finally, variation in the cellular receptor proteins for other physiological mediators that are similar to adrenaline is to be expected and chemical analogues of them would be expected to be selectively acting.

The only serious defect of salbutamol given by inhalation is its four-hour duration of action, because this is not long enough to control the attacks of asthma that are common during the night and early morning, or for convenient twice-daily maintenance treatment of chronic disease. After the Ware group had tried unsuccessfully to improve on salbutamol by a variety of different pharmacological mechanisms, Jack's thoughts turned again to adrenaline analogues in 1981. He concluded that if his explanation of variations of beta-stimulant activity was right, the required drug might be found in a new adrenaline analogue with high $beta_2$-selectivity and sufficient chemical affinity for the $beta_2$-receptor protein to form a stable complex which persisted for at least eight hours. The new drug would have to stick very firmly at its receptors and would therefore be a larger molecule than salbutamol. The outcome was salmeterol hydroxynaphthoate (GR 33343G), which was also made by Larry Lunts. Given by inhalation in doses as low as 50 or 100 micro-grammes, it is effective for at least 12 hours. Twice-daily dosage is therefore all that is required, together with inhaled beclomethasone dipropionate if necessary, to control asthma in the great majority of patients. The drug is performing well in short- and long-term clinical trials and, if there are no unexpected snags, it may be expected to replace salbutamol as the world's most commonly used asthma treatment.

In 1972 Brittain and Jack supported the suggestion of Patrick Humphrey, a newly recruited PhD pharmacologist, that they investigate the role of 5-hydroxytryptamine (5-HT) in migraine. 5-HT is also a phys-iological mediator, which is, *inter alia*, a nerve transmitter in the brain and the gut, and causes contraction of smooth muscle in the bronchi and most blood vessels, though a few of the latter are relaxed by it. The migraine project was very much in the Ware tradition: it was aimed at a common condition which was inadequately treated by available medicines. After years of work, Humphrey, with the help of Alec Oxford's chemistry group, produced an effective treatment for migraine called GR 43175 (sumatriptan), which appears to be effective by

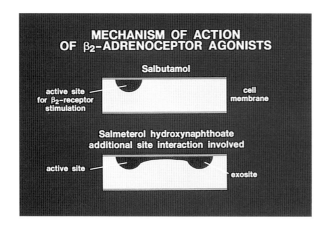

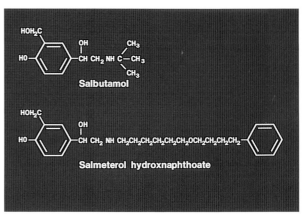

selectively mimicking the constricting action of 5-HT on blood vessels in the cranial circulation. If the clinical studies progress smoothly, Glaxo hopes that it will be a major advance when it comes on to the market.

The 5-HT programme has also produced a second new drug, GR 38032 (ondansetron), which is effective because it antagonises the effects of 5-HT by selectively blocking its receptors in the gut and close to the vomiting centre in the brain and thereby prevents the awful vomiting caused by the toxic drugs used to treat cancer. Ondansetron is therefore expected to improve the quality of life for cancer sufferers.

In conclusion, the research begun at Ware in 1962 has already played an important role in the growth of Glaxo and this influence seems likely to continue. For many of those individuals who joined Allen & Hanburys both before and after 1958, the results have been gratifying. Cyril Maplethorpe, too, lived to see the realisation of his dream of a major research establishment at Ware. Fittingly, his portrait hangs in the entrance hall of one of the new buildings, a circumstance that pleased him very much.

In 1990 Allen & Hanburys celebrates its 275th anniversary. There may have been larger pharmaceutical companies, and there may have been firms, that, at least for some periods, were more profitable and successful – but there are few companies, even outside the pharmaceutical industry, that have been in existence as long as Allen & Hanburys. The company has spanned the development of the British pharmaceutical industry. In retrospect, the history of the firm can be seen to fall into four main phases. In the first, from 1715 to the 1850s, the business at Plough Court was dominated by the Quaker philosophy of its partners, who made the most of their Society's reputation for quality and honest dealing. It was a period of moderate business success for the firm, due partly to the Quaker belief that making money was never an end in itself, and moderate scientific advance, reflecting the relatively limited knowledge of the British industry at a time when medicines were based on plant products. But the firm's reputation grew, alongside that of its famous partners, such as William Allen. In the second phase, between 1850 and the 1920s, Allen & Hanburys expanded rapidly in line with the burgeoning of the economy and adopted the stance of a "Universal Provider". It was an era characterised by high sales, moderate profits,

*In 1990 Allen &
Hanburys will move to
Stockley Park.*

and the first sign of the development of science-based products: though,
like other British chemical firms, Allen & Hanburys lagged well behind
their European and American competitors. In the third phase, between
the 1920s and 1950s, Allen & Hanburys settled into an undynamic period
as a conservative family-run firm, long on prestige and "service" to the
customer, but short on growth and scientific application. In the final
phase from about 1960 to the present day, the trend for rationalisation
and merger within the British pharmaceutical industry rejuvenated Allen
& Hanburys. As part of Glaxo, the firm enjoyed the most spectacular
growth in its history, with an exemplary record of research. Marketing
and international strategy were at last given adequate attention, with
obvious effects, and the firm also rid itself of much of the detritus of the
past, such as its non-pharmaceutical interests. The result is that Allen &
Hanburys is now a market leader in the U.K. in its chosen field of

233

Glaxo Group Research at Ware. This new multi-million pound Pharmacy Building, opened in 1989, was built to house Pharmaceutical Science and Pharmaceutical Analysis.

respiratory medicines. As part of Glaxo, it illustrates the success of the British pharmaceutical industry within the last twenty years, which is now challenging the hegemony of the German and American market leaders.

NOTES

Abbreviations

Chapman-Huston and Cripps	D. Chapman-Huston and E.C. Cripps, *Through a City Archway: The Story of Allen and Hanburys 1715-1954* (London, 1954).
Cripps	E.C. Cripps, *Plough Court: The Story of a Notable Pharmacy* (London, 1927).
DBB	D.J. Jeremy and C. Shaw (eds.), *Dictionary of Business Biography* (5 vols, London, 1984-6).
DNB	Leslie Stephen and Sydney Lee (eds.), *Dictionary of National Biography* (63 vols, Oxford, 1885-1933, plus supplements, to date).
RPSGB	Royal Pharmaceutical Society of Great Britain

Introduction: Of Pills, Potions and Medical Men: Allen & Hanburys and the Beginnings of the Pharmaceutical Industry

1   See generally L. McCray Beier, *Sufferers and Healers: The Experience of Illness in Seventeenth-Century England* (London, 1987); and R. and D. Porter, *In Sickness and in Health: The British Experience 1650-1850* (London, 1988).

2   L. G. Matthews, *History of Pharmacy in Britain* (Edinburgh & London, 1962), p. 113. See also *Kremer and Urdang's History of Pharmacy*, revised by G. Sonnedecker (Philadelphia, 3rd edn., 1963); G. E. Trease, *Pharmacy in History* (London, 1964).

3   I. Loudon, *Medical Care and the General Practitioner 1750-1850* (Oxford, 1986), quoted p. 67.

4   See Laurence Dopson, "State of London Chemists' Shops in the 18th and Early 19th Centuries", *Chemist and Druggist* 163 (1955), pp. 718-21. Interestingly, the Royal College of Physicians' censors visited Allen & Hanburys (then William Allen & Co) in the 1820s and noted that it was "an excellent House".

5   "Counter Practice", *Pharmaceutical Journal* 4 (December 1844), p. 248.

6   J. Bell, *A Concise Historical Sketch of the Progress of Pharmacy in Great Britain* (London, 1843), p. 89. This work is reproduced in Volume 1 of the *Pharmaceutical Journal* (1841).

7   Loudon (n. 3), quoted p. 64.

8   Bell (n. 6), p. 8.

9   E.A. Wrigley and R.S. Schofield, *The Population History of England, 1541-1871: A Reconstruction* (London, 1981).

10   *Pharmaceutical Journal* 4 (December 1844), pp. 247-8.

11   R. Porter, *Health for Sale: Quackery in England 1660-1850* (Manchester, 1989); C.J.S. Thompson, *The Quacks of Old London* (London, 1928); A.C. Wootton, *Chronicles of Pharmacy* (2 vols., London, 1910). See also: J.K. Crellin, "Dr. James's Fever Powder", *Transactions of the British Society for the History of Pharmacy* 1 (1974), pp. 136-43; W.H. Hefland, "James Morison and His Pills: A Study in the Nineteenth Century Pharmaceutical Market", *Transactions of the British Society for the History of Pharmacy* 1 (1974), pp. 101-35.

12   Cf. Ward, *DNB*.

13   Bell (n. 6), p. 98.

14   Thomas Beecham (1820-1907), who styled himself "Dr", built his success on a herbal or laxative pill and a cough pill, which he sold from a small shop in St. Helens from about 1860. Jesse Boot, 1st Lord Trent (1850-1931), was born into a family of "medical botanists" and began selling proprietary medicines in Nottingham in 1874. See: Beecham, Boot in *DBB*; S. Chapman, *Jesse Boot of Boots the Chemists* (London, 1973); R. Cooter (ed.), *Studies in the History of Alternative Medicine* (London, 1988); and C. Stockwell, *Nature's Pharmacy: A History of Plants and Healing* (London, 1988).

15   For this account of the firm's early days I have drawn largely on Cripps and Chapman-Huston and Cripps.

16   J.G.L. Burnby, "A Study of the English Apothecary from 1660 to 1760", *Medical History*, Supplement No. 3 (1983), p. 50.

17   A. Raistrick, *Quakers in Science and Industry* (London, 1950); D.J. Jeremy (ed.), *Business and Religion in Britain* (Aldershot, 1988).

18   See: "John Bell & Co", *Pharmaceutical Journal* 182 (1959), pp. 454-6; T.D. Whittet, "The Firm of Corbyn and Stacey", *Pharmaceutical Journal* 228 (1982), pp. 42-8. For details on another Quaker apothecary, see J.G.L. Burnby, "Life and Travels of Thomas Pole, Anglo-American Apothecary", *Pharmaceutical Journal* 229 (1982), pp. 751-7. Other pharmaceutical firms had Dissenting roots. The father of Jesse Boot was a dedicated Wesleyan preacher, and his son's sympathies always lay with evangelical Nonconformity.

19   C.J.S. Thompson, *The Mystery and Art of the Apothecary* (London, 1929), pp. 262-4.

20. John H. Davies (ed.), *The Letters of Lewis, Richard, William and John Morris of Anglesey* (2 vols., Aberystwyth, 1907-9), vol. 2, pp. 336-7.

21. A.N. Gamble, *A History of the Bevan Family* (London, 1924), p. 39.

Chapter 1:   Joseph Gurney Bevan Takes Command

1   Seven letter-books cover the period of Bevan's management of the firm (Allen & Hanburys' Archive, A-G, 5 January 1775 – 11 January 1806). The books are indexed and mostly fairly legible. I have drawn extensively on this correspondence for this chapter and all of the uncited quotations are from this source. I have also consulted Bevan's "Inventories of Drugs", 1776-94, a volume held by the RPSGB.

2   R. Bevan, *A Short Account of the Last Illness and Death of Joseph Gurney Bevan. A Member of the Society of Friends* (London, 1815), p. 4.

3   J.G.L. Burnby, "A Study of the English Apothecary from 1660 to 1760", *Medical History*, Supplement No. 3 (1983), pp. 50-1.

4   S.S. Stander, "A History of the Pharmaceutical Industry with Special Reference to Allen & Hanbury, 1775-1843" (London MSc., 1965), quoted p. 98.

5   For details on Bevan's prices, see the anonymous article "Wholesale Prices in the Eighteenth Century", *Chemist and Druggist* 62 (1903), pp. 179-83.

6   Stander, "History" (n. 4), pp. 55-6.

7   *Extracts from the Letters and Other Writings of the Late Joseph Gurney Bevan; Preceded by a Short Memoir of His Life* (London, 1821), pp. 11-12.

8   *Short Account* (n. 2), p. 4.

9   *A Short Account of the Life and Writings of Robert Barclay* (London, 1802); *Memoirs of the Life of Isaac Penington: to which is Added a Review of His Writings* (London, 1807).

Chapter 2:   Science and Enterprise: Plough Court under William Allen and John T. Barry

1   A.W. Slater, "Howards, Chemical Manufacturers, 1797-1837: A Study in Business History" (London MSc., 1956). See also "Howards of Stratford and Ilford", *Chemist and Druggist* 84 (1914), pp. 115-23.

2   Again, all uncited quotations in this chapter are from the company letter-books in the Allen & Hanbury Archive. Four letter-books cover the period 1815-49. The RPSGB also has three volumes of Plough Court records from the Allen period: "Laboratory Calculation Book, 1795-98"; "Stock Book 1810 and 1811"; and "Cost Price Book, 1824-44".

3   Jonathan Liebenau, *Medical Science and Medical Industry: The Formation of the American Pharmaceutical Industry* (London, 1987), pp. 11-17.

4   *Memorials of Christine Majolier Alsop,* compiled by M. Braithwaite (London, 1881), p. 41, quoted in Cripps, p. 30.

5   *Life of William Allen with Selections from his Correspondence* (London, 1846), vol. 1, p. 3. The following two quotations are also

from this source, vol. 1, pp. 22-3, 29-30. The editors of this volume only reproduced those sections of Allen's letters that they considered to be morally uplifting; the correspondence then appears to have been destroyed.

6   See Leslie G. Matthews, "An Unrecorded William Allen Caricature", *Medical History* 15 (1971), pp. 305-6. It was rumoured Allen had married for money (an unlikely event perhaps, given Allen's already considerable wealth), which gave rise to the jibe: "To be sure the Beef is rather old, but then the Gristle's made of gold".

7   See Allen in *DNB*; Helena Hall, *William Allen, 1770-1843, Member of the Society of Friends* (Haywards Heath, 1953); *William Allen: His Life and Labours* (London, 1865). All of these works give almost exclusive attention to Allen's public career.

8   Robert Owen, *The Life of Robert Owen by Himself* (London, 1857, reprint 1971), pp. 95, 141, 235.

9   S.W.F. Holloway, "The Orthodox Fringe: The Origins of the Pharmaceutical Society of Great Britain", in W.F. Bynum and Roy Porter (eds.), *Medical Fringe and Medical Orthodoxy 1750-1850* (London, 1987), pp. 129-57; C.P. Cloughly, J.G.L. Burnby and M.P. Earles, *My Dear Mr. Bell: Letters from Dr. Jonathan Pereira to Mr. Jacob Bell, London, 1844 to 1853* (Edinburgh, 1988); Leslie G. Matthews, *History of Pharmacy in Britain* (Edinburgh & London, 1962), pp. 118-27.

10   Joshua Fayle, *The Spitalfields Genius: The Story of William Allen* (London, 1884), pp. 36-7.

11   Cripps, p. 26 *et seq.* for the following quotations and information. See also Chapman-Huston and Cripps for a detailed account of Allen's scientific career. Besides the material in the Allen & Hanbury Archive, the Royal Society also has an album of letters from Allen to the scientist Robert Were Fox (1789-1877) during the period 1809-40.

12   Ian Inkster, "Science and Society in the Metropolis: A Preliminary Examination of the Social and Institutional Context of the Askesian Society of London, 1796-1807", *Annals of Science* 34 (1977), pp. 1-32. The Greek equivalent of Askesian means "training".

13   Cripps, p. 28.

14   S.S. Stander, "A History of the Pharmaceutical Industry with Particular Reference to Allen & Hanbury, 1775-1843" (London MSc., 1965), pp. 79-81.

15   The lease is printed as Appendix II in Cripps, pp. 214-19.

16   F. Mohr and T. Redwood, *Practical Pharmacy: The Arrangements, Apparatus, and Manipulations of the Pharmaceutical Shop and Laboratory* (London, 1849), pp. 21-2. See also Samuel F. Gray, *The Operative Chemist* (London, 1828).

17   Working at Plough Court was not quite as arduous as this suggests. Allen did allow some time for the cultivation of the mind. In 1812 he wrote, concerning the activities of the shopmen: "I allow each of

the shopmen one afternoon in a week to themselves – by rising early in a morning they have an opportunity of studying if they are so inclined."

18   Stander (n. 14), pp. 164-5.

Chapter 3:   Expansion under the Hanburys, 1850s-1893

1   Peter Mathias, *The First Industrial Nation: An Economic History of Britain, 1700-1914* (London, 2nd edn., 1983), p. 221 ff., p. 419.

2   On Beecham, Boot, Eno and Holloway, see *DBB*.

3   Jonathan Liebenau, "Marketing High Technology: Educating Physicians to Use Innovative Medicines", in R.P.T. Davenport-Hines (ed.), *Markets and Bagmen: Studies in the History of Marketing and British Industrial Performance, 1830-1939* (Aldershot, 1986), pp. 82-101.

4   Amy A. Locke, *The Hanbury Family* (2 vols., London, 1916).

5   Sir Cecil Hanbury, *La Mortola Garden* (London, 1938). The Gardens, no longer owned by the family, have now fallen into neglect. See "Up the Garden Path", *Sunday Telegraph*, 7 May 1989. On Frederick J. Hanbury, see: (ed.), *The London Catalogue of British Plants* (London, 11th edn., 1925); (with Edward S. Marshall) *Flora of Kent* (London, 1899); "Frederick Janson Hanbury ... Some Observations on His Work as a Botanist, with Notes and Pictures of the Remarkable Gardens at His Residence, Brockhurst, East Grinstead", *Chemist and Druggist* 87 (1915), pp. 157-61.

6   Daniel Hanbury, *Science Papers, Chiefly Pharmacological and Botanical. Edited with a Memoir by J. Ince* (London, 1876); Friedrich A. Fluckiger and Daniel Hanbury, *Pharmacographia: A History of the Principal Drugs of Vegetable Origin Met with in Great Britain and British India* (London, 2nd edn., 1879). The following manuscript collections have material relating to Daniel's prodigious researches: the Allen & Hanbury Archive at Greenford has 16 volumes of his Scientific Notebooks (1843-75); the RPSGB holds correspondence and papers (1856-75) on Indian, Chinese and South American materia medica, his large collection of books, and his incoming correspondence from the botanist Richard Spruce; while the Royal Botanic Gardens, Kew, has ninety of his letters (1848-65) to Sir W.J. Hooker.

7   E.J. Shellard, "Daniel Hanbury: One of the Founders of Pharmacognosy", *Pharmaceutical Journal* 214 (10 May 1975), pp. 417-21. See also "The Life and Work of Daniel Hanbury (1825-1875)", part six of Shellard, "A History of British Pharmacognosy", *Pharmaceutical Journal* 227 (1981), pp. 774-7.

8   Chapman-Huston and Cripps, pp. 155-6.

9   For details of one druggist in Highgate that relied on Allen & Hanburys, see A.E. Bailey, "Early Nineteenth Century Pharmacy", *Pharmaceutical Journal* 185 (September 1960), pp. 208-12.

10   Cripps, p. 100.

11   Chapman-Huston and Cripps, p. 176.

12   From Dodd's speech at the Allen & Hanburys' bi-centenary,
      reported in *Chemist and Druggist* 87 (1915), pp. 53-5.
13   Chapman-Huston and Cripps, p. 180.
14   Thomas Percival, *The Works, Literary, Moral and Medical of
      Thomas Percival* (4 vols., London, 1807), vol. 3, p. 355.
15   Cripps, p. 102.
16   Richard Bennett and J.A. Leavey, *A History of Smith & Nephew
      1856-1981* (London, 1981).
17   W.R. Dunstan and A.F. Dimmock, "Estimation of Diastase", *Phar-
      maceutical Journal* 38 (1879), pp. 733-5.
18   *Chemist and Druggist* 42 (1893), p. 145.
19   *Chemist and Druggist* 62 (1903), p. 563.
20   "A Visit to Messrs. Allen & Hanburys' Works", *Chemist and
      Druggist* 22 (1880), p. 14.
21   Judy Slinn, *A History of May & Baker 1834-1984* (Cambridge,
      1984).

Chapter 4:   Allen & Hanburys Limited: The Universal Provider

1   Glaxo Group Archive, Allen & Hanbury Minute Books. I have
     used these documents, alongside the Reports for the Annual
     General Meetings, as the major source for the firm's history during
     the period 1893-1940. All uncited quotations are from this source.
2   Albert Mason, "The 'Old Firm' Huddled by the Railway Track",
     The Bulletin No. 300 (September 1964), pp. 20-2.
3   "Operation Tables: Design Through the Ages", *The Bulletin* No.
     307 (May 1965), pp. 24-7.
4   Chapman-Huston and Cripps, p. 212.
5   Cripps, p. 199.
6   These developments can only be lightly sketched in here. For a
     much more detailed treatment, see W. Sneader, *Drug Discovery:
     The Evolution of Modern Medicines* (New York, 1985), a book I
     have found especially useful. See also the series of articles by Miles
     Weatherall, "Science and the Discovery of Drugs", *Pharmaceutical
     Journal* 237 (1986) – 238 (1987).
7   It was William Whiteley, the famous Victorian department store
     owner, who used this phrase as a slogan. However, I have found it
     perfectly appropriate for Allen & Hanburys' policy at this time.
     Shortly after I wrote this chapter, I found that Charles W. Robinson
     in his autobiography, *Twentieth Century Druggist* (Beverley, 1983),
     had also used this phrase in describing one of Allen & Hanburys'
     competitors, Evans Medical. This firm also had a vast range of
     products, which Robinson describes as the company's "strength and
     its bane".
8   See G. Jones (ed.), *British Multinationals: Origins, Management
     and Performance* (Aldershot, 1986).
9   Chapman-Huston and Cripps, p. 200.
10   Cornelius Hanbury marked the change by joining the Church of
     England. In his "Recollections" he stated: "As the children

advanced in years I became less & less satisfied that they should have the very limited religious instruction which they received at the Friends' Meetings, & I accordingly sought information as to the teaching to be had elsewhere."

11 Sir Paul Girolami, "The Development of Glaxo", unpublished Business History Unit (London School of Economics) seminar paper, 18 June 1985, p. 4.

12 G. Macdonald, *One Hundred Years Wellcome 1880-1980* (London, 1980). See also J. Liebenau, "Industrial R & D in Pharmaceutical Firms in the Early Twentieth Century", *Business History* 26 (1984), pp. 329-46; Miles Weatherall, "Research in the Pharmaceutical Industry: 19th Century", *Pharmaceutical Journal* 242 (1989), pp. 543-5.

13 M. Robson, "The British Pharmaceutical Industry and the First World War", in J. Liebenau (ed.), *The Challenge of New Technology: Innovation in British Business Since 1850* (Aldershot, 1988), pp. 83-105.

14 *Chemist and Druggist* 88 (1916), p. 43.

Chapter 5: The Firm Between the Wars

1 Again all uncited quotations in this chapter are from the Allen & Hanbury Minute Books and the Reports at the Annual General Meetings.

2 F.B. Smith, *The Retreat of Tuberculosis 1850-1950* (London, 1988), p. 189.

3 Cripps, p. 126. See also "A & H Laboratories for Analysis and Research", *Chemist and Druggist* 102 (1925), pp. 920-1.

4 M. Bliss, *The Discovery of Insulin* (Toronto, 1982). In 1925 a Nobel Prize was awarded to Banting and Macleod. Banting shared his portion of the prize with Best; and Macleod shared his with Collip. See also "Forty Years of Insulin Therapy", a series of articles in the *Chemist and Druggist* 179 (1963), pp. 487-504.

5 David O. Evans, "Recollections of 'Vere Street'", *Pharmaceutical Journal* 196 (1966), pp. 510-11.

6 Cripps, p. 131.

7 "Round the Factory with Notebook and Camera: No. 4 – Pastilles", *Plough Magazine* (October 1926), p. 16.

8 On Glaxo's history, see *Gold on the Green: Fifty Glaxo Years at Greenford* (Greenford, 1985); and Sir H. Jephcott (compiler), *The First Fifty Years* (1969).

9 Jephcott (above), p. 91.

10 For biographical details on Jephcott, see R.P.T. Davenport-Hines entry in *DBB*. There is also a less detailed treatment in *DNB*.

11 See W. Sneader, *Drug Discovery: The Evolution of Modern Medicines* (New York, 1985), pp. 227-47.

12 E.K. Samways, interview with the author.

13 H.G.L. Lazell, *From Pills to Penicillin: The Beecham Story* (London, 1975), pp. 4-5.

14   "Our Overseas Branches: No. 2 – Durban, South Africa", *Plough Magazine* (April 1926), p. 14.

15   F.W. Gamble and Norman Evers, "Advances in the Manufacture of Pharmaceutical Products, 1910-1935", *Pharmaceutical Journal* 134 (1935), pp. 541-3.

Chapter 6:   An End and a Beginning, 1940-58

1   Quoted in J. Slinn, *A History of May & Baker 1834-1984* (Cambridge, 1984), p. 125.

2   R. Hare, *The Birth of Penicillin* (London, 1970). See also: G. Macfarlane, *Alexander Fleming: The Man and the Myth* (London, 1984); and D. Wilson, *Penicillin in Perspective* (London, 1976).

3   W. Breckon, *The Drug Makers* (London, 1972), pp. 23-4.

4   H.G.L. Lazell, *From Pills to Penicillin: The Beecham Story* (London, 1975). See also the account by T.A.B. Corley in *DBB*.

5   C. Webster, *The Health Services Since the War. Vol. I: Problems of Health Care: The National Health Services Before 1957* (London, 1988), pp. 222-7.

6   Chapman-Huston and Cripps, p. 221.

7   "Birth of an Industry", *Chemist and Druggist* 145 (1946), pp. 590-1.

8   This quote and subsequent uncited ones are from the Allen & Hanbury Minute Books and the Reports of the Annual General Meetings.

9   Dr. D. Jack, *Pharmaceutical Journal* 231 (1983), p. 734. See also Maplethorpe's obituary in the same journal on 5 November, pp. 547-8.

10   See, for example, Maplethorpe's address "The Future Pharmacist: Efficiency and Pharmaceutical Equipment", *Pharmaceutical Journal* 156 (1946), pp. 68-9.

11   Chapman-Huston and Cripps, p. 235.

12   "A New Sterile Unit at Ware", *Chemist and Druggist* 167 (1957), pp. 558-9.

13   J.C. Hanbury memo to R.D. Smart, 27 October 1965.

14   R.P.T. Davenport-Hines, Jephcott entry in *DBB*.

Chapter 7:   Allen & Hanburys and the Chemotherapeutic Revolution

1   W. Breckon, *The Drug Makers* (London, 1972), p. 29.

2   Sir Paul Girolami, "The Development of Glaxo", unpublished Business History Unit (London School of Economics) seminar paper, 18 June 1985, p. 2.

3   Author's interview with E.K. Samways.

4   For details of Evans and the Glaxo takeover, see C.W. Robinson, *Twentieth Century Druggist: Memoirs* (Beverley, 1983), pp. 192-5. Duncan, Flockhart & Co was founded in Edinburgh in 1820 and specialised in anaesthetics. Allied Laboratories were London-based and had joined the Edinburgh group in 1959.

5   "Report of a Group Appointed to Study Certain Pharmaceutical Manufacturing Procedures", 27 September 1968.

6   "Pastille Manufacturing Department", *Allenburys Bulletin* (June 1966), p. 25.

7   "A & H (Surgical Instruments) Ltd", *Allenburys Bulletin* (October 1966), pp. 24-9.

8   H. Jephcott, "The Glaxo Research Organisation", in Sir John Cockcroft (ed.), *The Organisation of Research Establishments* (Cambridge, 1966), pp. 148-67.

9   R.P.T. Davenport-Hines, "Glaxo as a Multinational Before 1963", in G. Jones (ed.), *British Multinationals: Origins, Management and Performance* (Aldershot, 1986), pp. 137-63.

10   The following account and quotations rely heavily on information and handwritten notes generously supplied to me by Dr. David Jack.

11   D. Jack, "The Challenge of Drug Discovery", unpublished Centre for Medicines Research Lecture (1988), p. 14.

12   Quoted in D.J. Lane and A. Storr, *Asthma: The Facts* (Oxford, 2nd edn., 1987), p. 25. See also W.E. Brocklehurst, "Asthma: A Long and Continuing Story", in M.J. Parnham and J. Bruinvels (eds.), *Discoveries in Pharmacology* (New York, 1984), vol. 2, pp. 647-78.

13   Author's interview with Dr. Roy T. Brittain.

14   D. Hartley, D. Jack, L. Lunts, and A.C.H. Ritchie, "New Class of Selective Stimulants of Beta-Adrenergic Receptors", *Nature* 219 (1968), pp. 861-2. See also L.C.H. Lunts, "Salbutamol: A Selective Beta$_2$-Stimulant Bronchodilator", in B.J. Price and Stanley M. Roberts (eds.), *Medicinal Chemistry: The Role of Organic Chemistry in Drug Research* (London, 1985), pp. 49-67.

15   W. Sneader, *Drug Discovery: The Evolution of Modern Medicines* (New York, 1985), p. 171.

Chapter 8:   Allen & Hanburys Ltd in the 1980s

1   Data on the industry is collected in the Association of the British Pharmaceutical Industry, *The Pharmaceutical Industry and the Nation's Health* (London, 1988).

2   W. Breckon, *The Drug Makers* (London, 1972), p. 216.

3   Daniel Hanbury stated the industry's standpoint in 1867: "The greatest ignorance prevails as to the reason for the cost of the medicines which are retailed by druggists, and the most erroneous notions are entertained as to the druggists' profits. Why it is asked should this little vial of arsenical drops be charged at 2/6 when it does not cost more than 2d? The fact is that the price of the medicine is often *chiefly made* up of the premium or fee that is paid for the intelligence, skill and care that the pharmacist is called to display – almost in fact as with the lawyer or physician, whose fees are not altered by the price of ink and paper." Hanbury to Dr Waring, 27 August 1867, Scientific Notebook, vol. 9, pp. 110-11.

Allen & Hanbury Archive, Greenford.

4   For criticisms of this nature, see Joe Collier, *The Health Conspiracy* (London, 1989). The author is the son of the late Allen & Hanbury pharmacologist, Dr. Harry Collier.

Source: This chronology is based partly on Raymond L. Hanbury, "The History and Development of Allen & Hanburys Ltd, 1715-1965", unpublished typescript (1965).

CHRONOLOGY

1715   The old Plough Court pharmacy was established. Silvanus Bevan, apothecary, leased the premises from John Osgood.

1725   Silvanus Bevan took over the second lease of the premises which showed that the business was flourishing. He was elected Fellow of the Royal Society. Timothy Bevan, his younger brother, came to London and was apprenticed to him.

1731   Timothy took up his Freedom of the Society of Apothecaries. Shortly afterwards, the two brothers went into partnership as Silvanus & Timothy Bevan, Apothecaries, Lombard Street.

The marriages of Timothy Bevan

(i) 8 September 1735 to Elizabeth Barclay of London
(d. 30 August 1745)

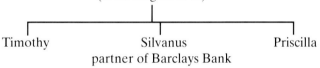

Timothy   Silvanus   Priscilla
                    partner of Barclays Bank

(ii) January 1752 to Hannah Gurney of Norwich

Joseph Gurney Bevan

1766   The two eldest surviving sons of Timothy Bevan, Timothy and Silvanus, were taken into the partnership, which was henceforth styled Timothy Bevan & Sons, Druggists and Chymists, Plow Court, Lombard Street.

1767   Silvanus, the son, retired and became a partner of Barclays Bank.

1773   Timothy, the son, died, but his father continued for two years.

1775   The father retired in favour of his third son, Joseph.

1792   Joseph took on William Allen as his confidential clerk.

1794   Joseph was succeeded in the business by Samuel Mildred, son of Daniel Mildred of Mildred & Roberts.

1795   William Allen was taken on as partner by Samuel Mildred, the firm becoming Mildred & Allen.

1797   Mildred retired, selling out to Allen for £525. The latter immediately took on his friend, Luke Howard, and the firm was re-styled as Allen & Howard. Allen supervised Plough

Court; Howard worked at the manufacturing laboratory which was established at Plaistow.

1804   John Thomas Barry entered Plough Court.

1805   The laboratory moved to Stratford.

1806   The partnership was dissolved and Luke set up on his own as Luke Howard & Co.

1807   Allen was elected to the Fellowship of the Royal Society.

1808   Daniel Bell Hanbury entered Plough Court under Allen and Barry.

1813   Cornelius Hanbury joined Plough Court under Allen and Barry.

1818   Barry, who had for some time been in charge of the manufacturing laboratory, was made a partner with Allen, and the title was changed to William Allen & Co.

1822   *The marriages of Cornelius Hanbury*

(i) 20 February 1822 to Mary Allen (d. 1823 in childbirth)
|
William Allen Hanbury

(ii) 1826 to Elizabeth Sanderson
┌──────────┴──────────┐
Cornelius   Charlotte

1824   Daniel Bell Hanbury and the elder Cornelius Hanbury were taken into partnership, the firm becoming Allen, Hanburys & Barry. At that time Allen was fifty-four, Barry, the second senior partner, thirty-five, Daniel Bell, thirty, and Cornelius twenty-eight.

1841   Allen helped found the Pharmaceutical Society and was elected its first president. Barry and Daniel Bell Hanbury were also founder members, and the latter was its treasurer from 1852-67. Cornelius the younger was treasurer, 1876-8.

The marriages of William Allen

(i) 13 November 1796 to Mary Hamilton (d. shortly after the birth)
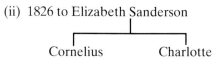
Mary (married Cornelius Hanbury, the elder, in 1822)
(ii) 1806 to Charlotte Hanbury of Stoke Newington (sister of Cornelius's father, Capel) (d. 1816 in Geneva)
(iii) 13 March 1827 to Grizell Birkbeck (widow), who d. 1835

1841   Daniel Hanbury, eldest son of Daniel Bell Hanbury, entered Plough Court. Though engaged in the business for a number of years, he pursued a scientific career, becoming a Fellow of the Royal Society in 1867 and a member of its Council in 1873.

1850   Cornelius Hanbury, the younger, entered Plough Court.

1856   John T. Barry retired and Daniel Hanbury and Cornelius Hanbury, the younger, were admitted to the partnership. The present name of Allen & Hanburys was adopted.

1858	The elder Cornelius retired.
1860	Cornelius, the younger, sent an assistant, John Tuttle, to establish a cod-liver oil factory in Newfoundland. The oil was refined at Plough Court. By 1914 seven further cod-liver oil refining factories were opened – five in Norway, one in Aberdeen and another in Hull. In 1903 refining was conducted temporarily at Bethnal Green, but later at Aberdeen.
1868	Daniel Bell Hanbury retired.
1870	Daniel Hanbury retired and Cornelius Hanbury became the sole partner.
1872	Frederick Janson Hanbury, the elder son of Cornelius, joined the firm. Together they developed the manufacturing side of the firm and concentrated on the introduction and marketing of a wide range of specialities, such as cod-liver oil, malt products, pastilles and jujubes, milk foods for infants and a number of products under licence from other companies, particularly in America. They also established foreign subsidiaries after the turn of the century.
1873	The new Plough Court was built as a result of major replanning of the Lombard Street area.
1874	Frederick J. Hanbury entered into partnership with his father.
1875	Daniel Bell Hanbury died at the age of fifty.
1876	Frederick J. Hanbury visited the USA.
1878	A factory was opened at Bethnal Green as a manufacturing laboratory under William Ralph Dodd and his assistant, George Wessendorff.
1880-5	A workshop and forge for making surgical instruments were installed at Bethnal Green, and instrument makers were brought from Sheffield to begin production.
1884	Messrs. F. Forrest & Co of Melbourne were appointed agents.
1885	A pharmacy was opened at No. 7 Vere Street to strengthen contact with the West End medical community.
1893	The firm was incorporated as Allen & Hanburys Ltd, with Cornelius as chairman, and his son, Frederick, on the board.
1894	W. Ralph Dodd was elected to the board. Arthur J. Firkins was sent out to Australia. George Reddick of Messrs. Reddick & Co (East India Merchants) was appointed representative in India. A depot was opened at Calcutta. A showroom and workshop were opened at 48 Wigmore Street.
1896	A mill site was acquired at Ware, Hertfordshire.
1898	Buryfield was acquired at Ware for the expansion of a new Allen & Hanbury factory and the production of Foods and Malts was transferred there under the direction of W.R. Dodd. F.J. Hanbury visited Canada and the USA and appointed agents in Toronto and New York.

1900	The company's first agents in South America were appointed. F.W. Gamble became manager at Vere Street. The production of jujubes, pastilles and capsules was transferred to Ware. John Netherway was appointed company secretary.
1901	A West End wholesale department was added to the Vere Street pharmacy.
1902	The New York agency, was transferred to Niagara Falls. F.J. Hanbury, accompanied by two of his sons, Reginald and Capel, visited Canada for a third time, and established a subsidiary company with its distributing centre at Toronto.
1904	Depots were opened, in turn, in Cape Town and Durban and rapid development of the company's activities took place in South Africa.
	Reginald J. Hanbury, MRCS, LRCP, and F. Capel Hanbury, Ph.C., were elected junior directors of the company.
1909	A subsidiary company was formed in South America, based in Buenos Aires, but political disturbances and the First World War prevented growth.
1912	Operations were begun in Russia. The Johannesburg surgical instrument branch was opened. Frederick J. Hanbury, Ph.C., FLS, FES, was elected vice-chairman. His sons, Reginald and Capel, were appointed senior directors, with the former assuming responsibility for the medical department and for the surgical division of the company.
1913	The lease of No. 6 Vere Street was obtained.
1914	Frederic W. Gamble, Ph.C., was elected a director.
1914 et seq.	A factory was established in farming country at Lindsay, Ontario, and began manufacturing "Allenburys" Milk Foods.
1915	The bi-centenary of Allen & Hanburys was celebrated by the presentation to F.J. Hanbury of his portrait painted by Percy Bigland; W.R. Dodd was presented with a silver centrepiece and a silver cabinet.
1916	John Netherway, FCIS, became a director. Cornelius Hanbury died on 11 April at the Manor House, Little Berkhamstead, leaving £180,186 gross.
1917	W.R. Dodd died suddenly from typhoid fever on 4 December in Cheshunt, Hertfordshire. F. Capel Hanbury assumed responsibility for the production of foods and pharmaceutical products.The Bolsheviks confiscated the Allen & Hanbury plant in Moscow. The following dividend on the ordinary shares was passed to compensate for this loss.
1918	The Bethnal Green factory was hit by a German bomb and severely damaged.
1920	Turnover of the company passed the £1 million mark.

1922	Completion of the rebuilt Bethnal Green factory, with a new analytical laboratory.
1923	Allen & Hanburys began the manufacture of recently discovered insulin on behalf of the Medical Research Association and in partnership with The British Drug Houses Ltd.
1924	A new cod-liver oil factory was opened in Aberdeen.
1928	Synthetic vitamin D was added to the "Allenburys" foods.
1931	The company opened a creamery near Glastonbury.
1934	Allen & Hanburys' "Haliborange" and "Halibol" were introduced.
1935	Reginald J. Hanbury, director of the firm, died at his home at Woldingham at the relatively early age of fifty-seven.
1937	F. Capel Hanbury succeeded his father as chairman of the company.
1938	Frederick J. Hanbury, chairman of Allen & Hanburys for over forty-one years, died on 1 March at his home at East Grinstead.
1939	"Sterivac" manufacture commenced at Ware.
1940	The famous Model E operating table was introduced. The Bethnal Green factory was severely damaged by enemy bombing and manufacturing was transferred to Ware. Plough Court suffered bomb damage and in a little over a year the site had been vacated by Allen & Hanburys.
1943	John C. Hanbury, MA (Cantab), BPharm (Lond), Ph.C., ARIC, was elected a director.
1944	F.W. Gamble retired as managing director. He was succeeded in the post by C.W. Maplethorpe, Ph.C., FRIC, MIChemE.
1946	J.C. Hanbury was appointed vice-chairman. W.J. Rennie, ACA, became company secretary. John Netherway retired. Lea Valley Dairies Ltd was formed.
1947	W.J. Rennie and W.M. Clayson, Ph.C., and G.T. Gamble, FIBST, were appointed directors.
1948	F.W. Gamble died during his retirement.
1950	A new Allen & Hanburys' factory was opened in Congella, Durban. Dr F. Arnold Robinson was appointed research director.
1951	Allen & Hanburys offered £1 million 4 percent first mortgage debenture stock. The issue was eleven times over-subscribed before the day was out. F.J. Conduit, Ph.C., and F.A. Axe, ACA, were elected directors. John Netherway, the former secretary of the company, died in his eightieth year.
1952	203,500 ordinary shares of £1 each were issued to existing ordinary share holders in the proportion of five new shares for every three previously held.
1953	The boards of the overseas subsidiaries were reconstituted, under the direction of C.W. Maplethorpe and W.M. Clayson.

A fire destroyed the Congella factory. The Allenburys' Infant Foods were discontinued.

1954   F. Capel Hanbury retired as chairman and was succeeded by his son, John C. Hanbury.

1957   A new sterile-filling block at Ware was opened. F. Capel Hanbury died on 21 October.

1958   G.T. Gamble resigned his directorship. The Wigmore Street premises were evacuated on the expiry of the lease and the display of surgical products was transferred to Vere Street. The board of Allen & Hanburys Ltd wrote to its ordinary shareholders recommending that the offer received from Glaxo Laboratories Ltd, to exchange three ordinary stock 10/- units for each £1 Allen & Hanburys' share, be accepted. C.W. Maplethorpe was elected a director of Glaxo Laboratories Ltd; Herbert Palmer BCom (Lond.) became a director of Allen & Hanburys Ltd. E.K. Samways BSc, BPharm, FPS, FRIC, was elected a director of Allen & Hanburys Ltd. Allen & Hanburys Ltd announced that a contract had been won with the Imperial Welfare (Darou Pakhsh) Organisation to manufacture pharmaceutical products in Iran. Allen & Hanburys (N.Z.) was incorporated in New Zealand with headquarters at Wellington. Glaxo (Canada) Ltd and Allen & Hanburys Co Ltd of Canada were merged as Glaxo-Allenburys (Canada) Ltd. The company remained a subsidiary of Allen & Hanburys Ltd.

1959   A new block at Bethnal Green was completed (externally). New directors' offices and a new boardroom for the company were housed on the third floor. "Steriflex" disposable plastic products were introduced. "Dictol", a lungworm vaccine, was launched after collaborative work with Glasgow University. Lea Valley Dairies Ltd was sold.

1960   Glaxo-Allenburys (Export Ltd) was established with headquarters in London to take over the export activities of Glaxo Laboratories Ltd and Allen & Hanburys Ltd. The directors appointed were: Sir Harry Jephcott, H.W. Palmer, C.W. Maplethorpe, W.J. Hurran, R. Greenwood, and R.A. Langridge. Glaxo-Allenburys (Aust) (Pty) Ltd, Glaxo-Allenburys (South Africa) (Pty) Ltd, and Glaxo-Allenburys (Nigeria) Ltd were set up.

1961   Glaxo Laboratories Ltd acquired Evans Medical Ltd. R. David Smart BA (Cantab) was elected a director of Allen & Hanburys Ltd. The Indian branch of Allen & Hanburys Ltd ceased to trade in pharmaceutical products and its activities were taken over by Glaxo Laboratories (India) (Private) Ltd. It continued, however, to sell and distribute surgical goods. At an Extraordinary General Meeting of Glaxo Laboratories Ltd a resolution was passed that the name of the company be changed to Glaxo Group Ltd. A new subsidiary company,

Glaxo Laboratories Ltd, was formed to conduct the manufacturing and trading activities which had previously been carried out under that name. Another new subsidiary, Glaxo Research Ltd, was created with responsibility for research and development. Allen & Hanburys Ltd ceased to be a subsidiary of Glaxo Laboratories Ltd and became a subsidiary of Glaxo Group Ltd. R.A. Langridge was appointed managing director of Glaxo-Allenburys (Export) Ltd, and Raymond Greenwood was appointed deputy managing director.

1962   The name of R.E. Harding & Co (Ghana) Ltd, a subsidiary of Glaxo Laboratories Ltd, was changed to Glaxo-Allenburys (Ghana) Ltd, and it became a subsidiary of Glaxo Group Ltd. C.W. Maplethorpe was elected vice-president of the Pharmaceutical Society of Great Britain. Dr. David Jack BSc, PhD, FPS, FRIC was appointed a director of Allen & Hanburys Ltd with responsibility for research, in succession to F. Arnold Robinson. Edinburgh Pharmaceutical Industries Ltd became a subsidiary of Glaxo Group Ltd.

1963   A new factory was acquired by Allen & Hanburys Ltd at Portsmouth for producing hospital equipment, which began trading as Swanbrig Engineers Ltd. H.I.M. the Shah of Iran officially opened the £1.5 million pharmaceutical factory near Tehran in Iran. C.W. Maplethorpe MSc, FRIC, FPS, MIChemE was elected President of the Pharmaceutical Society of Great Britain, the first partner or director of the firm to hold this position since William Allen in 1841. Sir Harry Jephcott retired from the chairmanship of Glaxo Group Ltd and was succeeded by Sir Alan H. Wilson FRS. Allen & Hanburys (Surgical Engineering) Ltd was incorporated to take over the surgical activities of Allen & Hanburys Ltd. Its subsidiaries were: W.H. Deane (High Wycombe) Ltd; Eschmann Bros & Walsh Ltd; Swanbrig Engineers Ltd; and Wardco Ltd. A team was set up by Sir Alan Wilson to study the rationalisation of the pharmaceutical production of Allen & Hanburys Ltd, Evans Medical Ltd, and Glaxo Laboratories Ltd.

1964   C.W. Maplethorpe was re-elected president of the Pharmaceutical Society of Great Britain. The board of Glaxo Group Ltd decided that the speciality sales companies of Duncan, Flockhart & Co Ltd and Allied Laboratories were to cease being the responsibility of Edinburgh Pharmaceutical Industries Ltd and were to be associated with the pharmaceutical business of Allen & Hanburys Ltd. The drug and speciality business of Allen & Hanburys was to be unified executively with that of Evans Medical Ltd, excluding the latter's wholesaling activities.

1965   The 250th anniversary of the founding of the business at Plough Court. C.W. Maplethorpe retired as managing director of Allen & Hanburys Ltd, to be succeeded by David Smart.

1966	Glaxo International Ltd was formed to co-ordinate the overseas activities of Glaxo Group Ltd.
1968	Austin Bide, deputy chairman of the Glaxo Group, appointed a committee under the chairmanship of E.K. Samways to study pharmaceutical manufacturing within the Group.
1969	Allen & Hanburys Ltd introduced salbutamol ("Ventolin"), a treatment for asthma.
1971	Maurice J. Smith was appointed director of Allen & Hanburys Ltd, in succession to David Smart.
1972	Glaxo Holdings p.l.c. was formed to control the activities of Glaxo Group Ltd. Glaxo strengthened its position in Japan by buying a 50 percent interest in Shi Nihon. Allen & Hanburys Ltd introduced an inhaled steroid, beclamethasone dipropionate ("Becotide") for the treatment of asthma.
1973	John C. Hanbury retired as chairman of Allen & Hanburys Ltd. Sir Alan Wilson retired as chairman of Glaxo Holdings, and was succeeded by Austin Bide. Allen & Hanburys' pharmacy at Vere Street was closed.
1974	John C. Hanbury was knighted. Allen & Hanburys Ltd launched "Beconase" (beclamethasone dipropionate) as a treatment for allergic rhinitis (hay fever).
1978	Sir Harry Jephcott died on 29 May. Glaxo acquired Meyer Laboratories Inc, a small but vigorous marketing concern in Fort Lauderdale, Florida, as part of an initiative to penetrate the American market. Maurice J. Smith retired as managing director of Allen & Hanburys Ltd.
1979	Glaxo's research activities at Greenford and Ware were unified as Glaxo Group Research Ltd, with Dr David Jack as its chairman and chief executive. Jack also became a director of Glaxo Group Ltd.
1980	Sir Austin Bide retired as Glaxo chairman and was succeeded by Paul Girolami, who had been Group Financial Director since 1968. Ranitidine ("Zantac") was introduced under the Glaxo brand-name as a new anti-ulcerant drug.
1982	Allen & Hanburys' administration was transferred to Greenford, where Horsenden House had been built as a site for Glaxo Operations. The Bethnal Green premises were closed.
1983	C.W. Maplethorpe died on 26 October at Hertingfordbury, Hertford.
1987	Dr David Jack retired as a board member of Glaxo Holdings p.l.c. Dr Richard B. Sykes was appointed chief executive of Glaxo Group Research Ltd.
1988	"Zantac" became the first drug in history to pass the £1 billion per annum sales mark.
1990	275th anniversary of Allen & Hanburys Ltd.

BIBLIOGRAPHY

I – Manuscripts and unpublished sources

Allen & Hanburys Ltd
Allen & Hanburys has had an admirable policy of retaining all its important documentation. This has resulted in a voluminous Archive, which is presently split between two sites. At the Greenford Archive the most important items are the firm's early Quaker letter-books, covering the period 1775-1849. The Archive also holds several volumes of William Allen's correspondence and the Science Notebooks of Daniel Hanbury. An extensive collection of trade catalogues, house magazines (such as *Plough Magazine* and the *Allenburys Bulletin*), photographs, engravings, advertising material and artefacts are also held at Greenford.

Most of the firm's business documentation after 1893 – including minute books, accounts, reports of the overseas subsidiaries – is deposited in the Glaxo Group Archive, London. This collection also includes, *inter alia*, the "Recollections" of Cornelius Hanbury and documentation from Plough Court, such as the dispensing books.

Royal Botanic Gardens, Kew
Daniel Hanbury's letters (1845-65) to Sir W.J. Hooker.

Royal Pharmaceutical Society of Great Britain
The RPSGB has several items relating to Plough Court and the work of Daniel Hanbury: "Inventories of Drugs 1776-94"; "Laboratory Calculation Book, 1795-98"; "Stock Book 1810 & 1811"; "Cost Price Book 1824-44"; Daniel Hanbury's correspondence and papers, mainly relating to Indian, Chinese and South American materia medica (1856-75); and the correspondence (1856-75) of Richard Spruce to Daniel Hanbury.

Royal Society
William Allen letters (1809-40) to Robert Were Fox.

Dissertations and typescripts
Girolami, Sir Paul. "The Development of Glaxo", Business History Unit (London School of Economics) seminar paper (June 1985).
Hanbury, Raymond L. "The History and Development of Allen & Hanburys Ltd, 1715 to 1965" (March 1965).
Jack, David. "The Challenge of Drug Discovery", Centre for Medicines Research Lecture (1988).
Stander, Simon S. "A History of the Pharmaceutical Industry with Special Reference to Allen & Hanbury, 1775-1843" (London MSc., 1965).

Slater, Arthur W. "Howards, Chemical Manufacturers, 1797-1837: A Study in Business History" (London MSc., 1956).

II – Published Sources

Journals
Chemist and Druggist (London, 1859+).
Chemistry and Industry (London, 1951+).
Pharmaceutical Journal (London, 1841+).

Articles
Brocklehurst, W.E. "Asthma: A Long and Continuing Story", in Michael J. Parnham and J. Bruinvels (eds.), *Discoveries in Pharmacology* (New York: Elsevier Science Publishing Co, 1984).

Burnby, Juanita G.L. "A Study of the English Apothecary from 1660 to 1760", *Medical History,* Supplement No. 3 (1983).

Crellin, J.K. "Dr. James's Fever Powder", *Transactions of the British Society for the History of Pharmacy* 1 (1974).

Davenport-Hines, Richard P.T. "Glaxo as a Multinational Before 1963", in Geoffrey Jones (ed.), *British Multinationals: Origins, Management and Performance* (Aldershot: Gower, 1986).

Ganellin, C. Robin. "Discovering New Medicines", Messel Medal Address, 1988, *Chemistry and Industry*, 2 January 1988.

Hartley, D.; Jack, D.; Lunts, L; and Ritchie, A.C.H. "New Class of Selective Stimulants of Beta-Adrenergic Receptors", *Nature* 219 (1968), pp. 861-2.

Hefland, William H. "James Morison and His Pills: A Study in the Nineteenth Century Pharmaceutical Market", *Transactions of the British Society for the History of Pharmacy* 1 (1974).

Holloway, S.W.F. "The Orthodox Fringe: The Origins of the Pharmaceutical Society of Great Britain", in W.F. Bynum and Roy Porter (eds.), *Medical Fringe and Medical Orthodoxy 1750-1850* (London: Croom Helm, 1987).

Inkster, Ian. "Science and Society in the Metropolis: A Preliminary Examination of the Social and Institutional Context of the Askesian Society of London, 1796-1807", *Annals of Science* 34 (1977).

Jephcott, Harry. "The Glaxo Research Organisation", in Sir John Cockcroft (ed.), *The Organisation of Research Establishments* (Cambridge: At the University Press, 1966).

Liebenau, Jonathan. "Industrial R & D in Pharmaceutical Firms in the Early Twentieth Century", *Business History* 26 (1984), pp. 329-46.

Liebenau, Jonathan. "Marketing High Technology: Educating Physicians to Use Innovative Medicines", in R.P.T. Davenport-Hines (ed.), *Markets and Bagmen: Studies in the History of Marketing and British Industrial Performance, 1830-1939* (Aldershot: Gower, 1986).

Lunts, L.H.C. "Salbutamol: A Selective $Beta_2$-Stimulant Bronchodilator", in Barry J. Price and Stanley M. Roberts (eds.), *Medicinal Chemistry: The Role of Organic Chemistry in Drug Research* (London: Academic Press, 1985).

Matthews, Leslie G. "An Unrecorded William Allen Caricature", *Medical History* 15 (1971).

Books

Association of the British Pharmaceutical Industry. *The Pharmaceutical Industry and the Nation's Health* (London: ABPI, 1988).

Beier, Lucinda McCray. *Sufferers and Healers: The Experience of Illness in Seventeenth-Century England* (London: Routledge & Kegan Paul, 1987).

Bell, Jacob. *A Concise Historical Sketch of the Progress of Pharmacy in Great Britain* (London: Pharmaceutical Society, 1843).

Bennett, John Hughes. *Treatise on the Oleum Jecoris Aselli, or Cod Liver Oil, as a Therapeutic Agent in Certain Forms of Gout, Rheumatism, and Scrofula: with Cases* (London, 1841, but another edn. *With an Appendix for 1847* (Edinburgh: Maclachlan, Stewart & Co, 1848)).

Bennett, Richard; and Leavey, J.A. *A History of Smith & Nephew 1856-1981* (London: Smith & Nephew, 1981).

Bevan, Joseph G. *A Short Account of the Life and Writings of Robert Barclay* (London: William Phillips, 1802).

Bevan, Joseph G. *Memoirs of the Life of Isaac Penington: to which is Added a Review of His Writings* (London: William Phillips, 1807).

Bevan, Joseph G. *Extracts from the Letters and Other Writings of the Late Joseph Gurney Bevan; Preceded by a Short Memoir of His Life* (London: William Phillips, 1821).

Bevan, Rebecca. *A Short Account of the Last Illness and Death of Joseph Gurney Bevan* (London: William Phillips, 1815).

Bliss, Michael. *The Discovery of Insulin* (Toronto: McLelland & Stewart, 1982).

Breckon, William. *The Drug Makers* (London: Eyre Methuen, 1972).

British Pharmacopoeia. Published under the direction of the General Council of Medical Education. (London: Spottiswoode & Co, 1864).

Chapman, Stanley. *Jesse Boot of Boots the Chemists* (London: Hodder & Stoughton, 1973).

Chapman-Huston, Desmond; and Cripps, Ernest C. *Through a City Archway: The Story of Allen & Hanburys 1715-1954* (London: John Murray, 1954).

Cloughly, C.P.; Burnby, J.G.L.; and Earles, M.P. *My Dear Mr. Bell: Letters from Dr. Jonathan Pereira to Mr. Jacob Bell, London, 1844 to 1853* (Edinburgh: British Society for the History of Pharmacy, 1988).

Collier, Joe. *The Health Conspiracy: How Doctors, the Drug Industry and the Government Undermine Our Health* (London: Century Hutchinson Ltd, 1989).

Cooter, Roger (ed.). *Studies in the History of Alternative Medicine* (London: Macmillan Press Ltd, 1988).

Cripps, Ernest C. *Plough Court: The Story of a Notable Pharmacy* (London: Allen & Hanburys Ltd, 1927).

Davies, John H. (ed.). *The Letters of Lewis, Richard, William and John Morris of Anglesey* (2 vols., Aberystwyth: privately published, 1907-9).

Fayle, Joshua. *The Spitalfields Genius: The Story of William Allen* (London: Hodder & Stoughton, 1884).

Fluckiger, Friedrich A.; and Hanbury, Daniel. *Pharmacographia: A History of the Principal Drugs of Vegetable Origin Met with in Great Britain and British India* (London: Macmillan & Co, 2nd edn., 1879).

Gamble, Audrey. *A History of the Bevan Family* (London: Headley Bros., 1924).

Gold on the Green: Fifty Glaxo Years at Greenford. Ed. by Clifford Turner. (Greenford: Glaxo Pharmaceuticals Ltd, 1985).

Gray, Samuel Frederick. *The Operative Chemist: Being a Practical Display of the Arts and Manufactures which Depend upon Chemical Principles* (London: n.p., 1828).

Guibourt, Nicolas J. B. G. *Histoire Abrégée des Drogues Simples* (Paris: L. Colas, 1820).

Hall, Helena. *William Allen, 1770-1843, Member of the Society of Friends* (Haywards Heath: Charles Clarke, 1953).

Hanbury, Sir Cecil. *La Mortola Garden* (London: Oxford University Press, 1938).

Hanbury, Daniel. *Science Papers, Chiefly Pharmacological and Botanical. Edited with a Memoir by J. Ince* (London: n.p.?, 1876).

Hanbury, Frederick J. (ed.). *The London Catalogue of British Plants* (London: G. Bell & Sons, 11th edn., 1925).

Hanbury, Frederick J.; and Marshall, Edward S. *Flora of Kent . . . With Notes on the Topography, Geology and Meteorology . . . of the County . . . With Two Maps* (London: F.J. Hanbury, 1899).

Hare, Ronald. *The Birth of Penicillin* (London: Allen & Unwin, 1970).

Jephcott, Sir Harry (compiler), *The First Fifty Years: An Account of the Early Life of Joseph Edward Nathan and the First Fifty Years of His Merchandise Business that Eventually Became the Glaxo Group* (n.p.: Glaxo, 1969).

Jeremy, David J. (ed.) *Business and Religion in Britain* (Aldershot: Gower, 1988).

Jeremy, David J.; and Shaw, Christine (eds.). *Dictionary of Business Biography: A Biographical Dictionary of Business Leaders Active in Britain in the Period 1860-1980* (5 vols., London: Butterworths, 1984-6).

Jones, Geoffrey (ed.). *British Multinationals: Origins, Management and Performance* (Aldershot: Gower, 1986).

Kremer and Urdang's History of Pharmacy. Revised by G. Sonnedecker. (Philadelphia: J.B. Lippincott Co, 3rd. edn., 1963).

Lane, Donald J.; and Storr, Anthony. *Asthma: the Facts* (Oxford: Oxford University Press, 2nd edn., 1987).

Lazell, H.G. Leslie. *From Pills to Penicillin: The Beecham Story* (London: Heinemann, 1975).

Liebenau, Jonathan. *Medical Science and Medical Industry: The Formation of the American Pharmaceutical Industry* (London: Macmillan, 1987).

Liebenau, Jonathan (ed.). *The Challenge of New Technology: Innovation in British Business since 1850* (Aldershot: Gower, 1988).

Life of William Allen with Selections from His Correspondence (3 vols., London: Charles Gilpin, 1846).

Locke, Amy A. *The Hanbury Family* (2 vols., London: A.L. Humphreys, 1916).

Loudon, Irvine. *Medical Care and the General Practitioner 1750-1850* (Oxford: Clarendon Press, 1986).

Macdonald, Gilbert. *One Hundred Years Wellcome 1880-1980: In Pursuit of Excellence* (London: Wellcome Foundation Ltd, 1980).

Macfarlane, G. *Alexander Fleming: The Man and the Myth* (London: Chatto & Windus, 1984).

Magendie, François. *Formulaire pour La Préparation et L'Emploi de Plusieurs Nouveaux Medicaments* (Paris: Mequignon-Marvis, 1821).

Mathias, Peter. *The First Industrial Nation: An Economic History of Britain, 1700-1914* (London: Methuen, 2nd edn., 1983).

Matthews, Leslie G. *History of Pharmacy in Britain* (Edinburgh & London: E. & S. Livingstone, 1962).

Memorials of Christine Majolier Alsop. Compiled by Martha Braithwaite. (London: Samuel Harris & Co, 1881).

Mohr, Francis; and Redwood, Theophilus. *Practical Pharmacy: The Arrangements, Apparatus, and Manipulations of the Pharmaceutical Shop and Laboratory* (London: Taylor, Walton & Maberly, 1849).

Owen, Robert. *The Life of Robert Owen By Himself* (1857; reprinted London: Charles Knight, 1971).

Page, John. *Receipts for Preparing and Compounding the Principal Medicines Made Use of By the Late Mr. Ward* (London: H. Whitridge, 1763).

Percival, Thomas. *The Works, Literary, Moral and Medical of Thomas Percival* (4 vols., London: J. Johnson, 1807).

Pereira, Jonathan. *The Elements of Materia Medica* (London: n.p., 1839).

Pharmacopoeia Bateana (London, 1699).

Porter, Roy. *Health for Sale: Quackery in England 1660-1850* (Manchester: Manchester University Press, 1989).

Porter, Roy; and Porter, Dorothy. *In Sickness and in Health: The British Experience 1650-1850* (London: Fourth Estate, 1988).

Raistrick, Arthur. *Quakers in Science and Industry* (London: Bannisdale Press, 1950).

Robinson, Charles W. *Twentieth Century Druggist: Memoirs* (Beverley: Galen Press, 1983).

Slinn, Judy. *A History of May & Baker 1834-1984* (Cambridge: Hobsons Ltd, 1984).

Smith, Francis B. *The Retreat of Tuberculosis 1850-1950* (London: Croom Helm, 1988).

Sneader, Walter. *Drug Discovery: The Evolution of Modern Medicines* (New York: John Wiley & Sons, 1985).

Stephen, Leslie; and Lee, Sydney (eds.). *Dictionary of National Biography* (63 vols, Oxford: Oxford University Press, 1885-1933; plus supplements, to date).

Stockwell, Christine. *Nature's Pharmacy: A History of Plants and Healing* (London: Century Hutchinson Ltd, 1988).

Talbor, Robert. *The English Remedy, or, Talbor's Wonderful Secret for Curing Agues and Feavers* (London: n.p., 1682).

Thompson, Charles J. S. *The Quacks of Old London* (London: Bretano's, 1928).

Thompson, Charles J.S. *The Mystery and Art of the Apothecary* (London: John Lane, 1929).

Trease, Geoffrey. *Pharmacy in History* (London: Baillière, Tindall & Cox, 1964).

Webster, Charles. *The Health Services Since the War. Vol. I: Problems of Health Care: The National Health Services Before 1957* (London: HMSO, 1988).

William Allen: His Life and Labours (London: n.p., 1865).

Wilson, David. *Penicillin in Perspective* (London: Faber & Faber, 1976).

Wootton, A.C. *Chronicles of Pharmacy* (2 vols., London: Macmillan & Co, 1910).

Wrigley, E.A.; and Schofield, R.S. *The Population History of England, 1541-1871: A Reconstruction* (London: Edward Arnold, 1981).

INDEX

operating tables 98, 132, 175, 179
opium 14, 25
"Opren" 230
orciprenaline 213
Osgood, Salem
"Ostelin" 148
Owen, Robert 42

"P" Building, Ware 172-3
Page, John 11
Pakistan market 181
Palmer, Herbert 195, 202
"Paludrine" 167
Parke Davis 164, 167, 183
Pasteur, Louis 57
pastilles 79, 91, 140-2, 170-1, 179, 197-8
patent medicines 10-12, 28-9, 35
Pelletier, Pierre-Joseph 46
"Penbritin" 167
Penington, Isaac 31
penicillin 163-4, 165, 167, 171-4, 189
Penicillin Chemical Committee 171
Pepys, William Haseldine 47
Pereira, Jonathan 61
Pfizer 164, 167, 172, 208, 220, 223
Pharmaceutical Society of Great Britain 8, 11, 43, 61, 64, 72, 79, 99, 174, 179
Pharmacy and Poison Act 126
phenylketonuria 184
The Philanthropist 42
Phillips, Richard 47
pills 139
"Piriton" 184, 202
Plough Court 14, 16, 52, 55-6, 67-72, 95-6, 169 and passim
Pope, Alexander 16
Poynter, Desmond 208
Price, Barry 221
"Propaderm" 216
propranolol 217
Priessnitz 11
Pritchard, Brian 217
"Prontosil Rubrum" 160
Prosser, James 81
"Pyopen" 167

Quakers 14-15, 18-33 passim, 115
quacks 10-12
Quare, David 15
Quare, Elizabeth 15
quinine 12, 46

Radford, Harry 174
Radford, William 91, 174

ranitidine 221, 225
Redwood, Theophilius 61
Rennie, W. J. 173
Rheum 13
Rhodes, Deryck 208
rhubarb 13
Richards, David 217, 221
Richards, Glyn Owen 172
Riddick, George 112
Riker & Co 211
Ritchie, Alec 208
Robertson, James 27
Robinson, F. Arnold 182, 206
Royal College of Physicians 1, 2
Royal College of Surgeons 6, 157
Royal Free Hospital 38
Royal Jennerian Institution 47
Royal Society 49, 65
rusks 140

St. Bartholomew's Hospital 123, 132
St. Mary's Hospital, London 163
St. Mary's Hospital, Manchester 98
St. Thomas's Hospital 21, 47, 98
salbutamol 213-15, 227, 230-1
salmeterol hydroxynaphthoate 231
Salvarsan 102, 120, 122, 160
Samways, E.K. 170, 182, 195, 197, 202, 205
Sandoz 223
Sanitas Co 73, 93
sassafras 13, 38
"Sauerin" 102
Savery 6
Schering Corporation 184
Scott 159
Selitrenny, S.S. 115
senna 13, 25
Shah of Iran 201-2
Sharland & Co 181
Shin Nihon 203
Sierra Leone slave colony 43-4
Simpson, Margaret 170
Simpson, Wilfred 208, 216
slavery 30, 45
soap 119
Smart, David 199, 203, 205
Smith, Ian 195
Smith Kline & French 167, 193, 206, 220, 223
Smith, Lester 182, 190
Smith, Maurice 203
Smith, William D. 26
Snell, Eric 216
Society of Apothecaries 2, 14, 52